D0467616

San Diego Christian College
2100 Greenfield Drive
El Cajon, CA 92019

Speaking Shakespeare

Also by Patsy Rodenburg

The Right to Speak
The Need for Words
The Actor Speaks

822.33
H
R687s

Speaking Shakespeare

Patsy Rodenburg

SPEAKING SHAKESPEARE
Copyright © Patsy Rodenburg, 2002.
All rights reserved. No part of this book may be used
or reproduced in any manner whatsoever without written
permission except in the case of brief quotations embodied
incritical articles or reviews.

First published by PALGRAVE MACMILLAN™ in 2002
175 Fifth Avenue, New York, N.Y. 10010 and
Houndmills, Basingstoke, Hampshire, England RG21 6XS.
Companies and representatives throughout the world.

PALGRAVE MACMILLAN is the global academic imprint of
the Palgrave Macmillan division of St. Martin's Press, LLC and of
Palgrave Macmillan Ltd. Macmillan® is a registered trademark in
the United States, United Kingdom and other countries. Palgrave is
a registered trademark in the European Union and other countries.

ISBN 0-312-29420-4

First edition published in the United Kingdom by Methuen 2002.

Library of Congress Cataloguing-in-Publication Data available
from the Library of Congress

First PALGRAVE MACMILLAN edition: August 2002
10 9 8 7 6 5 4 3 2 1

Printed in the United States of America.

To W.S. and A.F.

'Haply I think on thee – and then my state,
Like to the lark at break of day arising
From sullen earth, sings hymns at heaven's gate:
For thy sweet love remember'd such wealth brings
That then I scorn to change my state with Kings.'

Contents

Part 3: **The Imaginative**

Part 4: **The Speeches**

Part 5: **Checklists**

Acknowledgements

Conversations and insights with Ralph Fiennes, Antony Sher, Greg Doran, Ruth Padel, Kristin Linklater, Tina Packer, Michael Howard, John Roberts, Judi Dench, Cicely Berry, Daniel Grans, Di Trevis, Fiona Shaw, Harriet Walter, Simon Russell Beale, Alakanada Samarth, Nick Hytner, Cecil O'Neal, Brigid Larmaur, Deborah Warner, Sam Mendes, Trevor Nunn, Olympia Dukakis, Wallace Shawn, Sue Lefton, Jane Gibson, Genista McIntosh, Jonathan Kent, Terry Hands, Ronald Eyre, Jude Law and Declan Donellan.

Complete support from Lesley Murdin, Antonia Francheschi, Mary Carter, Paula Chitty, Wendy Allnut, Angie Fairclough, Robert and May Freeburn, Rick Scott and Elizabeth Ingrams.

And finally this book wouldn't exist if not for all my students past and present at the Guildhall School of Music and Drama, and my brilliant editor Max Eilenberg.

Preface

Speaking Shakespeare is based on the following principles:

- To understand any play text fully you have to speak it.
- To release its full power you have to commit through the body, breath and word.
- You have to trust the words and know what those words mean.
- To access the power of a play you have to know how it's constructed.
- You can't act Shakespeare until you can speak him.

The book was born several years ago, one Monday afternoon in a rehearsal room at the Royal National Theatre.

Forty-five actors had gathered to work with a brilliant Shakespearean director, whose insights into the playwright's intricate forms and language were inspiring and illuminating. As the afternoon progressed, however, it became clear that many of the younger actors were growing restless. They seemed inattentive, and even bored. This struck me as not just curious but strangely graceless, and so I questioned their apparent indifference later that week. It transpired that they were bored because they had no idea what the director was talking about. He was referring to things beyond their ken. They had no idea of what an iambic or an antithesis was, or the difference between a thought and a line; and they didn't seem to have realised that such knowledge might be necessary.

Few of those actors had ever played Shakespeare as part of their training; and if they had, it seemed to have involved little or no discussion of the mechanics of Shakespeare's writing.

As a result, I realised, they couldn't follow the director because they had never been given the basic tools even to start work on Shakespeare. In place of that basic training, they needed a manual.

Speaking Shakespeare is an attempt to address that need. A practical training guide on how to begin to speak and understand Shakespeare, it lays out the work that an actor should ideally have done and come to know before even entering a rehearsal space and facing a director.

Part 1 Foundation Craft

'Take pains; be perfect.'

(A Midsummer Night's Dream, I. ii)

Foundation Craft

At the Guildhall School of Music and Drama I don't teach my students Shakespeare until their second year. The reason is pragmatic: until the body, breath, support, voice and speech muscles are thoroughly worked and tuned it is extremely hard to realise and release such physical and sensual texts.

First year work on language sensitises the students to structure, rhythm, imagery and poetry. Language must be important to them – a powerful tool. This means they have to explore how they use language and how language affects them. Many of them have to rediscover the potential of language to make concrete and transform inner and outer worlds. Within a year of language-based exercises they begin to understand how powerful and poetic their own language can be. They realise what an armoury they have at their disposal.

In the first year they learn to memorise accurately and effortlessly so that the momentum and precision of great texts is honoured. There is no substitute for learning texts fully and completely. My students learn passages from complex texts every week. They learn mediaeval, Elizabethan, Metaphysical, eighteenth-century and Romantic texts: they touch base with Chaucer, Spencer, Donne, Milton and Pope. The important part of this training is to learn accurately and to practise regularly. I want them to feel the language – the words, thought structures and images – flowing in their bloodstreams, a familiar part of them rather than something baffling, strange or difficult.

This grounding in language is particularly important for Shakespeare. The passionate exchange of ideas and feeling through words has always been the blood and oxygen of English-speaking theatre, a theatre built on heightened poetic text. In this Shakespeare is the master. His plays are highly structured works in which the forms support and the words release the action. The language is active and intense: here the action is in the word – not merely described by it, not behind it or under it. The words create the world of the play through the articulation of sound, rhythm, structure and sense. As they are spoken, they bring the world into being. They must be spoken before they can be acted.

Speaking Shakespeare requires more than simply memorising texts. It needs a profound understanding of language and how it works. Actors have to engage fully with language before it can engage an audience. They must be able to connect to, experience and imagine the words concretely. They need to understand and internalise the physical operation of certain structures in rhythm and form, and work to realise them. The language must penetrate them, filling them with its power. The production and release of the word has to be so ingrained in their bodies, voices and imaginations that they can access the play, the character, the thoughts and the story without effort. Think of an actor as a swan that is crossing a river. The webbed feet are working away underneath the waterline whilst the grace of the bird appears above it. But to do this the actor needs to prepare body, voice and speech muscles – to acquire highly developed speaking skills; skills in body work, voice production and articulation; skills that enhance the text, not block it.

These are the areas this book will explore and develop.

Much of the work is basic and to older actors – those over forty – may be so obvious as to seem patronising. But it is necessary because so many younger actors believe loose concepts or generalised emotions are enough to guide them through Shakespeare. They have no sense that the heart of the plays lies in the concrete detail of the language. They don't know – and too often don't appear to care – what an iambic pentameter is, or the difference between a verse line and a thought contained within the verse.

For actors who lack basic training such as this, any proper realisation of the plays is problematic – and this is ironic, for not only does Shakespeare write powerful and beautiful plays, but his forms are actor-friendly. It could be said that in the end, if you trust him, he is easier to speak than a screenplay. As you learn to decipher the text, you quickly discover that he is on your side. He's a great support, not a hindrance.

You will get accustomed to me using the phrases 'the evidence of the text' and 'the givens'. The evidence of a text is what there is in the text – acting and character clues. The givens are the physical forms you cannot ignore, such as the breaking of a rhythm, the line length, the thought structure, the words themselves. The givens are as indispensable as learning the text accurately. They must be acknowledged even if you choose later to deny them. There is nothing wrong with actors breaking rules – provided they know the rules exist.

I will also be using the word 'rule'. Academic rules can block creative spontaneity but these acting rules will harness energy, focus mind and heart, and finally transform the actor. They are like a safety harness that enables you to climb the mountain or a map that guides you. As children listening to stories we are reassured by certain formulas. We know that 'Once upon a time' will eventually be followed by 'And they all lived happily ever after'. Between those two phrases, the most direful adventures can occur, but because the story is framed by a familiar structure we can experience horrors in the knowledge that all will eventually be well. The same applies to rhythm, form and rhyme. They are all tools that help us go deeper into a story, and guide us through it.

Structure helps define and release specific emotions. Theatrical structure is physical and as you allow the different physical structures of any of Shakespeare's plays to enter you, you will find yourself changing and transforming.

It's also true that all the basic rules I describe are broken by Shakespeare. As you learn to detect these broken rules you will see he is sending you acting notes. Look, he is saying – fragmentation is dramatic. See what happens when a line breaks half way through, or the rhythm starts to falter. It snags attention – it's like a broken heartbeat or even a broken heart. So too a shift from prose to verse, or vice versa, is dramatic, the equivalent of moving from dialogue to song in a musical or from jazz into Bach.

In all great plays the structures of the language reveal the meaning within the work. These structures are in fact organic to human communication – they have evolved from the human need to communicate in different ways: for efficiency, refinement, wit, a sense of fun. And the more we need to communicate with others, the more the form focuses us. In this way form equals content.

Characters in Shakespeare think and speak in structured thoughts. They care about speaking and it is important for them to express ideas well. In acting them you will have to think and respond very rapidly. You will speak, think and feel on the word, the thought, the line, not – as most real-life speakers do – ponder and then speak or speak and then ponder. Your existence is in the moment and on the word and thought.

It fires through your mouth and is made real through the word. As you speak you will need your emotions to change as the music does. Characters in Shakespeare never get emotionally stuck, like needles on vinyl records. On the contrary, Shakespeare requires you actively to transform your emotions as you speak.

Great poetic language is only in part to do with intellect. Not for nothing do we have to learn the speeches 'by heart'. They should occupy your whole being, body and breath. You will need to feel and completely respond to the heartbeat that drives them: the iambic pentameter. This fundamental Shakespearean verse rhythm returns the energy of speaking so that if you follow it you will never fall off a word or a line, never sound uninterested or disengaged. It is a rhythm of verse and speech that requires you to be vital and energised.

In order to speak Shakespeare you will need passion, energy and courage. You will need oxygen – to fuel and sustain the long thoughts and powerful emotions without suffocating yourself or the plays in the attempt to speak them. The ability to pursue long and structured thought patterns should appear effortless. You should feel that athletic thinking and passionate discussion are a part of your world: that the progression of ideas chasing solutions is a vital part of your existence.

Vivid and metaphorical language should be made concrete and your own. You must experience every image as you speak it. Your own poetic awareness must be released and married to Shakespeare's. This will need real energy supported by the breath so that as you enter the heightened world of need, passion and insight you don't resort to pushing, shouting, generalising or denying the energy of the form and the word.

If language has entered the bloodstream, it can be readily accessed rather than hauled up into the actor's mouth or skidded over as though it is meaningless. The word is the character's way out – body, heart and mind meet in the word. Don't travel lightly over the text, or play it naturalistically. Actors who think the words are irrelevant have few options in playing Shakespeare. They trowel emotion like a varnish over the text, break it up into digestible fragments that make nonsense of the whole, or play it so naturalistically that the audience can't hear it.

You will need to be able to speak clearly and efficiently – the speech muscles have to respond to highly defined and defining language. Clarity will always be essential. Every syllable, vowel and consonant should be in your mouth, not half there or forgotten. Hardly a single character in Shakespeare mumbles. You will need a clear, uncluttered, open, flexible and expressive voice to serve these texts. The movement of the voice that is called range is merely the physical manifestation of passion in either feeling or thought. A dull, restricted voice is unreal in terms of feeling. The more passionate the idea or excited the feeling, the more flexible your voice should be.

I once worked in an acting studio in America where a huge poster on the wall proclaimed: 'The word comes last'. The opposite is true in Shakespeare – in him the word is the beginning and end. The voice serves the word and the word serves the voice. Both should be in place before you enter a rehearsal room.

The Craft

If the preparation has been thorough, work on the text will not be obstructed by the actor worrying about his or her breath, voice or speech muscles. Technically weak actors preoccupy the audience with the question 'will they make it?' The focus of any performance should be on the word, the story and the play, not whether or not an actor will make it through. Thorough preparatory technical work frees both actor and audience, and gives one the right to speak Shakespeare and the other the chance to hear it.

In the past, this kind of knowledge was part of the actor's basic repertoire. Today, it's a craft neglected in most training establishments. In repertory companies it used to be learned by osmosis, passed on by older actors to younger ones, honed by constant practice and repetition. Nowadays, by contrast, even very celebrated actors enter Shakespeare blind and craftless. Even if they understand the rules and forms of the writing, they have often not practised them enough for the work to become unconscious and available without struggle.

Take this exchange, for instance:

> *Me*: If you can stand up straight when you address the audience and not shuffle, you will have more authority as Romeo and look less modern.
> *Actor*: I know – my teacher at school told me that, but I can't do it and act.

This is a case where the work has not been sufficiently embedded in the body. Repetition is needed to filter the head knowledge into the whole being. The teacher probably didn't have the hours needed to transform the actor. A good four-year stint in rep would equally solve the problem. Doing the work would free the actor.

Or another example:

> *Me*: You are pulling off the iambic rhythm, so the sense is being blocked.
> *Actor*: I'm always getting that note. I can only act in my rhythm.

Again, the actor has not spent enough time living in the iambic pentameter. It feels alien. It's nothing that work couldn't rectify.

The fact is that there are no short cuts in this work. Craft takes time and diligence. It's like the practice an athlete does to perfect a move and develop muscle memory: application, precision and repetition are required. Acting is more complex than a sport – it involves the complete engagement of a human being.

The work has to be done on a daily basis until eventually it becomes so internalised as to be virtually unconscious. This might mean you have to spend hours practising on your own in order to catch up with those actors who can access their voice and language with ease. You don't want to be one of those actors who drag a scene down and stop the emotional flow of the others because they can't speak or think accurately or quickly enough. Such 'back-footed' actors halt the energetic thrust of a scene. They can kill the performances of others and destroy scenes they might only have one line in. What they are doing is pretending to play Shakespeare; they are not actually doing it.

Of course, working alone is hard. Actors are social animals who often find working alone depressing and difficult. Musicians, by contrast, are used to working on their technique in isolation. They establish a daily routine of practice – which is exactly what the actor needs. It requires real discipline, but it is worth it. The sooner you do the work, the freer you will be. Talent is a commodity that needs focus through craft. No amount of talent will help you speak clearly if your speech muscles have not been worked and trained.

I once worked with a screen actress who was returning to the stage after a long break. She had to fill a theatre, and she said to me she thought it was all to do with intention. 'No,' I replied. 'I might have the intention of being a pole vaulter. I might see myself flying over that pole – but I couldn't do it unless I'd worked certain muscles.' Intention may be the start and even the end of the process, but in the middle there is work!

Communication

Many of our habits today are about non-communication. Perhaps we don't trust what we say or believe that others are listening. We're often frightened of committing to any powerful idea or passionate feeling. Our communication grows indirect, surrounded by an aura of studied casualness; we hesitate and mumble; we rely more and more on glibness, cynicism or denial.

This is not the energy at the heart of Shakespeare's world.

The world Shakespeare creates is full of inquisitive speakers and attentive listeners. His characters use their language to connect to the world, not to hide from it. They use it to survive, to probe, to explore, to quest. They are not afraid of profound expression. If they mock, it is direct and to the point, not under their breath. His is a world where everything appears new and interesting; where people enjoy speaking; where passion is attractive as opposed to faintly absurd. His characters' ears are twitching; their eyes are wide open, not glazed. It is in their best interests to be alert. They have to listen very carefully if they are to negotiate and survive the scenarios he puts them in.

In preparation for this whole directness in Shakespeare I encourage my students to own what they think and say. So, 'I'm *quite* scared' or 'I'm *quite* shocked' has to be shifted into 'I *am* scared' or 'I *am* shocked'. Equally, 'I feel, like, sad' and 'I feel, like, happy' will be more connected and direct when the 'like' is dropped.

It's important to understand that social habits of verbal, emotional and intellectual imprecision have real technical consequences for the actor today. On the most basic level, non-communication and inattention lead to underdeveloped muscles of voice and speech, flabby thinking and passion crusted over with rust. They lead to mumbled sentences and swallowed words, to inaudibility and the destruction of the iambic. They're matched by a physical coolness or shuffling: a completely unreal stance for anyone trying to engage with real curiosity and feeling. They're compensated for by a forced intensity where the actor whispers and hold the word inside, bottling and constipating the language – or alternatively by shouting in the attempt to manufacture passion.

The fact is that the actor who doesn't trust clarity or risk engagement cannot release Shakespeare's forms. We have to learn to care about our voices, our words, our ears and our ability to communicate and not be ashamed of caring. From the audience's point of view, anyone caring is fascinating and alluring. Unclear or unintelligent thinkers don't interest Shakespeare, as I believe they don't really interest anyone. Glibness and moaners, with their accompanying vocal habits of reduction and minor key or 'sigh' acting, don't appear in these plays. There are mean-spirited characters but they are vividly mean, not passive in their meanness. Half-voiced speakers hedge their bets and refuse to commit. Shakespeare is fully voiced and fully committed to every action undertaken.

We will return to this notion repeatedly. If we choose to appear to mumble, it must be a choice – not a matter of unexamined habit. A character can seem to devoice, shout or sound boring, but the speech still has to be clear to the audience. Such a choice takes enormous technique, and it is a filled decision, not a casual one.

For instance, you could interpret Polonius as an unlistening, uncaring politician who bores everyone by droning on and on. This might be an exciting way to approach him because these qualities are in the text – but they are there for a reason. He appears not to listen to Laertes' conversation with Ophelia, yet as soon as Laertes exits he reveals he has heard everything. Polonius knows when to pretend not to listen even if his way of speaking and sounds pompous and boring. In itself that is a great political technique used to wear down opposition. It's a choice – a choice based on survival. Polonius is not stupid. He has survived a very complex transfer of power between Hamlet's father and Claudius, and will sacrifice his daughter's feelings and his son's reputation to maintain that power.

Shakespeare strives constantly to communicate as clearly and intelligently as he can. He wants to tell a story, to explain, to witness the truth. All our reductive physical and vocal habits create a bond that holds the text, constraining and diminishing it. The actor struggles like a cat in a bag. Until the bag is opened, the play cannot begin. Start strong and clear in your body and voice when you make your choices.

Shakespeare will help you. Bad habits are often nurtured by the need to make unspeakable texts (like bad TV scripts) interesting. Faced with poor writing, it is only natural to throw in any effect that might help enable a disabled text. With Shakespeare by contrast, you can relax, trust and allow the text to shine through you. Let your habits go and as you do Shakespeare will hold you up. An act of trust and commitment will allow him to play and transform you. You will be held safely – re-energised and transformed.

I say transformed because what makes Shakespeare really great is his understanding of how we all work when we are most heightened, in our most life-changing and life-enhancing moments. In those moments we have all found clarity and expressed ourselves with passion, directness and articulacy. We have all had such experiences, if only in our dreams. Some people might have more memories of them than others, but somewhere – even if it's in a twilight zone – we all know what Shakespeare is asking us to do within the three to four-hour period of a play. We all know more than we think we know.

I was working recently in Los Angeles with a group of film actors. Most were convinced that Shakespeare was out of their reach. One in particular believed passionately that truth was never expressed with clarity in Shakespeare. And yet one day, while working on a sonnet, he suddenly became very engaged and clear.

He told me of a memory that had returned to him. He had a very unfulfilled relationship with his father, painful and uncommunicative. His father, whilst visiting, had started to shout at the actor's two-year-old son. Suddenly, he said, he'd found himself protecting his son and articulating with ferocious clarity his feelings towards his father. That truth was clear and unforced and direct, as it is in Shakespeare. Recalling it had given him access to the sonnet.

When we are heightened, when we need to communicate in order to protect or survive, we do so with real passion and urgency. We cannot afford to be unclear, reticent or imprecise. We may range from extremely sophisticated language to very crude utterances, but our words are active and formed through an acute need and their structure is built with equal care. This heightened state is the state Shakespeare is interested in. In Shakespeare, characters speak to survive. Perhaps the only bridge you have to cross in order to relate your own heightened awareness to that of Shakespeare is to understand that his characters explore these moments by voicing them clearly through precise and poetic language formed under pressure, and with full and equal attention to the world outside them.

The words we speak when we are heightened characterise us and as we change, our language changes with us. Ultimately we are what we speak and as our inner world meets the outer world these changes are mediated by the word. That is why the word is so important in Shakespeare, and why it is so important to serve the word. There is nothing casual or random about the writing of great plays. Each utterance has been honed appropriately.

There are many examples if we look around us that can help us realise our connection to the reality Shakespeare explores. Here are some stories from today's paper, as I write. A congressman in Washington is questioned over his alleged affair with a missing intern: Angelo in *Measure for Measure*. A widow describes how she pleaded with her young soldier husband to be careful in Macedonia days before he was killed: Kate Hotspur to her husband in *Henry IV Part I*. Businesses and investors fear falling shares and recession: Antonio in *The Merchant of Venice* wandering the streets, hearing how his ships have been lost at sea. A father goes to court to look at his daughter's killer: Titus facing his daughter's murderers.

Shakespeare works each of his story lines with tremendous human detail and then adds more ingredients to heighten us further. But at the heart of every play are personal truths we all know and politics we all administer or are marshalled under.

In Shakespeare:

- You speak yourself into consciousness.
- You experience the transforming aspects of language. The world and you change through the word.
- By the end of every speech, you and the world have changed for better or for worse.

Preparing the Equipment

There are three simple questions I ask any actor who wishes to play Shakespeare for the first time.

Are you prepared to work and put in time and energy?
Will you be diligent and give these plays your spirit, intelligence and heart? You have to know that when the great classical actors come

off stage having properly committed to a Shakespearean role, they are exhausted. This exhaustion is not only intellectual, emotional and spiritual; it is physical as well. Muscles in the body, breath, voice and speech have been worked, extended and stretched. You need to be fit and strong to cope with a Shakespeare work-out.

Do you have courage and are you frightened?

You should be frightened in the right way. Any imaginative and curious being exploring the human issues Shakespeare addresses will have a healthy dose of fear. Recognising your fear and working through it will gradually release the plays. At a technical level, letting bad habits go is frightening. To hold on to them is easy but reduces the text. Only when the fear is recognised and the denial stops, can the proper work begin.

Do you have enough humility?

You will need to stay open to the text, which requires respect and a lack of vanity. I've never met a great artist without humility. You should start by avoiding any discussion along the lines of 'I wouldn't say that', 'I don't believe that', 'I don't think my character would do that', 'Can we change this line?' or 'This scene is unreal.' Not only do such comments display an appalling lack of imagination, but they prove the actor's fear of working with trust. They are frightened of transforming, and only really want to play themselves – not another being. You cannot play Shakespeare unless you are of the species that can search and change.

Let's be absolutely clear.

- To speak Shakespeare you have to be fit.
- Not just physically fit, but throughout the body, breath, voice and speech muscles.
- You have to be fit intellectually and emotionally and awake in your spirit.
- You have to be passionate, political and curious.
- You have to keep up with a writer who operates through his words and forms on every human level.

To put it another way, in order to act Shakespeare, you have to be a complete human athlete – not just a footballer or a philosopher, but both. His plays are the most thorough work-out an actor can have, and they should be central to any actor's training. They challenge physically, intellectually and emotionally, and require access through the imagination to what it is to be human.

The Body

The Aims

- To open the body and free it of any tensions that could restrict the breath, voice and speech muscles, and to be centred, alert and aware.
- To clear the body to allow the text to pass through unimpeded – the actor is like a vessel for the text.
- To eliminate any tensions that block flexibility and hamper the audience's connection to feeling.
- To remove any tensions that will communicate wrong messages to an audience, physically or vocally. Characters should look and sound their parts.
- To achieve the state of readiness: the fully engaged mental and physical presence required in order to survive in heightened existence. This is what the actor needs to engage with the work, and should be the starting point of all rehearsal.

The Reasons

Most of our bodies today reflect either an almost complete lack of exercise or, at the opposite end of the spectrum, too much time in the gym: the over-worked, over-pumped physique that is cosmetic rather than natural. Actors start their training with bodies that are either physically weak and uncentred, or puffed up into a rigid shell. Neither state allows any physical flexibility, grace or passage of emotions. The more our bodies wither away through inertia or harden through too much gym work, the more difficult it becomes to engage and energise the power of the verse and language in Shakespeare. Equally important, neither condition would give us much chance of survival in Shakespeare's world.

Today most of us live in cities, our dwellings small boxes cut off from space and nature. This adds to the stunting of our physical and vocal imagination. It seems either to inhibit our bodies or make us occupy the space aggressively. Both positions lock and close us off from our surroundings. In Shakespeare's world this could be catastrophic. It was a dangerous place where men openly carried weapons, a volatile society where status was clearly defined and the crossing of boundaries a perilous activity. To be physically too casual could get you into trouble; and being too intrusive – a space invader – could get you severely challenged or punished. Imagine knocking into the volatile Tybalt in a bus queue.

In Shakespeare's time people not only walked vast distances, but did so on rough ground which automatically centres the body and keeps you alert. Any countryside walk we do today instantly gives us a different awareness of our body. When travelling distances, they rode horses for hours at a time and anyone who rides knows that you have to stay centred, breathing and alert.

Try lifting one of the swords a gentleman would carry – it's heavy. To fight with this would require the body being centred. A gentleman couldn't live moment to moment without drawing on his body as an instrument of survival. Life was hard: only the fit could survive.

This kind of physical alertness was as necessary in society as it was on the road or the battlefield. Many of Shakespeare's characters live at court, where the arrogance and power of young lords was harnessed by the demanding codes of courtly matters and manners. It was a social duty to be fit, graceful and alert. The English were known as 'the dancing English'. Elizabeth wouldn't employ any minister who couldn't perform a galliard – an extremely difficult and energetic dance.

Slouching or mumbling in front of a monarch or any high-placed benefactor was not an option. Imagine the risk of sounding so unclear that you are made to repeat yourself in front of a high status, all-powerful presence. You would speak up and out and not be caught off-guard by failing to listen or seeming inattentive. Insolence could be regarded as treason, which could mean beheading. Not listening, or not speaking clearly, could cost you your life.

When an actor looks disengaged on stage in the presence of a tyrant, it's not just unbelievable. It's a sign that the actor has lacked all imagination in thinking about the world of the play.

Servants too were expected to be attentive and hard-working. Shakespeare might make jokes about servants who don't work or are inefficient but the general order of the day was that they had to work. There are intelligent servants and unintelligent lords and vice versa, but they all speak to be heard and noted – they don't mutter or disappear. If they speak, it's for a purpose and that purpose has to be heard. The world Shakespeare's characters move in is very public – they're on show and switched on, not bored or lethargic. Even his intimate and private scenes are all about potent events and problems. When he investigates the domestic, it is at the moments when the domestic is in crisis. These are not relaxed scenes. Nothing in his plays is either casual or informal. Therefore casual or informal physical states are completely inappropriate.

Today, unfortunately, the fashion is 'cool': a physical statement of indifference or, at worst, apparent insolence. In 'cool' everything passionate or meaningful is being repudiated. I call this state *denial*. The general physical slump translates anatomically into breathing and speaking. You can't really take breath in this state. The voice is trapped and underpowered. The result is that lines and words fall away, back into the speaker. Ends of words are missed or ignored, and eye contact avoided. Speech becomes redundant, no more than a general vocal statement of withdrawal and hostility – or, in a charitable interpretation, of insecurity and fear.

There is a cool walk too. Urban sprawl means that many of us rarely experience real countryside. The rural life affects the body – your body is much more connected to itself. The perfect indication of urban physicality is the swaying, hip-hop walk that many young men adopt. You couldn't walk like that on rough ground. Observe anyone living and working in rural conditions: their movements are economical to avoid wasting energy. Try herding cattle hip-hop style! As soon as a character walks on stage, we should know all about his or her physical life. Wearing a period costume while keeping our modern urban walk is confusing, if not ridiculous. And it's totally inappropriate to Shakespeare unless you are very clear about what you are doing.

Every physical requirement or given in Shakespeare's writing is the direct opposite of 'cool'. The iambic, the word, the line, the thought structure urge you to move forward physically, emotionally and intellectually. You are speaking to engage, to solve and to confront. 'Cool' acting consequently kills the physical, emotional and intellectual spirit of Shakespeare. It denies the heightened circumstances of the play and the word. It is about non-engagement as opposed to engagement.

On the other side of cool is a physical stance that actors sometimes adopt in an attempt to appear heightened. This is the old favourite – the *bluff*. This position imposes a fake sense of power on the body and voice. Here the chest is heaved up, the back of the rib cage locked, the shoulders pulled back and the chin thrust forward. The shell of the body has been braced to appear strong and grand – but try fighting, walking on rough ground or riding like this and you will quickly realise how inefficient and unreal it is. It's hard to breathe and the tensions in the body lock the voice so it takes on a pushed quality. It is the sort of voice you can often hear in a theatre but not understand – all sound and fury, but no definition in the words. It splays out, unfocused, and can only express generalisations.

Energy is produced in the bluff state, but it comes from the wrong source. The text gets covered with a generalised varnish of power, which wipes out the subtleties of the language. There is a boom that eliminates any clarity of thought or feeling. It also makes the speaker sound insensitive and interferes with the actor's ability to listen and react in the moment.

You have to believe that unless you work on physical strength, flexibility and alignment, you will not be able to speak Shakespeare with any real authority or truth. The body is our house and the house must be in order to hold any heightened text.

There is a wonderful Shakespearean actor who has a passion for motorcycles – but he seems only to ride to rehearsal on his motorcycle when he is playing Shakespeare. For other plays he tends to arrive by car. When I asked him why, he grinned. 'Riding a motorcycle safely means you have to be alert, awake and in the moment – just what I need in rehearsing Shakespeare. It's my morning wake-up call. I dismount centred for Shakespeare.'

I have described the Shakespearean actor as an athlete and you too can be an athlete – in this sense, at any age. Many older, experienced actors are much fitter than the younger members of companies. Their fitness is in economy and precision: energy without effort.

Here is a very important point, which I will repeat in various forms throughout the book. As an acting *choice*, you can adopt the physical stance of denial or bluff. These stances will work as long as the flexible, clear energy of engagement is held in your body beneath them. The stance is only inappropriate when you lock or clutter the breath and voice in your body and lose awareness of the world within and without you. Flexible actors can do anything as long as their bodies are not locked and they remain alert and alive.

Movement coaches often say to me, 'Actors will work on their voices, but are reluctant to work on their bodies.' Believe me, without your body you have no voice!

The Work

In all my work I find it very instructive to experiment with the wrong way of doing an exercise. So play with adverse positions as well as the correct ones!

Centring the Body

At first, take time to feel each positioning. In time the whole process will only take a few seconds to do.

- Start with the connection you are making with the floor. Wear shoes that help you feel the floor or take your shoes off – trainers and heels are not helpful.
- Place your feet apart the width of your hips and parallel. Avoid the feet being too close together – denial – or too far apart – bluff.
- Feel the floor and feel the energy slightly forward on the balls of your feet. You should feel you could spring in any direction.
- Unlock any bracing of the knees and ankles.
- Unlock any clamping of the thighs.
- Put your hand just above your groin and try gently to release the abdominal muscles with the breath. As the breath enters, you should not stop it in the stomach or force it. Don't push the stomach out or hold it in. Allow the breath to release it. This is where the true power of your voice lies and where you connect to feeling and ultimately own the words you speak. Unless you are free here you will either be underpowered or forced.
- This area is also the place you move from.
- The spine should be up, not rigid or slumped. The slumped spine is denial. The rigid is bluff.
- If you sit forward on the edge of a chair you will begin to feel the moment when the spine finds its natural position.
- Keep your chest open, but not heaved up or sunken in. The hoisting or depression of the sternum (upper chest area) is a crucial indication of how open you are to an audience or to a text.

- Feel where you are tense. Playing Shakespeare places you in high pressure situations where tensions that seem unimportant in a life lived at low intensity will suddenly become a problem. Even the smallest and seemingly most innocent tensions, harmless in acting a low-key TV scene, can block and impede you and the play. Be aware of them. The two key areas that seem to be most problematic when actors enter Shakespeare are chest tensions and the abdominal holds.
- Now release the shoulders – don't hold or slump them. Swing your arms around as though you are gently throwing a ball underarm. You can do this with both arms separately or together. The important aspect of this exercise is after the swing to allow the shoulders to find their own place – that is, don't place or hold them. Any tension in the shoulders will block the breath and creep into the throat where after a few minutes on stage it will begin to close down your vocal range. Given the requirements of the breath to sustain the verse lines, long thoughts and passion in Shakespeare, even a small amount of shoulder tension will be deeply frustrating for you. And if you are playing a large role over three hours, there is going to be a massive problem if your vocal range is diminished – you'll be boring and very hard to listen to!
- Feel the centre of the body – the ribcage should be moving freely.
- Your head should be balanced on the top of the spine, not pushed forward, tucked in or pulled back. Let your head fall onto your chest and gently swing it from one shoulder to another. Shut your eyes and lift your head up. Only open your eyes when you feel it at the top of the spine.
- You must look out at the world, not away from it. I always like to start with the concept that Shakespeare's characters look directly at the world. They confront situations and the audience without shame. To survive, they don't pull away or push through with force, but stay open and alert.
- Your jaw should be released, not clenched: lips together, but the jaw released.
- Stay free of tension. Any tension or lock anywhere in the body will block the breath, voice and will also block your responses to language, your thoughts and your passions. Tension even stops you listening attentively – your concentration wanders.
- Flop over from the waist. Make sure the back of your neck is free, your jaw unclenched. Shake your shoulders free. Unlock your knees and stay on the balls of your feet. Try to release your spine and breathe into the abdominal area and back ribcage.
- Come up through the base of the spine. Allow your shoulders to

find their place. The head should come up last, balance effortlessly at the top of the spine and centre.

- Rock backwards and forwards and if you feel secure and able to keep your balance, you know that you are centred; if you totter, then the body is still holding extra tensions.

It's useful and fun to experiment at this point with adverse tensions. Locate some of the habitual tensions in your body and try rocking. You will notice how the tension, however small, knocks you off centre.

One of my favourite images when working with actors on Shakespeare is this. Shakespeare propels you into a rapidly changing and dangerous world. I suggest to actors that their world is changing, the earth moving and spinning in uncertain ways. In such circumstances you have to be more centred than normal – not braced or locked, which leads to 'presenting' Shakespeare rather than playing him. You have to be centred, a place of being alive, strong, flexible and vulnerable.

- So imagine yourself standing on ground that is moving. Think about this image when you next ride standing on the subway or underground. You will soon identify locks or tensions.
- Open yourself to the world both inside and outside your body.
- Without tightening your shoulders, swing your arms up to the gods. Allow the swing to start through your feet, knees and all the way up through the body. Look up, but stay very connected to the floor through the balls of your feet. An image that works for some people is that you are about to dive into a pool. You are going up but keeping forward and alert.
- Breathe and let your arms open to your sides with energy passing through to your fingertips and allow your head to find its position on top of your spine. You are now embracing the world. I call this position Da Vinci: it is the balanced, open human as depicted by Leonardo. You should feel energy flow out from your hands, through your feet into the ground and up through your head.

After doing this exercise you might feel the urge to pull away in some parts of your body. The Da Vinci position should make you feel open, but when you return your arms to your sides there might be a 'knee-jerk' sensation in parts of your body to withdraw. These reflexes are of enormous importance. They will recur, and as you become familiar with them they will alert you to the tension you have to deal with and give you the power to do so.

The open feeling you get from Da Vinci is strong, but it may also leave you feeling vulnerable as your physical tensions often act as a shell against the world. This vulnerability is particularly noticeable for the actor entering Shakespeare. The text has the power to shake you in such a way that you want to hide from or deny it – or you may distance yourself by holding it in such reverence that you can't stay open to it. To play Shakespeare we have to walk through dark and brilliantly sunlight landscapes. Stay open throughout.

Most unexpected, though, is a sensation I vividly remember from my own training. You may encounter it once you have found your centre. It is this: you are centred, perfectly placed – and yet you feel dead, vacant, spaced out. The reason is simple. Useless physical tensions often give you a sense of energy and effort that can feel exciting. Now that you have addressed them – freeing the old habits – you are left feeling naked and floppy. You need to replace them with the right tension or energy. I call it *the state of readiness*. It is an important concept, one that I've particularly introduced in teaching Shakespeare.

The State of Readiness

The state of readiness is a condition that is absolutely applicable to any character in Shakespeare. It's a place of survival. You can observe it in any unpampered creature; any animal aware of living; any sportsperson avid to win. The energy is efficiently centred in the breath and the breath support. All options are available – neither too relaxed (although you can appear relaxed) nor too tense. It's a place of poise and alertness.

Every character in every scene in Shakespeare either starts in or comes to be in this state. Sometimes they may have a few casual lines of unguarded 'normality' before the upheaval that will 'click' them into readiness; but that is all. The moment of the 'click' is critical, and revelatory. The readiness I am describing is a physical state of vivid alertness and presence that matches the heightened awareness and imagination of the Shakespearean character at this moment.

Juliet's first entrance is a good example. She is called for by her nurse:

> *Nurse*: Where's this girl? What, Juliet!
> *[Enter Juliet.]*
> *Juliet*: How now, who calls?
> *Nurse*: Your mother.
> *Juliet*: Madam, I am here.
> (I.iii)

Juliet's first line could be relatively casual but as soon as she hears it is her mother, there is surely a heightening of her being. The text tells us that they don't often communicate with ease. It might only constitute a small change initially, but as the scene progresses that physical heightening would intensify. Firstly, her mother seems to want to talk to her alone – unusual. Then she tells her to think of marrying. In this scene, Juliet starts to transform from a girl into a woman. As scene after scene develops, events are constantly raising the stakes in every way.

In *King Lear*, Edgar in his first scene has what seems a series of low-key exchanges with his brother until, taking in the import of what Edmund says, he is thrown into chaos and confusion.

> *Edgar*: How now, brother Edmund! What serious contemplation are you in?
>
> *Edmund*: I am thinking, brother, of a prediction I read this other day what should follow these eclipses.
>
> *Edgar*: Do you busy yourself with that?
>
> *Edmund*: I promise you, the effects he writes of succeed unhappily; as of unnaturalness between the child and the parent; death, dearth, dissolutions of ancient amities; divisions in state, menaces and maledictions against king and nobles; needless diffidences, banishment of friends, dissipation of cohorts, nuptial breaches, and I know not what.
>
> *Edgar*: How long have you been a sectary astronomical?
>
> *Edmund*: Come, come! When saw you my father last?
>
> *Edgar*: The night gone by.
>
> *Edmund*: Spake you with him?
>
> *Edgar*: Ay, two hours together.
>
> *Edmund*: Parted you in good terms? Found you no displeasure in him by word nor countenance?
>
> *Edgar*: None at all.
>
> *Edmund*: Bethink yourself wherein you may have offended him; and at my entreaty forbear his presence, until some little time hath qualified the heat of his displeasure, which at this instant so rageth in him that with the mischief of your person it would scarcely allay.
>
> *Edgar*: Some villain hath done me wrong.
>
> *Edmund*: That's my fear. I pray you have a continent forbearance till the speed of his rage goes slower; and, as I say, retire with me to my lodging, from whence I will fitly bring you to hear my lord speak. Pray ye go; there's my key. If you do stir abroad, go arm'd.
>
> *Edgar*: Arm'd, brother!
>
> *Edmund*: Brother, I advise you to the best.
> I am no honest man if there be any
> Good meaning toward you. I have told
> You what I have seen and heard – but
> Faintly; nothing like the image and horror
> Of it. Pray you, away.
>
> *Edgar*: Shall I hear from you anon?
>
> *Edmund*: I do serve you in this business.
>
> (I.ii)

By the line 'Some villain hath done me wrong', Edgar's heart must begin to beat differently. He grows alert as he listens to Edmund's description of their father's rage. Most children know this feeling – the fear and excitement that courses through us when we hear of a parent's anger, compounded with other sensations if we are unjustly accused. Edgar's physical readiness begins here and grows throughout the play. It is safe to say that if the two brothers were to fight now, at the beginning of their journey, Edgar wouldn't stand a chance. The physical click that starts here is what will grow and enable him eventually to defeat his brother.

Another example of this shift or 'click' into readiness is Prince Hal's first scene in *Henry IV Part I*. He talks with Falstaff and Poins in casual banter: the characters speak in prose. But by the end of the scene, Hal has moved into verse:

> *Prince*: I know you all, and will awhile uphold
> The unyok'd humour of your idleness;
> Yet herein will I imitate the sun,
> Who doth permit the base contagious clouds
> To smother up his beauty from the world,
> That, when he please again to be himself,
> Being wanted, he may be more wond'red at
> By breaking through the foul and ugly mists
> Of vapours that did seem to strangle him.
> If all the year were playing holidays,
> To sport would be as tedious as to work;
> But when they seldom come, they wish'd-for come,
> And nothing pleaseth but rare accidents.
> So, when this loose behaviour I throw off
> And pay the debt I never promised,
> By how much better than my word I am,
> By so much shall I falsify men's hopes;
> And, like bright metal on a sullen ground,
> My reformation, glitt'ring o'er my fault,
> Shall show more goodly and attract more eyes
> Than that which hath no foil to set it off.
> I'll so offend to make offence a skill,
> Redeeming time when men think least I will.
>
> (I.ii)

The change in form is significant. Something has clicked in Hal's earlier exchanges with Falstaff, a physical and emotional knowledge that gives him a form of epiphany. Now he understands that he has been mixing with villains and will have to change. He is growing up. We will nearly all have a moment like that. We can drink, behave badly and rebel but one day some sense of survival will save us, make us pull ourselves out of that destructive company. Today is Hal's epiphany.

The state of readiness is not about being rigid or stiff. Once you have experienced it, you can even afford to slump as long as you still feel alert and engaged. There just has to be something happening inside you – inside your body, heart and head. But it's hard to sustain. I've said the Shakespearean actor needs to be an athlete. By that I don't mean that you have physically to sculpt yourself; rather that maintaining this state of readiness and engagement is exhausting. To stay 'clicked' and alert for three to four hours takes enormous energy, focus and concentration. It requires work and practice to develop: it has to be built up. Most students come equipped to stay concentrated for ten to twenty minutes. In order to sustain concentration for hours it has to be worked like any muscle: trained into the muscle memory.

Here's a simple example. If we drive a car well, we are always alert and engaged. If on a long motorway journey we find ourselves drifting and unfocused, we should stop the car before we kill someone. Acting is less dangerous than driving, but the feeling of readiness is the same. To put the hazards another way, imagine someone playing your life story and reducing all the great and important moments to a physical and vocal slump: everything that matters would be ironed out.

There are minutes, days and nights in all our lives that we will remember on our deathbeds or in our dreams. Shakespeare writes only about these moments, these states of readiness.

Here are a few simple exercises to make you feel this state and eventually be able to recapture it. It is, after all, known to us all – we have all experienced feeling switched on and fully alive. When you begin to touch and harness this feeling, it will be surprisingly easy to recapture it at will. You can prepare text, rehearse and, of course, perform with it.

- Walk around a room as though you have somewhere urgent to go. Feel centred on the floor without looking down. Feel the floor. You can walk swiftly – run into walking, walk slowly but with intent. What you can't do is shuffle or wander. You must feel focus and direction as you walk. After even a minute of this walking, you will feel more engaged and alive. At that point stop and centre, but feel all the energy of the walking in you – filling you. You will feel more ready, alert and more three-dimensional. Energy moves all around you. If an actor is in this state, even looking at his or her back will be exciting for the audience. There is no dead place in the body.

- Try pushing a partner or using a wall. If you really needed to push the wall down because someone you loved was trapped, you wouldn't lock shoulders and knees or be back on your heels. You would begin to touch the huge power you have in your breath and the lower abdominal area. You wouldn't physically indulge in the useless tensions of denial or bluff.
- Experiment with some of these useless tensions. See how weak you become and how displaced the breath energy is if you tense your shoulders or lift the upper chest. Lock your knees or hold your stomach in; go back on your heels. You cannot efficiently push with these tensions. As you unlock them, you begin to touch your whole power and feel the strength of the lower breath support. As you come away from the push and re-centre, try to keep the memory of the power in your body.
- At this point it will be interesting to note where you want to replace tension or pull back from your power – to deny it. These are the knee-jerk tensions that regularly crop up in your acting and block the text. They are your tensions, not the text's. Take note of them, for they can impede the power and the momentum of the verse and block the text's passion – which generally results in the actor pushing the voice when emotion is required. They appear if you strive falsely without real thought or imagination to become heightened.
- Repetition will be needed to feel constant readiness and address useless tensions. Repeat the walking. Go back and push. Return to centre. Keep experimenting with the freedom and power you feel in the walk or the push when you return to centre and readiness.
- Begin to be aware of the breath in these exercises.
- Another favourite physical activity that has the same effect as pushing is holding a chair above your head. Breathe. Feel the breath go down. At this point it is impossible or uncomfortable to tighten shoulders, chest, stomach, knees, etc. Your unnecessary tensions become apparent and useless. When you replace the chair on the floor, you will be able to observe centre and readiness in your body. Eventually you can energise sections of text by using the push or the chair to engage with a text as you speak it.

What you are doing is building up in your body *a memory of readiness* which will eventually embed itself in you and remain constant through you as you act Shakespeare.

As you grow acquainted with it, you will be able to transfer this feeling to any physical stance. I am not suggesting you have to speak Shakespeare in a perfectly centred way, but I do believe that the state of readiness is necessary to attempt his plays and be truthful to them. When your body has internalised this energy as a state of reality and truth, no physical habits of denial or bluff will block the play's energy.

Once you have this awareness you will be able – where it is a valid character choice – to slump or slouch but you will do so with life and energy. A slumped Iago should still be an alert predator. Goneril can be played in Versace and drink a vodka and tonic, but she still has to be working her main chance and playing for high political and personal stakes. As soon as Juliet sees Romeo, she holds him in the alertness of her body: even if she is draped on the balcony before he comes, she is filled with this awareness, this readiness. As Hamlet says, 'If it be now, 'tis not to come; if it be not to come, it will be now; if it be not now, yet it will come – the readiness is all'.

Shakespeare, like all great theatre, is about the life force of readiness. The audience might enter the theatre half dead and disengaged but the actor has to be on this level of energy and engagement throughout.

If you start to rehearse in this physical state, you have a chance of realising the plays. If you start internally and physically flaccid, the plays go down the drain. They disappear. Physical deadness kills the plays – they lose their vitality and muscle. Neither you nor the play have a chance. The sooner the actor engages physically, the sooner the play can be rehearsed.

- Use a section of Shakespeare to experiment. Speak the text from a state of readiness.
- Now speak it with the physical habits that deaden you.
- Return and speak it with readiness.

I'm willing to bet that already the readiness has begun to enliven your speaking and connect you to the text. It is also probable that your voice has more body, range and life in it.

There is a theatre cliché that it is dangerous to act alongside an animal or child. In reality the danger only exists where the actor is not in a state of readiness or is bluffing one. Animals and children are for the most part naturally in this state and will only upstage the disconnected, unready actor. The audience's eyes and ears are inevitably drawn to the more alert and vivid life force on stage. However hard and diligently the unready actor works, we won't want to look or listen. Crab the dog scratching itself with readiness is far more interesting than an actor playing Launce who is not really ready but pushing for truth and laughs – in other words, pretending.

Breath

The Aims

- To have a free, flexible and powerful breath system.
- To have a breath system that will respond to any length of thought, passionate feeling or epic space.
- To have a breath system that moves easily through the body without locks and can change rhythm and pace effortlessly.
- To have a breath system that can support a full range in the voice, change character and recover quickly and silently.

The Reasons

Oxygen and breath power the voice, feed the brain and fuel the heart. You are about to embark on some of the most passionately felt plays ever written, full of long and often complex thoughts. You will need oxygen to explore them. Your voice will need breath to be free, to have full range and to be propelled forward on the wave of the iambic, the line, the thought, the scene. You will need oxygen to be able to listen to and receive the language of other characters on the stage. You will need breath to explore the many specific emotions in a part, the reflections in a character's soul, the transformations they undergo. You will need to alter the rhythm of your breath. Every human being breathes differently and Shakespeare writes each character with a different rhythm of breath that changes as they change.

Without a free, powerful and flexible breath actors will often resort to shouting the text – power from the throat, not the breath and the whole body. They cannot sustain the energy of a thought: they break it up, rendering it nonsense to the audience, and shattering the rhythm and the music of the verse. Verse needs air. Without oxygen heightened passion sounds pushed and generalised. Alternatively, actors try to make the plays sound naturalistic, and discuss great world events as though they are chatting about what they ate for supper. This denial is not always to do with the imaginative failing of the actor but a physical inability to breathe sufficiently. The events in Shakespeare's plays are not mundane or unimportant. They should shock us – for good or ill – and when we are shocked we need oxygen or we pass out.

Without breath the voice will lack range. The internal power of the iambic, of the play's momentous structure will bleed away. Characterisation through the breath and its rhythm will be dispelled. Both actor and play will be suffocated and the text submerged and lost.

To breathe properly is to tap into the human source of all energy – oxygen. With breath you can stay in the moment, on the word and on the line. Actors overwork when they are not breathing. Real breath energy makes the actor work as effortlessly as can be.

The Work

We start with stretching the muscles that open the ribcage, to help keep the breath moving easily through the body with the breath muscles alive and exercised. These stretches must be done without any lifting or tensing of the shoulders or upper chest. They should engage muscles around the centre of the body – the ribs – and deeper into the lower abdominal area.

You have already explored the action of these muscles when you pushed a partner or a wall in the state of readiness exercise. In pushing, or holding a chair above your head, you will have begun to touch the important muscles of breath support.

Stretches
- Side stretches: stand centred, knees unlocked, and gently stretch to one side. Breathe. Do the other side. Each time you re-centre, you should feel wider around the ribcage.
- Repeat, but extend the stretch by pulling over with your arm. You can hold the wrist of the stretching arm to give a greater side-rib extension.

- Back stretches: the hug flopped over from the waist. Without tightening the shoulders, firmly hug yourself. With the hug in place, flop over for a breath. Keep your knees unlocked and the back of your neck free. You will feel the back open and muscles in the lower abdominal engage. Be careful as you stand up and centre. You might feel dizzy, but you should feel the back of the ribcage opening. Accompany each stretch by a calm, silent breath in through the nose and out through the mouth.
- The hug with squat: repeat the above exercise but in a deep squat position. This will open the deeper areas of breath.
- The prayer position: this opens the back and releases energy into the lower body. Get on to your hands and knees. Keeping your thighs unclamped, allow your bottom to collapse on to your feet. Release your body over until your head touches the floor. Keep your arms and shoulders relaxed. Breathe and you will feel engagement throughout your breath. After a few breaths, sit back onto your feet and you should feel the breath settle deep into your body.
- The abdominal release: feet wide apart, knees bent over feet, spine up. One hand above the groin, the other on the ribcage. Keep the ribcage moving as you feel the abdominal muscles release low into your body.
- Lie on your back with your knees hugged to you. Breathe. Release your arms but keep your legs dangling up and allow the breath to go deep into your body. Your breath muscles are being gently stretched open. The body is becoming more alive with breath. You should feel wider and calmer. The breath should feel low in the body, never high in the chest.

You have been stretching to get the breath into the body. As you do this you should begin to invest in a simple but profound notion of a *readiness in the breath*. Feel it first at the moment in the inward breath when you are naturally ready to act, to move, to speak; and then in the outward breath when you feel the natural desire to breathe in. Don't go beyond that moment. You will still have breath but it won't be enough to propel a vigorous speaking energy. To speak Shakespeare, you must work within these two realms. You should speak only when you are ready, and take breath when you and your body need it. If you go beyond these natural yet extended realms, you will find yourself in difficulty.

The sensation of readiness in the breath is actually very simple to discover, and very familiar. Gently breathe in. You will feel a point when you are ready. You felt it before just as you were about to push the wall. The moment before you push is the moment of readiness. Imagine throwing a ball. Just before you throw, the breath has settled into a position of readiness and you then throw with the breath, not before or after it. The ball is propelled on the breath as is the voice and the word.

It is equally true that when you breathe out, there is a distinct moment when you know you should breathe in – a natural place in the body at which it needs breath. If you go beyond it you will be squeezing and forcing the breath and your voice.

To speak without readiness in the breath is not only unnatural. It apologises, with a pushing that signals no true right or power to speak; or it is a panic moving towards to hysteria. It is a sign of weakness, a physical reflection of low self-esteem, a symptom of impotence. It is not the norm in Shakespeare. His characters suffer all sorts of doubts, but they do not suffer from an inability to breathe or speak. Speaking is their release and their solace, not their horror. They are heightened and alive in their breathing and speaking; it's very hard to feel alive on a half breath or a locked one.

Vocalising the Breath Capacity

When the breath has been stretched, you should build up your capacity. Remember that long thoughts and passionate feeling require more breath. As this build-up continues, check that you are not tightening shoulders or chest. Check that you only start the release when you feel the breath in your body (the point of readiness) and don't go beyond your breath – that is, lose contact with the breath muscles and squeeze the breath out, constricting your vocal equipment. Work and stretch within the confines of ease.

These exercises can be performed walking, running, throwing a ball against a wall, pushing a wall. Your breath capacity will improve rapidly. Start the exercises two weeks before you begin a rehearsal period, particularly if you've been working on film or TV. Remember you are constantly aiming at a place of ease so that your technique releases the text rather than your lack of technique blocking it.

- Breathe in and gently release on an *s* for ten seconds. If you run out before, don't despair: work will increase your capacity. Build up the release to twenty and then to thirty-five seconds. This might take six weeks of diligent but gentle practice.

- Now control this capacity by using a *z* or *v* (without jaw tension) over twenty to thirty seconds. Aim to keep the sound strong, steady and sustained.

Next strengthen the ease and flow of your recovery ability for long and short demands on the breath. As the pressure builds on your breath system, be extra vigilant about shoulder and chest tensions, gasping and panic breaths. There will also be a tendency for the breath to creep higher in the body – keep it low.

Remember you shouldn't hear yourself breathe in or out – aim for silence. You can work with breath through your mouth or your nose. The mouth breath is generally connected to shorter thoughts and a more panicked feeling. It can dry your voice if used too much. The nose breath takes time and is connected to longer thoughts, more considered and a deeper preparation in feeling. You should be able to use both and mix and match them.

- Release on *z* as far as you can go, but recover before any squeezing happens. The muscles around the ribs and abdominal areas are working, not the spine or chest collapsing.
- Go as far as you can again and then recover.
- If you try three of these and don't feel tense, carry on.
- If you can do seven with ease, then you are getting fit and prepared for Shakespeare.

Now prepare the fast but low recovery of breath.

- No tension in the upper body.
- Count aloud 'one', recover, then 'one, two', recover, then 'one, two, three', and so on up to fifteen.
- Build up speed, pace and ease of the breath coming in – no gasping.
- Speak a speech with the ease of a full breath as opposed to a held, a gasped or no breath. Keep breathing with ease throughout.

The difference, I hope, will be clear. Finally, try learning speeches while making a conscious effort to breathe easily. The text will enter you faster and be learned more efficiently.

By now your breath capacity will have increased, you will feel an ease of recovery, and you will be attuned to the physical knowledge of when you are ready to speak with the breath and when you need it. Try to ensure that you have reached this state before you even go to rehearsal. The fitter your breath is before rehearsals start, the further your work will go. Too many actors use rehearsals to get fit and therefore miss out on the valuable experimental work and time they should provide.

Support

The breath should now be working, and we need to address the muscles that support the breath.

Support is the physical connection from the muscles of the ribcage and lower abdominal area to the breath.

The breath fuels and powers the voice. The support muscles fuel and power the breath. No committed sound or utterance can be freely made without support.

Support is the most natural process – a baby's scream is supported. Animals don't make sound without it. In theory, if you are breathing naturally you will be supporting your voice. Yet I frequently encounter actors who know how to breathe, but fail to use that breath to support their voices. Their breath systems lock or deflate too quickly.

You can breathe and not support the breath. If you do this on a Shakespearean text, you will exhaust yourself. You can often observe actors working so hard with their breath but not getting anywhere because the breath isn't supporting the voice with the appropriate muscles. It's like swimming and trying to propel yourself through the water with splayed fingers – all splash and little movement. Without support you cannot free your voice, think, feel fully, or power a heightened text.

You will have supported your voice naturally whilst pushing a wall or throwing a ball – if you can't throw a ball or push effectively, you are not using support.

Along with the physical state of readiness I have described, and equally importantly, there is a *breath support readiness*. It enables you to speak on the breath, not before or after or without the breath support. Support is active centre: there is no true state of readiness without it. It is not only an active speaking energy, but an active listening one. No one on the stage of a Shakespearean play can afford to be inactive. You can be still and active, but what you cannot be is still and internally dead.

The Aims

- To support the breath constantly at every moment in a play – through the word, the line, the rhythm, the thought and the intense passion of the work.
- To listen and respond with support.
- To start and end with support.

The Reasons

Without support you cannot power your voice or any of the energising forms, structures and givens in these plays, and it is extremely hard to own ideas, feelings, individual images or words.

Unless you start each line with support, you cannot be 'in the moment'. If you try to support the breath after you start to speak, or hold the support before, you will be off the line and out of the moment. The same is true if you rush to speak before the support is there, or deflate – sigh – before speaking. In each case you will either be squashed by the text or push falsely through it, covering the words with generalised emotion.

But if you support the breath you will have the chance to communicate with ease, emotional truth, power and specificity.

The Work

- Gently breathe in until you feel an active state of readiness on the breath. It should be a very clear feeling.
- Sometimes swinging the arms as though you are about to throw a ball or spear will help this feeling. It is a moment when the breath settles in the body: not a lock, but a moment of suspension.
- Breathe in; feel the active support; breathe out when you sense the support is under the breath.
- Throw a ball as the breath settles, on the breath and with the breath. The ball is being sent on the support.
- For another exercise to aid this sensation, push gently against a wall to feel the breath settle and then feel the release as you release from the wall.

Now experiment with not using support. You will find that if you come off the breath support, you will come off the moment in the text. See if you recognise your own habit of not supporting.

- Breathe in and hold support before speaking. You will be behind the impulse of the line.
- Breathe in and speak without getting full support, before the full power is there. You will be rushing ahead of the text.
- Breathe in and then deflate before speaking. You will be de-energising the text and word.

By trying out different support habits, you will learn to recognise when you are failing to support – and when you are on your support.

It might, as a deliberate choice, be possible to play certain characters in Shakespeare without support. It would be hard to make yourself heard but with work the choice could be achieved. For instance, it is possible to imagine playing a powerful monarch or tyrant this way. Their power means they don't have to work: everyone around them has to, but they can sit back and wait for the world to come to them.

I recently tried this notion with an actor playing Richard II. We thought no effort, no support, was a possible Richard norm. To begin with he rehearsed the first scene this way but as Bolingbroke and Mowbray entered eighteen lines into the play, the temperature rose and Richard became under threat. As his throne began metaphorically to wobble, he needed to be alert and engaged – and immediately the actor found himself switching onto support. Being off support is not safe when the world spins unexpectedly. But it was useful to think that this might have been the first time in many years that Richard had had to be so heightened. The long-term inattentiveness that is part of being off support might have lain at the root of his present difficulties. It was the sign of a complacency all too ripe for questioning.

At first it may take some time to support the voice but that will change with work. Support is a muscular sensation in the breath and voice; without it, it is very hard to feel the muscular structures of word, line, rhythm and thought as you speak. With support and the breath low in the body, you will eventually be able to speak faster in the moment than without it.

- Take a line of text and build it up word by word using breath and support – for instance, 'I left no ring with her' from *Twelfth Night*

(II.ii.): breathe, 'I', breathe, 'I left', breathe, 'I left no', breathe, 'I left no ring', breathe, 'I left no ring with', breathe, 'I left no ring with her'.

By supporting you will gain not only vocal clarity and ease, but an emotional connection to the words and the thoughts and feelings within them. When you deliberately place oxygen under a word it begins to live in and with you. This reality can be explored by speaking a speech first without breath or support and then with both. You will gain a whole arena of sound and sensation with the support as well as a greater understanding of the words. As soon as you support, you become active and on the words, travelling through and with them.

Support is active. Even when you are silent, as long as you actively support the breath you will be alert and alive. In order to listen you must have support. The muscular exchange of air keeps you connected to yourself and the world. Try learning a text with support. You will learn it more quickly and know it more profoundly. Try to prepare any heightened text actively not passively. Rehearse with support and you will engage with other actors, yourself and Shakespeare immediately. Observe the next time someone doesn't listen or engage with you – they will probably not be supporting the breath.

Freeing the Voice

The Aim

- To produce a free and unconstricted voice that can move with ease and express any emotion or idea without pushing or straining.

There is a common misconception about a free voice. A free voice isn't necessarily beautiful or elegant; it is one that will move with the intention and sound appropriate to the content of the text. This means a free voice can be ugly or beautiful as required. A free voice is further able to express all the structured energy within a text. If the voice isn't free it cannot play the iambic – for instance, it will either ignore or overstress the beat.

Vocal tension blocks the actor from the text, and the audience from both actor and text. A locked voice interferes with speaking and listening – giving out and taking in. Speeches end up either pushed and shouted or swallowed and de-energised: the vocal equivalents of bluff and denial. In either case, the audience might observe the actor going through some vague ordeal but they can't guess what it might be. It might be interesting for a scene or two but it can never illuminate a play.

Vocal freedom is essential in heightened speaking with highly energised verse lines and passionate expressions of thought or heart. It is essential to sharing – and these plays were written to be shared.

The Reasons

Shakespeare's world is a world of speakers, a world that enjoys language and the exchange of ideas. It is a place full of vocal colour, definition and silence, where speaking is an art. Our world by contrast is full of noise, imprecision and stress, where it's a struggle to hear or be heard. Our modern voices tend to be held and tight – tight jaws, riddled with urban stress. We either fight the world vocally, pushing aggressively at it, or avoid committing ourselves to speech, underusing our voices. Both options reduce the range and enjoyment of the voice. Tension locks sound and words into the speaker. We have to unlock sound in order to release every quality embedded in Shakespeare's language. Trying to release Shakespeare while vocally constricted could, at worst, physically damage your voice. More likely, you will just not be heard – or be so difficult and unpleasant to listen to that the audience will switch off. You risk reducing the text to one energy, one focus and therefore one dimension. Without freedom you cannot excavate the clues Shakespeare has sown in his text.

Perhaps a single-energy delivery would be acceptable in a short, modern play with short speeches, minimal dialogue and simple language – perhaps! But to expect an audience to sit through a three-hour play with long speeches, elaborate thoughts and rich complex language, all delivered in one dimension, is too much to ask.

The Work

As we progress, you will realise that we are building on foundation stones that need to be permanently in place. The work you've already done on physical centre and freedom, breath and support is constant and essential to the following work. Please keep checking that these things are securely present.

Even if you are naturally physically free and have good support, you might still constrict the voice – trap it in the body, so that sounds and words cannot leave you unimpeded. There are a few people who have naturally free voices that never feel blocked or tight, but they are a species under threat. Such freedom rarely survives the bruising nature of life.

There are several common ways of constricting the voice. Try to identify any that apply to you – you may have more than one.

- *Tension*: lodged somewhere in the throat, jaw, tongue, mouth or even the back of the neck. After long or athletic voice use, this tension might tire the voice or make it husky, covered in mucus –

the body's emergency procedure to protect against misuse – or feel as if some friction has occurred. It is possible that this tension never worries you if you are playing less demanding texts or usually act in TV or film. The vigorous nature of Shakespeare requires fine vocal tuning and strong support. Even the smallest vocal blockage will inhibit the voice and the text and make it impossible to sustain a three-hour journey through a play.

- *The push*: a general strain in the throat that can build up into the jaw and neck. Your face also tightens so speech becomes harder. Artistically you probably feel there are very few options to explore in your voice: only loud or soft! The push is exhausting, and increases in intensity when you are required to be more emotional. It can sound aggressive.

- *The push down*: here the voice is held down in the throat and chest, often in an attempt falsely to lower the pitch. The whole instrument is muffled. Free movement is impossible as the voice has been stuck in place; it rumbles around in the speaker's body, which means that the definition of the word is unclear. This voice is often heard at the back of the theatre but the word is unclear or woolly. There will be very little range available: to move the voice, you will probably have to jump notes – there will be no fluidity. For power you need to bellow. It is extremely tiring and a waste of your energy. Bluffers tend to push down.

The push and the push down affect some actors' voices only when they are doing Shakespeare. They adopt these tensions for the Bard! This is probably connected to the belief that something extra has to be done when acting Shakespeare, that some extra effort is required. My experience is that such actors usually believe they are not really good enough for Shakespeare, so they have to put on a voice. If you are one of those, think again. Start with your free voice: it's enough.

- *Devoicing*: this constriction is one of half-voice. The speaker is moving towards a whisper. The voice sounds coated, as though it is hidden behind glass. It is almost impossible to hear over space as the nature of the tension removes all power from the voice – it sounds fuzzy and makes it extremely hard for the speaker to engage emotionally, access range or define a word. This habit is often adopted by deniers and can sound sentimental or self-centred. It is sometimes used to try and intensify the text, although the result only clutters it. Some actors think it helps to make the text more naturalistic and conversational. In fact, it merely underpowers the writing, the actor and the audience.

- *Swallowing or pulling back*: half a word or line escapes from the speaker, the rest is pulled back. Energy returns into the speaker, de-energising both the actor and the audience. It's very hard to stay interested if every sound is dissipated in this way. It is impossible to articulate words fully or vary stress and range. Verse lines fall and dip away – they droop. The iambic is reduced and the voice sounds pessimistic. It sounds as though the speaker is giving up or moaning as the line is constantly deflated.
- *Jaw and tongue tension*: these can be a knock-on effect of any of the habits described earlier – but equally the tension can start here. Speaking 'trippingly on the tongue' is impossible. Clarity of word and variety of voice are out of the question, vowels get squashed and the emotional content of words is diminished.

Any of these tensions makes it almost impossible to speak the verse, complete an iambic, sustain a line emotionally or clarify a thought. Not only do they frustrate the audience by making the text unclear, but the actor will often feel bottled up in the mouth and make things even worse by trying to push through the blockage – which only renders the text yet more impenetrable.

Problems like these may seem unimportant when you are not under enormous pressure, but with the stress of a press night or an inaudibility note from the director, they can develop into something fearsome. And of course it is common for actors to feel safe with their tensions. You are used to them; the way they make you work is comfortingly familiar. But in reality, they implode the text.

Working with less demanding plays, some actors can go for years without registering any vocal restrictions. Only when they encounter the multi-layered Shakespearean text do they feel the tensions blocking their voices. Then they may express frustration at their lack of vocal freedom with a comment like 'I'm more interesting than I sound': a telling description of how voice tension has locked in their creativity and prevented what they are experiencing inside from coming out. To bypass the problem many – and perhaps unconsciously – adopt a 'Shakespeare Voice': the voice parodied in comic routines when Shakespearean actors are mocked.

A free voice feels effortless. If you start free you can begin to understand where the text's tensions and conflicts lie in the word, the line, the rhythm and of course the content. If your voice is free we will hear the complexities of the text, not your voice. The text will change your voice but you should always start from yourself. Eventually your voice's freedom will need range and muscularity – but if you add these to a voice full of tensions, you are likely to end up with the dreaded 'Shakespearean Voice'.

Too often we are tempted, by the awe we have of Shakespeare, combined with the power of his forms and content, to cheat. Don't cheat. Trust your free voice. It can do the job.

Begin by starting to free the voice, working from the outside of the vocal apparatus – the face – inwards to the throat.

- Release all facial muscles. Massage them. Massage your jaw. Massage the back of your neck.
- Bunch up your face and allow the muscles to return gently without placing them. After a couple of attempts at this, your face and jaw will feel freer – breathe and support the breath throughout.
- Smile and, keeping the smile in place, open your mouth as wide as you comfortably can. You will feel your throat open, and you will probably want to yawn.
- Stretch your tongue out over your chin three times, allowing it to return and find its own place.
- Yawn.
- With breath and support speak on the edge of a yawn. Feel your throat stretch open.
- Breathe in and out silently through an open throat. You should begin to feel breath settle in the lower support area and make a connection through the body – with no blockages.
- With lips together and jaw unclenched, breathe and begin to hum gently without tension in throat or jaw. If tensions creep in through the freeing process, think of the yawn.
- As you hum, remember to support.
- Continue humming until you feel your voice is motoring along without any splutters.
- Play with different notes, but keep the whole process effortless.
- Move into a gentle 'mah, mah, mah' sound.
- Intone – a gentle, supported release of continuous sound.
- Now intone over a count of five.
- Then intone and move into speaking on the same breath.
- Repeat this at least five times. Intone into speaking over ten.
- Imagine the support coming through an open channel.

- Push gently against a wall if you cannot feel support.
- Speak a speech with this ease: it might be alarming as you are breaking deep habits, but persevere.
- Return to your habitual tensions, if any, and feel the difference.
- Go back to the place of ease.
- Breathe.
- Support.
- Vocalise with no constrictions in your throat, jaw or tongue.
- Feel nothing in your throat or your jaw.
- You should start to feel connections to the text through the support muscles in your rib and lower abdominal areas – not in your throat or face.

Placing the Free Voice

The Aims

- To place the voice forward and allow the sounds and words to flow from you and out of you.
- To sustain this forward placing.

The Reasons

You might have a free voice which isn't placed forward, so it stops somewhere in the mouth. You might have a free voice that gets part of the way out, but then falls back into you because it is not sustained – a common cause of the falling line. Without forward release the voice is difficult to hear distinctly. Even a microphone won't help. A microphone will only amplify what is there, and highlight what is not.

Without forward placing of the voice, it is impossible for the muscles of articulation to define each word. If the energy of the voice isn't forward in the mouth, the muscles have no reason to work. Without definition, it is impossible to end a word and complete the full weight of a syllable, and hence impossible to speak the iambic and release the full rhythm of the text.

Without sustained forward placing, the verse line will fall. It will be impossible to convey the sense of long thoughts to the audience, or to support and develop the growth of an argument. Similarly, without forward placing the emotional power of a speech or scene will flag. It will stop and need starting again.

The release of the voice and the placing of words into space have an emotional effect. When you place a word out of you – into space – you begin to create the thing itself. This is particularly compelling when the language is so concrete and sensual. When characters speak, it is an event: they are making things happen – speech is not separate from action. That is why a curse, for instance, is so potent and frightening.

If you place words into space, you cannot call them back – they are out there – so in placing them there, you have to commit to what you have said, thought and felt. No retreat is possible. You must have meant them! This is important, because when we come to examine structure we will see that the underlying forms Shakespeare employs invariably move us forward. There is a very clear progression: you speak something; it exists; you move forward, step by step, word by word, thought by thought and feeling by feeling. To speak is tangibly to shift and change. In this way, Shakespeare's characters speak themselves into consciousness.

It is therefore essential that the word be placed out of you in order that you can move on. The trouble with this placing is that it is frightening. It takes an act of pure commitment and courage to speak out. It is precisely because we understand the power and transformation involved in speaking out that we are frightened of it and will spend hours in rehearsal trying to avoid this form of commitment. Once it is out there, there is no going back. We need to remember that most of Shakespeare's characters are in some way trapped or pushed into a corner and that speaking out is often their only means of escape. Words are the conduits out of heightened feelings into change and resolve.

> *Claudius*: O, my offence is rank, it smells to heaven;
> It hath the primal eldest curse upon't –
> A brother's murder [...]
>
> (*Hamlet*, III.iii)

Claudius has just observed the re-enactment of his murder of his brother. He has stopped the play, calling for light. Light has been cast into his consciousness. Though of course he already knew that he killed the king, this is the first moment when he really acknowledges to himself the nature of his crime, and begins to face it. We can know something but only truly recognise it when we articulate it, when we speak it out in clear, specific language. In this speech, Claudius edges forward through words, and for the first time speaks his crime, admitting it to the audience and himself as he does so.

- First step, a general recognition: 'O, my offence is rank'
- Second step, and it's getting worse: 'it smells to heaven'
- Third step, a terrifying moral perspective: 'It hath the primal eldest curse upon't'
- Fourth step, the truth of the fact: 'A brother's murder.'

Having at last spoken it, Claudius can move on to debate the consequences of his action.

Unless you commit to the release of words into space, you cannot follow the psychological journey of a character or penetrate the emotional heart of the text, for both are located in the rhythm of the speaking.

The Work

- Use a point just above eyeline as a visual aid. Imagine you will project towards it in an arc.
- Breathe and think to that point.
- Now vocalise on an 'oo' to that point. Use your lips to focus the sound forward.
- When you feel the sound forward, change from an 'oo' into an 'ah' – but be careful not to pull away. 'Ah' is an emotional and committed sound, which encourages us to deny it and pull it back. Also, avoid pushing the voice or jutting your head forward, tensing in the throat or jaw.
- Imagine throwing a dart or a ball to the point.
- Remember breath support – push a wall if necessary.
- Feel that you finish the sound outside you so that it doesn't droop or fall off and back into you.

Sustaining the sound requires not just physical, but intellectual and emotional energy too. Claudius' 'O' is the start of the release that will lead him into self-knowledge.

- Open the whole of your body to this release: 'oo' into 'ah'.
- Open your arms on 'ah'.
- Send it out.
- Repetition is important. Dynamic vocal release and energy can feel strange and untruthful at first, so you have to work to feel its power and importance.

- Repeat this simple exercise with support and an open voice until it feels effortless and the sound simply leaves you.
- Take this release into a whole speech – you might need to push a wall, throw an imaginary ball or hold a chair above your head to locate the support, but you will begin to know when it's free and released. The words will leave you. They won't feel trapped inside.
- Intone a line of text. Intone and move into speaking on the same breath. The speaking should have the same energy as the intoning. You should feel there is a gear change that energises the speaking. Intone a whole speech, occasionally moving into speaking.

When you have intoned a whole speech with support and an open voice placing, you will begin to grasp how much energy free, heightened speaking involves. Now return to speaking the text with the same commitment. It might feel strange, too big, too committed, but it will almost certainly feel fuller and more energised. The word will be clearer and more physical, and you will be meeting the text anew with oxygen, vigour and vitality.

Consolidation

At this point we have worked on the following fundamentals:

- The body: centred, ready and open.
- The breath capacity: flexible and extended with a strong and connected support system.
- The free voice: placed forward and out.

We will consolidate and marry this work by speaking the prologue from *Henry V*. To aid you in this, I would like you to imagine that you are a member of a small touring troupe of actors. Before your company has arrived at this particular town, leaflets and posters have been circulated promising a re-enactment of the battle of Agincourt.

As the audience gathers, one actor has to begin the show by explaining that there isn't a cast of thousands and that the play is reliant on the audience's imagination. Straws are drawn to decide who is going to explain this – and you are chosen. The speaking of the prologue is consequently infused with the energy of an actor surviving in front of an audience.

As you walk out to begin, you must physically carry authority but not bluff. Bluff could patronise and alienate the audience – tomatoes could be thrown. You centre, breathe and wait until the audience settles. When there is a hush you start, in a state of readiness with support and breath. The voice must be free: any push or tension could communicate aggression and it is essential that you please this crowd – you want them on your side. Denial would be equally annoying for them, as they must hear, without effort, all you say, and understand their particular role in the performance.

The words should be sent out with a placed voice to touch each corner of the theatre.

To survive and captivate, you need control of your body, breath, support and voice.

Enter CHORUS

Chorus: O for a Muse of fire, that would ascend
The brightest heaven of invention,
A kingdom for a stage, princes to act,
And monarchs to behold the swelling scene!
Then should the warlike Harry, like himself,
Assume the port of Mars; and at his heels,
Leash'd in like hounds, should famine, sword, and fire,
Crouch for employment. But pardon, gentles all,
The flat unraised spirits that hath dar'd
On this unworthy scaffold to bring forth
So great an object. Can this cockpit hold
The vasty fields of France? Or may we cram
Within this wooden O the very casques
That did affright the air at Agincourt?
O, pardon! since a crooked figure may
Attest in little place a million;
And let us, ciphers to this great accompt,
On your imaginary forces work.
Suppose within the girdle of these walls
Are now confin'd two mighty monarchies,
Whose high upreared and abutting fronts
The perilous narrow ocean parts asunder.
Piece out our imperfections with your thoughts:
Into a thousand parts divide one man,
And make imaginary puissance;
Think, when we talk of horses, that you see them
Printing their proud hoofs i' th' receiving earth;
For 'tis your thoughts that now must deck our kings,
Carry them here and there, jumping o'er times,
Turning th' accomplishment of many years
Into an hour-glass; for the which supply,
Admit me Chorus to this history;
Who, prologue-like, your humble patience pray
Gently to hear, kindly to judge, our play.
[*Exit.*]

• Stand and centre, weight forward on the balls of your feet. Release
your shoulders. Feel that your spine is up, that your head is
balanced on the top of your spine and that you are looking out at
an audience seated in a semi-circle around and above you.

- Swing your arms up and then release them down to the Da Vinci position without shoulder tension.
- Breathe and feel the support low in your body. Feel the support's readiness.
- Allow your arms to return to your sides without reducing or squashing your spine or chest. You must look and sound appealing.
- Speak the speech with support.
- Imagine the furthest point in the theatre and release an 'oo' to that point. When you feel the energy of the support or voice beginning to fall away from the space and back into you, recover the breath.
- With this forward, free vocal energy and support, intone the whole speech and then immediately speak it with full physical breath support and vocal engagement.
- You should feel how much breath energy is required to make a free and forward delivery. Anything less committed will result in the collapse of the body and breath and a withdrawal of the voice – which would signal a carelessness to the audience.
- You should feel how free the voice has to be to allow energy to pass through the mouth into the word. Any sense of tension will result in vocal pushing or constriction, which will impede the text and place a barrier in the audience's ears.
- Swing your whole body with the breath support underneath the movement and throw the beginning of each line with this motion.
- 'O for a Muse of fire'. Let your voice freely out. Then speak the speech for meaning.

This has been your first Shakespeare work-out. As the muscles tune and strengthen up, you will be able to make many different choices regarding delivery and interpretation; but until these essential muscles are trained you have few choices available, and little ability to interpret any Shakespearean speech.

Deepening the Work

The Reasons

It is quite possible to serve Shakespeare on a limited level with just the body, breath, support, freeing and placing work. But further preparation will enable you to have more fun, with more colour and choice available to you. It will fine-tune your ability to vocalise and speak the plays. In this section, therefore, we will build on the foundations already established in order to use the voice imaginatively; to speak clearly with ease, freedom and variety; and to develop strong and flexible speech muscles.

Remember above all that the audience has come to *listen*. Of course, they also use their eyes, but the visual is secondary to the aural because the action is primarily in the word and this they can only fully experience through the ears. This is simply not possible if the actor is boring to listen to, struggling to make sense of the text or fighting so hard with technique that we observe *how* rather than why and what is spoken. It reduces the play to the limited range of the actor's own weaknesses, rather than taking us beyond into the rich and expanded horizons of the text's world.

When actors perform in musicals, it is understood that they can sing. When you perform a Shakespeare play, it should be understood that you can speak and be thrilling to listen to. Incoherence is not an option and neither is vocal dullness.

In performance:

- The audience must hear every word.
- They must be enticed to listen, and wooed with vocal passion.

- The expression of thoughts must be crystal clear.
- The precision of every aspect of the writer's forms and words must be honoured in the delivery.
- The audience must not be aware of the actor's technique.

Ensuring this will require the next body of work and preparation. Any diligent, willing actor can achieve it. We all have good, flexible and muscular voices if we choose to use them.

Range and Resonance

The Aims

- To develop range and resonance, extending vocal texture, tone and movement.
- To deliver intellectual and emotional passion in the voice.

The Reasons

The more access you have to your range and resonators, the greater the choices you have as you speak. The variety of your expressions will grow limitless and exciting. The muscular working of the speech muscles is the final act of communication. Think of the physical making of a word as the tip of an iceberg, which focuses the whole of our being – body, breath, voice, head, heart and spirit.

The Work

- Warm up the resonators of the head, nose, face and throat. You can do this by gently humming and then speaking into each area. Keep on support and keep the throat open.
- Start on the head and play with each resonator as you come down into the nose, face, throat and chest. Avoid sinking into the body: always think out. Use the focus of a point above eyeline to help you. Each area will have a different texture and quality.
- After isolating each area return to speak a text on your full voice. You should sound richer in tone – the whole voice will be more available to you.
- Avoid pushing either in the voice or down into the throat and chest.

- Think up to the point above eyeline to work your range. Warm up your range by sliding down through it from the top down – always thinking up to the point above and outside you. As you shift the range of your voice, you will need more awareness of support. Without tension, move down and up: gradually any breaks in the range will go.
- Try to keep your head still. Don't move it up and down. Don't sink into your body on the lower notes or pull up the body for the higher ones.
- Now experiment by speaking a speech and overdoing the range, and then return to a more normal delivery. You should find that the voice has more variety and body.
- Now speak a speech aiming to sound elegant, then beautiful.

These voicings might feel odd, but at this stage you are extending both your physical voice and your imaginative response to it. I am not suggesting that you 'put on' a voice when you act, but that the voice should be flexible enough to respond to any text or character demands. You are widening your vocal landscape.

Clear Speech

The Aims

- To have such control and freedom of all your speech muscles that you can speak highly complex structures of language with ease and clarity without the audience noticing your technique.
- To feel each word clearly in the mouth, so you can stay in the moment – not in front of it because you are skidding across consonants or behind it because the speech muscles are slow to respond.
- To feel the physical quality of sounds and words in the mouth so you can recognise and respond when Shakespeare creates difficult speech sections as acting notes. Unless you have confidence in your own ability to speak clearly, you won't know when he offers you a complicated passage as a clue to character and situation.
- To be able to speak any rhythm clearly and keep up with rapid thought without tripping over sounds or words.

The Reasons

Without muscular clarity no-one will understand what you are saying. Without complete clarity of word and syllable, the rhythm cannot exist. Without a complete physical connection to word and form you cannot stay in the moment on the text.

If you do not stay on the text you miss the acting clues written into the physical word constructions – the most basic of which is that if something is difficult to say, the situation itself is difficult or uneasy.

> *Paulina*: What studied torments, tyrant, hast for me?
> (*The Winter's Tale*, III.iii.)

The profusion of *t*'s and *d*'s is hard to speak, and deliberately so. Paulina is forcing herself to speak clearly either to control her tears, or possibly to stop herself hitting Leontes. She is pinning him down with consonants.

Clear speech will also illuminate the ways in which pace reinforces content.

> Weary with toil, I haste me to my bed
>
> (Sonnet 27)

Speak the whole line accurately and you will plod along on 'Weary with toil', and trot rapidly off to bed on 'I haste me to my bed'. It would be nonsense to speak the first part of the line quickly and the second slowly. You will not do so if you speak it clearly. You might well if you speak it sloppily.

The Work

- Work all the muscles of articulation with breath support, an open throat and a free jaw.
- Work the lips, tongue, mouth and soft palette.
- Try a series of *b*'s, *d*'s, *g*'s, *r*'s and *l*'s.
- Chew the face around.
- Without voice, mouth a text. Be particularly careful to shape every vowel physically and touch every consonant. Be diligent and experience the beginning, middle and end of every word.
- Return and speak the text on a full voice. You will begin to feel the language differently. The text is immediately easier to speak, to get your mouth around physically.

Doing this you will also begin to notice all the more those places where Shakespeare creates obstacles within the words. He tells you by their physical nature when to take care and when to move forward quickly. You will feel the word controlling you. Speech muscles in good working order reveal his intentions; rusty muscles miss the clues as they struggle inappropriately. The clearer the articulation is, the clearer the thought.

The pace and rhythm of the text will also be more evident. By speaking everything that is written, you will stay in the moment, in the action of the text. You might have started to feel the spring of the iambic.

Now let's isolate the vowels. The vowels will help you reveal the feeling in the text.

- With support and an open throat, and aiming to place vowels as far forward as you can, speak only the vowels in a text: no consonants. During this exercise, you may well feel more connected to the heart of a speech – it can be very emotional.
- Return to speak the whole text. You will meet the consonants with relief as they begin to give order to an emotional outpouring. Your voice and connection to the text will be full and heartfelt. Notice how longer vowels open the heart, shorter ones close it down.

> *Paulina:*   Woe the while!
> O, cut my lace, lest my heart, cracking it,
> Break too!
>
>   (*The Winter's Tale*, III.ii)

The first set of vowels – 'W*oe* the wh*i*le / *O*' – opens up the feeling. Then the vowels begin to close as Paulina struggles to maintain control. Consonants – *t*'s and *k*'s – work to hold her emotions, just as the corset she is wearing presses on her heart and might even break it – a final, painful opening of the sound and feeling in despair.

> No longer mourn for me when I am dead
> Then you shall hear the surly sullen bell
> Give warning to the world that I am fled
> From this vile world, with vilest worms to dwell.
>
>   (Sonnet 71)

The open set of vowels sounds like mourning, and then you hit the final word with a short vowel and a literal cutting off – 'dead'. It's over and you must stop mourning. You can hear the bell tolling in the second line through the vowels, but then notice how they shorten and close emotion and move you into the fourth line. Feel the disgust in this line as the vowels mirror the vile world and worms.

Form is content. Dead is dead in the speaking of the word 'dead'. If you mean and imagine what you say as you say it – not before, not after, but on and with the word – Shakespeare will act you. You do not have to act Shakespeare. He gives you all you need.

That is why many great Shakespearean directors say is there is no subtext in his text. It is what it is. 'Just speak it' is a note often given to actors. It means trust it, meet it, don't clutter it. These things are only possible if the text work marries completely with content. Feel, think and speak simultaneously, and all will be revealed!

Listening

It sounds basic but it's the first and last thing you must do. You must practise listening, not to your voice, but to the outside world.

Unless we listen in Shakespeare, we won't hear the richness of the language or follow complex thoughts and debates. Ideas develop and grow, they don't stay entrenched and constantly repeated. If we miss one part of a point, we won't be able to follow the next stages, which move us as they move forward.

I don't think we can really listen – hear with the full clarity we need – until we are physically free, breathing calmly, engaging support and open in the throat and jaw. Attention to ourselves and to the outside world can only be achieved in this open yet active state. Freedom in the ears needs freedom throughout the breath and vocal systems. When people are tight and tense in their bodies, or emotionally or intellectually, they are not really listening. They are receiving through filters, straining to hear.

These plays are about survival, and in order to survive we need to listen out. We all have memories of feeling threatened in ways that make us very alert to sound – if someone is following us, for instance. Our ears twitch open: if they don't and we remain sealed off from the world, the stalker will get us. Likewise in an important argument or debate, you are bound to lose if you don't pay attention. Even those who who find it convenient to appear partially deaf will suddenly hear very clearly when they think it matters. My grandmother claimed to be hard of hearing until we spoke about her – then she miraculously heard every word!

Hearing is often about will and need. Some of the most powerful people seem not to hear, until, that is, it matters. Just consciously reminding yourself each day to listen to others can improve your ability to hear.

To listen attentively is also to be gracious, compassionate and interested in humanity. If Shakespeare's work, in which these virtues shine through above all others, is anything to go by, he must have been an extraordinary listener.

The Aims

- To hear the plays clearly.
- To receive the language and ideas objectively.
- To sense aurally the physical structures of rhythm, stress and rhyme.

The Reasons

You must listen to stay in the play, in the moment, with the other players and the audience. The inability to listen cuts you off from the world. You need to stay attentive in your spirit.

Lorenzo in *The Merchant of Venice* explains to Jessica the power of listening:

> *Lorenzo*: The reason is your spirits are attentive;
> For do but note a wild and wanton herd,
> Or race of youthful and unhandled colts,
> Fetching mad bounds, bellowing and neighing loud,
> Which is the hot condition of their blood –
> If they but hear perchance a trumpet sound,
> Or any air of music touch their ears,
> You shall perceive them make a mutual stand,
> Their savage eyes turn'd to a modest gaze
> By the sweet power of music. Therefore the poet
> Did feign that Orpheus drew trees, stones, and floods;
> Since nought so stockish, hard, and full of rage,
> But music for the time doth change his nature.
> The man that hath no music in himself,
> Nor is not mov'd with concord of sweet sounds,
> Is fit for treasons, stratagems, and spoils;
> The motions of his spirit are dull as night,
> And his affections dark as Erebus.
> Let no such man be trusted. Mark the music.
>
> (V.i)

The Work

- This is hard to do in cities, but try to sit quietly for ten minutes every day. This helps to clean your ears. Then take this journey:
- Listen to yourself breathing for three minutes.
- Then move your hearing outside yourself.
- Note how many noises you can hear.
- Start from the closest to you and then move outwards.
- Reach out with your ears as far as you can.
- Do this exercise at different times of the day and night.
- Find opportunities to sharpen up your hearing. Certain environments are especially useful. Sitting in churches or libraries always activates the ear.
- Seek out unamplified music and singing.
- Turn the radio and TV down and still follow the programme.
- Eavesdrop on conversations across crowded rooms. Try to hone your ears to specific voices.
- When you hear a foreign language, listen for its music, its rhythm, stress and inflection. Hum those qualities.
- When you are listening to views not your own, try to stay open and not block what is being said by your own thoughts rising in your head.
- Try not to interrupt people; hear them out. Don't assume you know what they are about to say.
- Stay attentive in rehearsals.
- Stay attentive as an audience member.

All this focus requires huge stamina and concentration. At first you might only be able to achieve it for a few minutes at a time, but your concentration span will extend with work and you will notice rapid improvements in your hearing and awareness.

Hamlet's Advice

We have come to the end of the first stage of the work on preparing to speak Shakespeare. Let's look now at Hamlet's advice to his actors, and find common ground with what we have done so far.

Remember how important the play within the play is to Hamlet. He needs the performance to be strong and truthful to expose his uncle's guilt. It matters that the play is acted well. It is not a casual piece of entertainment: it is a carefully planned tool. If the actors are inaudible or slur their words, if their acting is untruthful or they bluff, it won't work. Hamlet knows that if they shout or push or are physically wooden and disconnected, Claudius will not listen, be engaged or moved. He knows that in order to catch the king, the play must be well spoken. Bad speaking or acting will give the audience the opportunity to 'switch off'. It is crucial that the message, however unpalatable, be given truthfully. If the actor comes out of the moment or is a caricature of a human being, the audience has been given permission not to listen, not to attend.

In all the basic preparation so far, we have been working to remove the physical constrictions in the body, voice, speech and ears, so that the text can come through freely and be heard deeply.

> *Hamlet*: Speak the speech, I pray you, as I pronounc'd it to you, trippingly on the tongue; but if you mouth it, as many of our players do, I had as lief the town-crier spoke my lines. Nor do not saw the air too much with your hand, thus, but use all gently; for in the very torrent, tempest, and, as I may say, whirlwind of your passion, you must acquire and beget a temperance that may give it smoothness. O, it offends me to the soul to hear a robustious periwig-pated fellow tear a passion to tatters, to very rags, to split the ears of the groundlings, who, for the most part, are capable of nothing but inexplicable dumb shows and noise. I would have such a fellow whipp'd for o'erdoing Termagant; it out-herods Herod. Pray you avoid it.
> *1st Player*: I warrant your honour.

Hamlet: Be not too tame neither, but let your own discretion be your tutor. Suit the action to the word, the word to the action; with this special observance, that you o'er-step not the modesty of nature; for anything so o'erdone is from the purpose of playing, whose end, both at the first and now, was and is to hold, as 'twere, the mirror up to nature; to show virtue her own feature, scorn her own image, and the very age and body of the time his form and pressure. Now, this overdone or come tardy off, though it makes the unskilful laugh, cannot but make the judicious grieve; the censure of the which one must, in your allowance, o'erweigh a whole theatre of others. O, there be players that I have seen play – and heard others praise, and that highly – not to speak it profanely, that, neither having th' accent of Christians, not the gait of Christian, pagan, nor man, have so strutted and bellowed that I have thought some of Nature's journeymen had made men, and not made them well, they imitated humanity so abominably.

1st Player: I hope we have reform'd that indifferently with us, sir.

Hamlet: O, reform it altogether. And let those that play your clowns speak no more than is set down for them; for there be of them that will themselves laugh, to set on some quantity of barren spectators to laugh too, though in the meantime some necessary question of the play be then to be considered. That's villainous, and shows a most pitiful ambition in the fool that uses it. Go, make you ready.

(III.ii)

Here are the stages of Hamlet's advice:

1. He asks for clear, effortless articulation – and just to prove it can be done, he speaks a tongue twister: 'trippingly on the tongue'.

2. He doesn't want them 'to mouth it', i.e. show effort in their performance. Over-enunciated and affected speaking encourages the audience to watch and listen to the actor's craft rather than the words spoken. Hamlet wants them interested in the play, not the actor's mouth.

3. 'Nor do not saw the air too much with your hand'. This is a brilliant description of a physically uncentred actor flaying about on stage. The less centred you are, the harder it is to control your arms or your stance – smooth movement requires a rooted centre. The more heightened and emotional the actor becomes, the more control is required. Only uncentred actors fidget or flap. When a centred actor moves from centre, the

movement will feel connected and part of the performance, aiding not hindering it.

4. Hamlet hates vocal pushing – it offends his soul and splits open the ears of the audience closest to the stage, growing to a crescendo as the emotional charge of the play intensifies. The violent imagery Hamlet uses to describe the 'robustious' actor brilliantly captures the approach of one who is unfree and locked in his voice and body. This is the actor who bluffs.

5. On the other hand, Hamlet doesn't want the actor to be too tame: in other words, devoicing and under-energised. This is the actor in denial.

6. He asks the actor to be taught by discretion: 'Suit the action to the word, the word to the action.' This is the perfect description of an actor being in the moment and on the text. Mean what you say as you say it: not behind or ahead of the word, but fully and imaginatively with it at the moment of speaking.

7. Stay true to humanity. Don't over-act, embellish or play for cheap laughs. It might amuse some members of an audience, but those with judgement and discernment will know it's false. Hamlet has heard abominable actors praised who have nothing human about their portrayal – 'imitated humanity so abominably' – but it is a kind of profanity to be that bad. Shouting and bellowing are not the way to portray a character.

8. Don't improvise or add words. Learn the text accurately or you will lose the plot. Parts of the audience might enjoy it, but any actor encouraged by this is merely pitiful and ambitious.

So Hamlet's advice, in brief, is perfectly straightforward. It is a set of basic rules for any actor, and we do well to note it before moving on: speak clearly and well; stay centred; don't push or shout; don't devoice; stay on the text; be truthful; learn accurately; and don't improvise.

•

We have now reached an important crossroads. What we have done so far is what I think of as the foundation work of a classical actor. It generally takes about a year before a student owns organically and can use unconsciously the basics of support, vocal openness and placing out. With real diligence, it is possible to achieve it in months rather than a year. For the experienced actor returning to Shakespeare after a long absence, it may take about a month to get the flow and freedom back into the body and for the work to become unconscious.

That is the stage I want my students at the Guildhall to have reached at the end of their first year. I don't start on Shakespeare before then because the frustrations are too great. It is so difficult to attempt his texts if you haven't got support or can't sustain an open sound. But once you have experienced this work it will begin to flow and feel good. You will sense when the equipment is free and moving easily as the text begins to act you rather than you struggling with the text. You will have become a vessel.

Part 2 Structure

'I have with such provision in my art
So safely ordered...'

(The Tempest, I.ii)

'Ha, ha! Keep time. How sour sweet music is
When time is broke and no proportion kept.'

(Richard II, V.v)

The Givens

Many directors despair that young actors have no idea about how to begin to tackle verse speaking. Unfortunately and ironically, it is also true that many directors themselves have little idea! The consequence is that in some rehearsals of Shakespeare, verse speaking is never even discussed. It's like a conductor who isn't worried that the orchestra can't play the notes, but spends rehearsals trying to find ways to disguise the fact from the audience – perhaps with flashy lighting effects, or high-concept designs or unusual staging; even by dressing the musicians in exotic costumes. Anything to deflect attention from the basic absence of craft.

To some extent it has become fashionable not to speak verse well and indeed some drama schools don't teach it. The consequence is that those directors who do care about verse won't employ graduates of certain programmes precisely because of their ignorance and lack of craft. But the crisis is greater still: too often, even actors who want to learn can't find out. Knowledge used to be passed down by example, with older actors teaching young ones, and the plays themselves teaching through constant immersion. If you are steeped enough in the plays, they will tell you how they want to be acted, and reveal why they are structured as they are. But now as the older generations disappear, the newer ones – and this includes leading actors – have nothing to teach the freshmen. Even if they have an intellectual knowledge of Shakespeare, they haven't played him enough to own the work.

There is another problem: some actors feel that any formal education in Shakespeare's verse structure will suffocate their imaginative response to the work. This of course represents a profound misunderstanding. Knowledge of how a play is structured can only enhance the imagination and make the acting of it easier. It's a problem that really started in the late 1960s and early 1970s when there was a backlash against form and classical verse speaking. This was partly because younger actors at the the time felt there was no emotional engagement in the old style of speaking; and in many ways they were right. Well-spoken performances devoid of passion often rendered these powerful plays tame. Beautiful speaking had encased them and made them museum pieces that only appealed to certain self-satisfied audiences. They had become a well-played piece of music with nothing underneath.

The revolt against the perfect but dry coincided with a new political awareness shared by some actors and directors who felt uneasy with the middle-class aura that permeated 'classical theatre'. Clarity and a beautiful sound were demoted in favour of more naturalistic ways of speaking, even if this sometimes seemed to reward incoherence or led to verse being rendered as prose with no definition, no rhythm and no structure. And yet it is absolutely true to say that the adventurous, more imaginative approach to Shakespeare did pay dividends. The Royal Shakespeare Company in the late 1970s and early 1980s produced wonderfully spoken and emotionally exciting work. This was largely due to the fact that the actors who abandoned rigid verse speaking still had the concepts of verse embedded in them. They had encountered these rules at school, at university, at drama school; and they had worked alongside and been taught by actors who spoke the verse forms perfectly. They knew the rules they were breaking, and consequently an exciting marriage could and did take place: verse speaking that had spontaneity in it and was filled from beneath with emotion and the actors' imaginative connection to the word.

Today it is different. In the absence of an organic understanding of verse internalised through long experience, emoting, shouting, pushing and over-stressing are commonly used to convey meaning. It's a triumph of content over form – but unfortunately the content can't be understood without the form. The result, for an audience, is all too often a display of sound and fury – but no sense.

When I first started teaching in the 1970s, I often came across great actors who admitted that they didn't really understand the content of Shakespeare's speeches, but found a way through by accurately following the form of the verse. At the time, I worked as an apprentice to a brilliant – and slightly terrifying – classical voice coach. Her teaching was based on a similar principle. There was no intellectual or psychological exploration of the text. She believed that if you followed form, the emotional and intellectual life written into the text would automatically be released. At first I was sceptical. My own training had been based more in the new way – giving priority to thought and emotion – but I had to acknowledge, while working with that coach and those actors, that a strict observance of form did fully engage them and release the text.

Subsequently, I worked in many Eastern theatre traditions and found that the same approach applied. It was equally true, I later discovered, in the very different world of the New York City Ballet. There the genius choreographer George Balanchine had a similar way of working. He insisted that only by dancing his steps accurately would emotion and thought be released. He didn't want a discussion on feeling: he wanted his form expressed, because the expression of form would have emotional consequences.

So a full respect for form is nothing new; rather, in our current state of theatre, it's more like an ancient knowledge in danger of extinction. But the most important thing to stress about it is this: the knowledge of form is not just an intellectual awareness but one that must be fully incorporated in the body and voice of an actor. Only then will it serve its purpose.

We are about to trace two threads of work, both of which have to be in place to serve the text. The first thread I call 'the givens': the physical structures that shape the story and the sense and organise the chaos of passion.

The second thread is the imaginative exploration of the text: the imaginative connections created by the words themselves which release the specific quality of the verse – the emotion, the image, the concrete detail of the world and the character.

If you follow the first thread only, you will be clear but dry; follow only the second and you will be connected and passionate but make no sense. Weave them both together and you will create the tapestry.

The givens move you and the audience forward, and clarify. They lead you through chaos.

The imaginative connects you vertically to the depths of language, and engages you and the audience with passion.

The Word

The word is the most fundamental of the givens. Without proper attention to the word you will undermine any play. Approximate understanding of the word can result only in approximate interpretation of a part, expressed in generalised acting rather than specific playing. The exact order of the words is vital. Jumble them around, even one word out of order, and you can radically change the plot of the play. And you'll very likely make it harder on yourself. It's often the case that an actor who has particular difficulty in remembering or playing a Shakespearean line will find on checking the text that they have mis-learned it.

Heightened text is structured text. Shakespeare's structures move you forward word by word. Each word represents a step on the road. Misplaced steps will trip you up; you will lose your way. Similarly with mumbled text – if your speech muscles are not worked out and speaking clearly is an effort, you will block the flow of the iambic and the thought so you will not be able to change pace or rhythm with the text.

These plays exist through language, and the whole of every word is important. You must speak the beginning, middle and end of each one, effortlessly – not swallowing word ends or skidding over multi-syllabic words. The physical nature of the word is the fabric of the play.

Each word is important within the flow of a thought, so the word has to serve both the iambic and the thought. If you speak every word without riding on the iambic energy or the thought, you will sound clear but stuck and staccato, and make no connected sense. To achieve clarity and sense the word has to be spoken in the flow of rhythm and thought.

You must understand what each word means. Know every word and reference. Never enter a rehearsal 'sort of knowing' the meaning of a word. Be aware that some words have changed meaning over the years. Words are easily debased and their sense made flabby, so an exploration of the exact meaning of a word will often hoist acting up onto a higher level.

For instance, when Portia talks about 'these naughty times' in *The Merchant of Venice*, she means something far from light and trivial. She means evil times. When you realise this, the whole of her emotional struggle with her dead father's will becomes intense, vivid and tangible. It is a word appropriate to what a young girl would feel about having restrictions placed on her choice of husband.

> *Portia*:   O! these naughty times
> Puts bars between the owners and their rights;
> And so, though yours, not yours.
>
> (III.ii)

Similarly, research people and events from history.

> *Cassius*: Caesar cried 'Help me, Cassius, or I sink!'
> I, as Aeneas, our great ancestor,
> Did from the flames of Troy upon his shoulder
> The old Anchises bear, so from the waves of Tiber
> Did I the tired Caesar.
>
> (I.i)

In this speech Cassius reduces Julius Caesar – who would be king – to a mere mortal in order to help persuade Brutus to assassinate him. To do so he uses references to the founding of Rome – references that would quickly lodge in a Roman heart. But it's essential for the speaking of the lines to know the story of Aeneas. In three hundred years time, an actor might have to speak a line that refers to Jefferson and the Declaration of Independence. Research into both would be needed by the actor who hadn't heard of either!

Pay the same attention to the Bible and to Greek mythology. Shakespeare uses names and references from both with dramatic precision. Jupiter, Juno, Apollo – find out who they are. It will help you act more specifically. The audience might not know the references but the knowledge you attach to the name as you speak it will help fill your performance and in doing so help the audience comprehend. It's like friends talking about people you don't know – but you're interested because you know they know them!

Be curious whenever you don't understand. Every word tells you something. When Perdita in *The Winter's Tale* gives out flowers to her guests, you should know what each flower is, what it looks like and whether it symbolises anything.

> Here's flowers for you
> Hot lavender, mints, savory, marjoram;
> The marigold, that goes to bed with the sun
> And with him rises weeping; these are flowers
> Of middle summer, and I think they are given
> To men of middle age.

(IV.iv)

Research of this kind would be nothing unusual in preparing for a contemporary play, yet for some reason actors are often reluctant to do it for Shakespeare. When I worked on Sarah Kane's final play, *4.48 Psychosis*, the actors spent a whole day studying the list of anti-depressants she was prescribed. Each drug and its side-effects had to be researched. It should be the same with Perdita's flowers.

Having found the meaning of the words, trust it: don't imagine they conceal an opposing sense. I had a curious experience once with an actress working on Viola's speech from *Twelfth Night*: 'I left no ring with her; what means this lady?' The actress was making the most bizarre decisions in speaking this line. It soon transpired that she was approaching it from a perspective that had no anchor or reality in the play. Her feeling was that Viola had in fact left a ring – in other words, that 'I left no ring' was a lie. Accordingly, she was playing a meaning in complete contradiction to the sense of the words.

It was hard to stay calm. She obviously felt that any attack on her interpretation was an attack on her imagination as an actress. 'If she left a ring there, why does she then say "What means this lady?"' I ventured. Silence. 'Why don't you try the speech meaning what you say,' I coaxed. She did and eventually light started to dawn as she moved past the block: 'Oh, I see. If she didn't leave a ring, then maybe that's why she has to say the rest of the speech.' Yes indeed. Trust the text. It means what it says it means.

Be attentive to the physical qualities of words: they contain clues to meaning and pace. A *t* at the end of a word can sound precise or even violent. Open vowels are more emotional than shorter ones. The difficulty in speaking certain consonants and vowels together can reveal tensions in content and situation. Monosyllabic words often reveal a more direct simple line of communication than elaborate multi-syllabic ones – which take more time to speak and make you dwell longer on the word.

To realise the full word, you will need all the craft you've so far worked on. The voice must be placed forward in the mouth. Being in the state of readiness and on support – in the heightened state of survival – will clarify words naturally. You can speak Shakespeare in any accent, although those that have falling lines and back placing are harder to communicate in as you are swimming against the tide and vigour of the text. Some accents are less oral or bardic than others – but any culture that enjoys storytelling already has the energy that Shakespeare requires.

Finally, learn accurately, every word. The rewards of accurate learning are immense. You gain energy, passion, clarity, acting notes and safety. Speak every word and you are held in the moment and able to dance every step of the text without falling over. Speak every physical element of the words in the right order and you will be secure, confident, emotionally supported. Take fidelity to the word as your foundation, and you can begin to act and enjoy the whole of the text rather than fear it.

Exercises

> *Orsino*: If music be the food of love, play on,
> Give me excess of it, that, surfeiting,
> The appetite may sicken and so die.
> That strain again! It had a dying fall;
> O, it came o'er my ear like the sweet sound
> That breathes upon a bank of violets,
> Stealing and giving odour! Enough, no more;
> 'Tis not so sweet now as it was before.
> O spirit of love, how quick and fresh art thou!
> That, notwithstanding thy capacity
> Receiveth as the sea, nought enters there,
> Of what validity and pitch soe'er,
> But falls into abatement and low price
> Even in a minute. So full of shape is fancy,
> That it alone is high fantastical.
>
> *(Twelfth Night, I.i)*

Leontes: I am angling now,
Though you perceive me not how I give line.
Go to, go to!
How she holds up the neb, the bill to him!
And arms her with the boldness of a wife
To her allowing husband! [*Exeunt Polixenes, Hermione, and*
Attendants.
                    Gone already!
Inch-thick, knee-deep, o'er head and ears a fork'd one!
Go, play, boy, play; thy mother plays, and I
Play too; but so disgrac'd a part, whose issue
Will hiss me to my grave. Contempt and clamour
Will be my knell. Go, play, boy, play.
There have been,
Or I am much deceiv'd, cuckolds ere now;
And many a man there is, even at this present,
Now while I speak this, holds his wife by th' arm
That little thinks she has been sluic'd in's absence,
And his pond fish'd by his next neighbour, by
Sir Smile, his neighbour. Nay, there's comfort in't,
Whiles other men have gates and those gates open'd,
As mine, against their will. Should all despair
That have revolted wives, the tenth of mankind
Would hang themselves. Physic for't there's none;
It is a bawdy planet, that will strike
Where 'tis predominant; and 'tis pow'rful, think it,
From east, west, north, and south. Be it concluded,
No barricado for a belly. Know't,
It will let in and out the enemy
With bag and baggage. Many thousand on's
Have the disease, and feel't not. How now, boy!
(*The Winter's Tale*, I.ii)

Try the following speech exercises on these two speeches.

- Keep breathing and vocally open.
- Mouth each speech silently.
- Return to speaking the text on full voice.
- Just speak the vowels out aloud.
- Return to speak all the words.

On returning to speaking after mouthing, articulation and speaking will be easier and you may realise that parts of your speech equipment aren't working. Some sections of the text will have been harder to place in the mouth than others. After the vowel exercise, you are likely to feel emotionally more connected to the text.

You may not have known anything beforehand about Leontes or Orsino, but through speaking their words you will begin to understand something about them and their situations. Speaking Leontes feels physically aggressive and violent – even mean. Orsino is a more mellow sensation. Leontes' words are short and direct; Orsino's are physically more expansive. Leontes' state of mind is revealed more in the monosyllabic words, Orsino's in the polysyllabic ones. Perhaps you might think that Orsino is merely playing at feeling, while Leontes' feelings are all too frighteningly real.

Doing the word exercise you will also have discovered that Leontes moves faster than Orsino. Orsino's pace is more leisurely; he takes his time. Similarly, Leontes' iambic rhythm is fractured and disturbed while Orsino is more even and balanced. You can even see it in the physical shape of the speeches on the page. Run your eyes over the layout and imagine it as a landscape. If you were to walk in Orsino's, you would be among gently rolling hills, passing meandering rivers on a pleasantly warm day until 'Enough, no more' – and then you'd return to the amble. By contrast, Leontes is in fierce, jagged country, with crags and chasms and twisting paths and extreme temperatures – dangerous, difficult and demanding.

Pay attention to the shapes of words: they will tell you much more than you might have expected.

Alliteration, Assonance, Onomatopoeia

As you explore the physical nature of words, you quickly unearth some of the most fundamental joys in the making of language. These verbal pleasures are rooted deep in our history like ancestral sounds and voices harking back to its very birth of the English language. They include:

- *Alliteration*: the grouping of consonants together;
- *Assonance*: the grouping of vowels together;
- *Onomatopoeia*: a word that sounds and feels as it means, expressing by its sound the thing it represents.

Some years ago I was teaching a workshop at a boarding school. It was the first day of term and boys were being dropped off for the term by their parents and siblings. As the dreaded moment arrived and parents got ready to leave their sons, the tension was palpable. One twelve-year-old broke down, and I heard him say to his parents, 'Oh no don't go.' He spoke with assonance and from his heart. The feel of the line was so delightful and apt that his younger brother took up the line and started to chant, 'Oh no don't go'.

Onomatopoeia is locked into our sensual, physical understanding of language and its meaning. Words that shock us only do so because they feel as they mean when we speak them. Words that describe something without being onomatopoeic distance speaker and listener from the real power and meaning of the thing described. 'Uneven' is safer than 'jagged'. 'Assault' is clinical and distancing. 'Batter' makes you feel the blow and splatter of blood in your mouth.

Everyday words have something of this physical form and content locked into their spoken form. 'Take', for instance, withdraws into our mouths and stops on the *k* – unlike 'give' which moves forward and goes on and out with the *v*.

Return to Leontes in *The Winter's Tale*. His whole speech teems with violent and sexually salacious sounds expressed through alliteration, assonance and onomatopoeia. Leontes' violent jealousy at his wife's infidelity with his best friend vomits up into his mouth. Here are just some of the richnesses of sound that cram his words:

- I am angling now
- Though you perceive me not how I give line
- Go to, go to!

The short matching vowels in 'Though you' and 'Go to, go to' act as a relentless tapping in the mouth and brain while 'now' and 'how' give length, casting the fishing line to trap them on the water.

> Inch-thick, knee-deep, o'er head and ears a fork'd one!
> Go, play, boy, play; thy mother plays, and I
> Play too; but so disgrac'd a part, whose issue
> Will hiss me to my grave. Contempt and clamour
> Will be my knell.

The vowels match in 'Inch-thick' and again in 'knee-deep'; and the short vowel in 'Inch' echoes two lines later in 'disgraced' and 'issue', and then in 'will' and 'hiss'. As soon as vowels are repeated in this way, the words that contain them are woven together – not necessarily through sense but sensually. In the same section feel the *s*'s in your mouth sloshing around.

> but so disgrac'd a part, whose issue
> Will hiss me to my grave.

The alliteration on the *s* finally manifests fully in the onomatopoeic 'hiss'. Then the release factor of the *s* is transformed into the strong explosive *k* sound in 'contempt and clamour'. The insidious release of the *s* continues and is joined by the *sh* to heighten sensually the disgusting description of neighbours seducing wives. In the middle of all eighteen sounding *s*'s is 'sluiced', vividly rendering the act itself:

And many a man there is, even at this present
Now while I speak this, holds his wife by th' arm
That little thinks she has been sluic'd in's absence,
And his pond fish'd by his next neighbour, by
Sir Smile, his neighbour.

At this point in the speech, there is a physical hardening in Leontes' mouth as stronger consonants begin to dominate in alliteration: 'gates... gates... against'; 'bawdy planet...predominant,' and ''tis powerful, think it'; 'barricado for a belly'; 'bag and baggage'.

After all this turmoil, the last three words of the speech have open vowels: 'how now boy'. Their gentleness is in sharp contrast to the fierce physical struggle you have felt in your mouth hitherto. It is as though you are sighing out in exhaustion after a traumatic purge of a pain and fury.

In *A Midsummer Night's Dream*, there is a play within the play. The mechanicals are amateur actors, and Quince – a carpenter – has adapted the well-known tragedy of 'Pyramus and Thisbe'. Like many immature writers, he has used every poetic device in his adaptation, including rhyme, alliteration, repetition, onomatopoeia and assonance. Part of the humour in this play is that the poetic devices used do not serve the meaning – rather, they clutter it up. Form here does not equal content but obscures it.

Bottom has to act the main part of Pyramus. Bottom might be a good actor but he has a disabling text to work with – although one other aspect of all these poetic devices is that they make the learning of a text easier. Remember, this play has only been rehearsed once – only a portion was worked before Puck's interference. Clear form aids memory (which is very useful for Snug the joiner, who is 'slow of study').

> *Pyramus*: Sweet Moon, I thank thee for thy sunny beams;
> I thank thee, Moon, for shining now so bright;
> For, by thy gracious, golden, glittering gleams,
> I trust to take of truest Thisby sight.
>   But stay, O spite!
>   But mark, poor knight,
> What dreadful dole is here!
>   Eyes, do you see?
>   How can it be?

O dainty duck! O dear!
    Thy mantle good,
    What! stain'd with blood?
Approach, ye Furies fell.
    O Fates! come, come;
    Cut thread and thrum;
Quail, crunch, conclude, and quell.
[...]
O wherefore, Nature, didst thou lions frame?
Since lion vile hath here deflower'd my dear;
Which is – no, no – which was the fairest dame
That liv'd, that lov'd, that lik'd, that look'd with cheer.
    Come tears, confound;
    Out, sword, and wound
The pap of Pyramus;
    Ay, that left pap,
    Where heart doth hop,
[*Stabs himself.*]
Thus die I, thus, thus, thus.
    Now am I dead,
    Now am I fled;
My soul is in the sky.
    Tongue, lose thy light;
    Moon, take thy flight.
[*Exit Moonshine.*]
Now die, die, die, die, die.

                                                    (V.i)

Even a Shakespearean novice speaking this out loud would know that the writing does not serve Pyramus, who believes his love is dead and then commits suicide. Speaking the text makes you laugh. The sounds, the rhymes and the struggles to complete the rhymes, the abundance of the alliteration, the pettiness of the onomatopoeia are silly. You don't need to be an expert to realise the silliness because it feels silly as you speak it. There's nothing shocking or offensive in the writing, it just doesn't work. And yet what is supremely moving about Bottom the actor is that faced with this text he still acts his heart out.

Let's stay with the stage and speak Jaques from *As You Like It*. In this example, you might have to search harder for the alliteration, assonance and onomatopoeia simply because they are so wedded to meaning and effect. Here form is in service to and harmony with content.

Jaques: All the world's a stage,
And all the men and women merely players;
They have their exits and their entrances;
And one man in his time plays many parts,
His acts being seven ages. At first the infant,
Mewling and puking in the nurse's arms;
Then the whining school-boy, with his satchel
And shining morning face, creeping like snail
Unwillingly to school. And then the lover,
Sighing like furnace, with a woeful ballad
Made to his mistress' eyebrow. Then a soldier,
Full of strange oaths, and bearded like the pard,
Jealous in honour, sudden and quick in quarrel,
Seeking the bubble reputation
Even in the cannon's mouth. And then the justice,
In fair round belly with good capon lin'd,
With eyes severe and beard of formal cut,
Full of wise saws and modern instances;
And so he plays his part. The sixth age shifts
Into the lean and slipper'd pantaloon,
With spectacles on nose and pouch on side,
His youthful hose, well sav'd, a world too wide
For his shrunk shank; and his big manly voice,
Turning again toward childish treble, pipes
And whistles in his sound. Last scene of all,
That ends this strange eventful history,
Is second childishness and mere oblivion;
Sans teeth, sans eyes, sans taste, sans everything.

(II.vii)

Feel how the speech abounds with powerful onomatopoeia, sometimes with an extra enhancement of alliteration: 'mewling', 'puking', 'whining', 'shining', 'creeping', 'sighing', 'woeful', 'quick in quarrel', 'shrunk shank'. In fact the more you mouth the consonants and speak the vowels, the more the subtle variations of these devices appear – and always serving to dramatise Jaques' descriptions.

Later I will be looking at how language – including its physical qualities – helps characterise. Here Jaques speaks of theatre as an analogy of life and adopts a theatrical style of speaking to match his topic; but he also lists the negatives of each stage of our existence. We feel life through his view of the world as frustrating and difficult. The baby mewls and vomits: it doesn't gurgle or laugh. Boyhood means the tedium of school. The lover is unrequited. These perspectives not only characterise Jaques intellectually, but the sound and physical texture of the words he chooses reinforce his meaning so that we feel it in our mouths and ears.

Each observation is woven together with subtle alliteration or assonance until the final stage of life in the last line. Then the repetition of 'sans' with its short vowel is in sharp contrast to the long vowels of 'teeth', 'eyes' and 'taste'; but the last word 'everything' finishes the account with a long vowel sandwiched between two short ones. Notice how the word 'everything' has no *s* in it – no escaping air. The other word in the line without an *s* is 'teeth', but that is effectively linked to 'sans' as a second syllable while 'everything' is a three-syllable word without the *s* – the air. Throughout the previous seven words there is a gentle hiss, like air coming out of a wilting balloon: 'Sans teeth, sans eyes, sans taste, sans...'. 'Everything' ends the line and collapses devoid of oxygen and life.

The sound game Jaques plays contrasts with the literal meaning of the words – 'sans' has the *s* of life and air but means without, while 'everything' lacks air but is the opposite of without. Nonetheless, as you speak that final line and reach 'everything', you sense a finality in the word's shape if not its meaning. It makes you rest and you can sense the silence that follows, hovering in space as the final note of a symphony hangs before the conductor relaxes his arms and the audience applauds.

Throughout the play, you sense Jaques' power of delivery and the respect and awe he is held in – when he speaks he is attended to because he will create verbal and sound conundrums in his audience's ears.

- With full breath support and an open voice take your time and speak this speech again.
- Pay particular attention to the sound and tune within each word.
- As you touch the end of each word make sure there is clarity but also allow a flow of energy through the end of the word into the next.

By the time you finish speaking, I am confident you will have found or begun to sense a rhythm as you speak: a heartbeat. There is a tune to this speech. You have ridden on the iambic.

Rhythm

The Iambic

The fundamental rhythm of Shakespeare's verse is the iambic. This life-giving beat is the first and last we hear – that of our heart. It releases the physical pace and momentum of the verse, and illuminates the meaning through the stress. It also charts the heartbeat – including the stoppages or skips – of the character.

Two syllables are needed to create an iambic and the stress falls on the second: *de dúm*. The iambic can cut across two words – 'to bé' – or be lodged within one – 'disgráce'. A Shakespearean verse line generally has five iambics within it – consequently ten syllables a line. Called the iambic pentameter, this is the template of English dramatic verse construction. We might think of this regular iambic pentameter line as the standard shoe size. However, much of what is most interesting in Shakespeare's verse involves variations on it, variations you must learn to identify. Regular or not, the rhythm of his lines is completely aligned and married to meaning and emotion.

> When I do count the clock that tells the time.
>
> (*Sonnet 12*)

- Count the syllables in this line: there are ten.
- Hum the line. Can you feel the *de dúm*? How the iambic flows and highlights 'I', 'count', 'clock', 'tells', 'time'?
- Beat the line and speak it, feeling the energy of the rhythm hover over those five words.

You have spoken a perfectly regular iambic pentameter line whose rhythm reveals its own quality – the steady relentless ticking of a clock.

However the pure regularity of such a line is relatively rare, although it is the point of departure for all Shakespeare's verse.

Perhaps because it is so uncommon in its pure form, many directors seem reluctant to discuss it in rehearsals. And yet it has to be explored and understood before you can experience and respond to the many variations and irregularities that Shakespeare moulds into his line.

The director Ron Eyre told me once how, as a four-year old, he'd seen the sea for the first time. His parents asked if he wanted to go in to paddle. He replied, 'When it stops.' I liken Shakespeare's verse to the sea. Though it never stops, the waves on the surface change. The iambic is a wave, sometimes small and almost still, sometimes mighty. Waves can break, white horses appear, ripples spray and eddies disturb the surface. They can hurtle towards the shore or amble slowly up it. When they're regular – like the iambic pentameter – you can swim easily on them; when they're rough, you will be thrown off.

The genius of Shakespeare is such that as long as you follow his rhythm, you will be on and in the meaning of the text. To do this, you have to accept the sea and the weather conditions as they are. It would be impossible to swim in a rough sea and pretend it was calm – you might try but you would probably drown. Likewise you can't try to make an irregular line regular – but you still have to remember the basic form to feel the disturbances within the line. With 'When I do count the clock that tells the time' you are gently and regularly bobbing along. Here's the second line of the sonnet: 'And see the brave day sunk in hideous night'.

- Count the syllables. There are eleven; they are no longer regular or safe; the wave has broken.
- Hum the line: do you feel any changing energy around the words 'sunk' and 'hideous'? You bob along through 'And see the brave day', and then sink on 'sunk'. The 'in' begins to pull you up but you meet ripples on 'hideous'.
- Beat the line while speaking it out. Observe how the shifts revealed in the humming are created in two distinct ways. 'Sunk' is on the wave of the iambic but makes its difference felt through shape; 'hideous' breaks the iambic. Both have to be acknowledged to communicate the form's alignment with meaning. If you try to force the iambic pentameter to fit both lines, the first makes sense but the second is intellectually and emotionally flattened. Alternatively, if you ignore the iambic pentameter you fail to

harness not only the power of the sea but the communication, through the harnessing of that power, of the precise points of tension at 'sunk' and 'hideous' within the irregular second line.

Here is a basic process to start your verse-speaking journey:

- Count aloud the syllables of verse lines. Note whether they are regular or not: ten syllables, or more or fewer. Even if they are regular ten-syllable lines, note if a word is heavily weighted.
- Hum the lines – this will reveal the tune, the waves and their size and texture.
- Get to know the iambic. Start to beat *de dúm* into the lines. Allow the *dúm* to pull you up and out. Don't pull it into you. The iambic is a returning and optimistic energy.
- Begin to feel the iambic, but try not to make a word or a line fit the iambic if it doesn't want to.
- Even when it does fit, feel any word or phrase that might trip you up, slow you down or speed you up. *De dúm* can become *dúm de* or *de de dúm* or *dúm de de*. There may be rocks below the surface of the sea!

As you begin these exercises you may find you need to exaggerate the beat to feel it. It's like a pianist using a metronome to practise. The metronome doesn't come on to the concert platform – but the rhythm does, and that rhythm holds the performance together. Similarly you might have to over-explore the rhythm before it rests easily in your voice and breath.

At school every week I was made to learn not only poems, but verses from the King James bible. I had no idea what most of the words meant, and soon realised that rhythm could help me learn them. One day I was given Sonnet 116 to recite. I'd failed to learn it accurately and was kept in after school until I got it right. After a bit, I had the insight to beat it out to myself and succeeded in learning it through its rhythm and musicality. After a meaningless, passionless – but perfectly accurate – recital of the sonnet, I was eventually allowed home. Years later, on returning to that sonnet with thought and feeling, I understood the power of the iambic and its anchoring support beneath a text – it is the foundation to build on. It helped me, and it will help you.

Apply the process to Sonnet 29.

> When in disgrace with Fortune and men's eyes, (*ten syllables*)
> I all alone beweep my outcast state, (*ten*)
> And trouble deaf heaven with my bootless cries, (*eleven*)
> And look upon myself, and curse my fate, (*ten*)

The investigation of the syllables tells you immediately that there is an irregular third line. The first disturbance is on 'trouble' – trouble is troubled; then 'deaf heaven' attempts to climb back onto the wave, but 'bootless' gives another dose of friction. There is a distress in the uselessness of your cries.

Now let's look at the regular syllabic lines and feel where there is a swell that enlightens sense.

> When in disgrace with fortune and men's eyes

There seems to be a certain texture and music around the words 'disgrace', 'fortune' and 'men's eyes'. It's a perfectly scannable line, it's even, the *de dums* carry on beneath the whole, but there is a different energy and timbre around these words: the wave is a different shape and formation here. This is partly because the iambic is scanning whole words but it is also due to the swell gathering in the context of the line through 'When in' and 'with'.

The second line is also regular but there is a different wave shape under 'all', 'beweep' and 'outcast'.

> I all alone beweep my outcast state

The swell underneath 'all alone' reinforces within the rhythm the isolation in the words. It's as though you are lifted on top of a wave before you swoop down between waves to 'beweep', only to be swept out on 'outcast' and eventually land on firm ground on 'state'.

The fourth, regular line – 'And look upon myself, and curse my fate' – moves quickly, landing on 'myself' before a strong wave that pushes you down on 'curse', after which 'my' bobs you up so you can land on 'fate'. In this line 'myself' and 'curse' feel singled out with a distinctive energy and shape.

Now, put the iambic on the back burner and speak the four lines with the emphasis on sense. You will find that there is a marriage between the meaning and the places that stood out as having a particular texture in the iambic pentameter. The point is that while every word in Shakespeare is important, if every word is equally stressed or unstressed we will make nonsense of the text. Every note of music is important in a song but some phrases catch and move us more. We are alerted to them by the beat.

It is important to remember this, however: to achieve the iambic and find the shifting textures within it, the voice has to be free. The iambic might be the energetic power *behind* the voice, but what we hear *in* the voice as we stress words differently is inflection and pitch. An unfree voice can only over- or under-stress an iambic pentameter line even if the actor knows all about the rhythm and meaning it.

Students are often amazed that Shakespeare could do so much working from such a simple foundation. Indeed, it's not a wonder that he could access the form so effortlessly, given how much his education would have exposed him to it. The real marvel is how he focused the iambic and transformed its power from character to character, play to play. He understood it so well that he could break and extend it to astonishing effect. In his hands it determines pacing and focuses action, it reveals character, shifting as humans move and change. And as Shakespeare grew and changed as a writer, so he became more adventurous. Just look at the verse lines of his early plays, then compare them to the later ones.

Consider, for example, two men in emotional distress: Romeo, from an early play, and Leontes from the later *The Winter's Tale*. Work the basic process on their speeches.

> *Romeo*: Hadst thou no poison mix'd, no sharp-ground knife,
> No sudden mean of death, though ne'er so mean,
> But 'banished' to kill me – 'banished'?
> O friar, the damned use that word in hell;
> Howling attends it; how hast thou the heart,
> Being a divine, a ghostly confessor,
> A sin-absolver, and my friend profess'd,
> To mangle me with that word 'banished'?
> (*Romeo and Juliet*, III.iii)

Though Romeo is in high passion, all the lines bar one are ten syllables. Nonetheless, as you hum and beat them out, you will begin to feel how the shape and size of the iambic waves highlight Romeo's pain, as do the changes and breaks in the rhythm. Thus, 'poison mix'd' swells under you, before you fall to 'no', only to be propelled forward onto 'sharp-ground knife'. Then in the second line 'sudden' is an abrupt wave that heads towards and lands on 'death' – after which 'though ne'er so mean' surges you forward and away from it again. In the third line the weight of 'banished' resonates twice: feel how the word is hard to harness. Sense too the trip in the iambic on 'to kill me', moving you forward quickly until you are encased again in the weight of 'banished'.

Ride the rest of the speech and attune yourself to the shifts beneath the waves and the changes of rhythm within the iambic.

> *Leontes:*   Is whispering nothing?
> Is leaning cheek to cheek? Is meeting noses?
> Kissing with inside lip? Stopping the career
> Of laughter with a sigh? – a note infallible
> Of breaking honesty. Horsing foot on foot?
> Skulking in corners? Wishing clocks more swift;
> Hours, minutes; noon, midnight? And all eyes
> Blind with the pin and web but theirs, theirs only,
> That would unseen be wicked – is this nothing?
> Why, then the world and all that's in't is nothing;
> The covering sky is nothing; Bohemia nothing;
> My wife is nothing; nor nothing have these nothings,
> If this be nothing.
>   (*The Winter's Tale*, I.ii)

Leontes only manages one ten-syllable line: 'Skulking in corners? Wishing clocks more swift'. His pounding heart beats a whole variety of rhythms: he is a very distressed man. It is just this rapidity of the movement within the disorder that will facilitate his ruthless actions later in the play.

Actors who have spent years speaking Shakespeare, night after night, have the iambic pentameter embedded in them. They obey its structure by instinct. Some are so tuned into it that they can improvise in it almost unconsciously.

Many young actors, by contrast, may know what the iambic pentameter is, but haven't had the chance to speak it regularly enough for it to sit easily in them. If you are one of these, you will have to work diligently to achieve the iambic energy and in doing so conserve the plays.

Everything in Shakespeare conspires to move and launch you forwards. Both Romeo and Leontes are being propelled forwards.

Characters are speaking to probe, confront, examine, educate or witness events and issues. All the words are necessary to penetrate events, thoughts and feelings.

Rhythm and stress affect tone and speaking energy. The second stressed syllable of the iambic – *de dúm* – takes you up and forward. It returns the energy of speaking and moves you forward on to the next word and into the next idea and line. It is not the rhythm most of us speak in today, which tends to be a reductive falling away: *dúm de*. The iambic is optimistic and curious. The reverse is pessimistic and apathetic.

As you climb on to and stay with the iambic, you are moving on a living energy that engages not only your voice and speech but your head and heart. It is a sea moving and surging underneath you. The iambic is a constant passionate pulse of energy. The second syllable sends a surge of blood through your body. Ideas and meaning become clearer as you begin to not only feel the heavy stresses but textures within those stresses.

Thus the rhythm helps you make sense and simultaneously enhances sense. But you should not feel that you have to scan so rigidly that you make no sense. The iambic is a powerful guide but in speech, rhythm and stress are not as important as obedience to the musical use of tone. The rhythm is about emphasis connected to thought: it serves speaking rather than restricts it; it aids flow, not blocks it. Locate the iambic to release its power; then allow it freedom to harmonise with the meaning and intention of the text. It should be as natural as walking.

In the line 'Be wise as thou art cruel: do not press' from Sonnet 140, for instance, it would be unnatural to hammer out 'cru-el' just for the sake of the beat. All that's needed is lightly to touch the sound of the double syllable in the word. Or in 'Thou art as tyrannous, so as thou art' (Sonnet 131), the three syllables of 'tyrannous' don't have to be stubbornly spoken, although they gather weight and power in the line.

Actors who overstress the beat at the expense of sense remind me of the Monty Python sketch in which people who had forgotten how to walk staggered around trying to learn again in a London park. Something equally absurd and unnatural happens if you are enslaved to rhythm. But as you feel more confident with the iambic and stagger less, you will begin to observe places where the text itself staggers and to feel the sorts of friction these irregularities create. These are powerful acting notes.

You will quickly begin to feel, for instance, where there is a break in the rhythm. It will have an immediate effect on pace, for pace emerges through the iambic. The rhythm of your heart physically dictates the pace at which you feel and move in your body, and that translates to the speed of your thought and speech.

> *Juliet*: Gallop apace, you fiery-footed steeds
>
> (III.ii)

Feel how the pace gallops. It would be extremely perverse to speak this line slowly.

> *Richard II*: I have been studying how I may compare
> This prison where I live unto the world;
> And, for because the world is populous
> And here is not a creature but myself,
> I cannot do it. Yet I'll hammer it out.
>
> (V.v)

In contrast, there is a measured pace within the iambic here as Richard begins to study the real state of his being. He is alone in a cell. He has time. But you can feel the excitement and change of gear and pace on 'Yet I'll hammer it out'.

The changing pace of the rhythm is plugged into every pace of the rhythm of life, so any breaks or shifts subliminally signal all sorts of emotional and intellectual alterations, sensuousness and humour.

> Let me not to the marriage of true minds
> Admit impediments. Love is not love
> Which alters when it alteration finds,
> Or bends with the remover to remove.
> O, no! it is an ever-fixed mark,
> That looks on tempests and is never shaken;
> It is the star to every wand'ring bark,
> Whose worth's unknown, although his height be taken.
> Love's not Time's fool, though rosy lips and cheeks
> Within his bending sickle's compass come;
> Love alters not with his brief hours and weeks,
> But bears it out even to the edge of doom.
>   If this be error, and upon me prov'd,
>   I never writ, nor no man ever lov'd.
>
> (Sonnet 116)

Feel how sturdy and regular the pace is in the first twelve lines – and yet within the overall pace there are many different textures. 'Let me not to the marriage of true minds': a fluent speaker will walk this steadily, but feel a surge at the beginning of the line that arrives on 'not' and moves on to 'marriage' and 'true minds'. A rigid speaker will make nonsense of the line, hitting 'me', 'to' and '-rriage' (to break up 'marriage'), and floundering in the attempt to make 'true minds' fit. The first rendering makes sense because it flows and feels the different pulses of the rhythm. Throughout the sonnet the iambic takes odd turns, but it always returns to order. And the odd turns always inform the meaning and enhance it.

Thus at the very end note how Shakespeare alters pace and rhythm, spinning a joke in the rhyming couplet that changes the whole temperature of the sonnet. The seriousness of the poem's theme is flipped over on to its back.

Great jazz musicians extemporise with feeling and sense, but they know structure and rhythm intimately: only then are they free to improvise. To leave a form you have to know how to exit and then how to enter it again. It takes knowledge and imagination. The imaginative actor without knowledge can't speak verse; the knowledgeable one without imagination can't make sense.

The iambic is the underlying rhythm. Its energy will sustain you through a play in the same way that you can carry on dancing for hours with an energetic drum beat, not realising you are tired. The iambic keeps you going.

- Take a verse speech
- Count the syllables of the lines.
- Hum the speech.
- Beat the whole speech, returning to the energy of the iambic.
- Observe variations and textures in the lines.
- Breathe and feel the iambic move up through your body. Remember to keep the rhythm moving up and out. Don't pull it in. The *dúm* should not be physically beaten or drawn into you. It is all up and out. If you squash the iambic, you quell the blood flow.
- Walk the rhythm. Go with it. You will have to shift your own walking rhythms to serve it. It can be fast or slow. The change of pace will change your walk. You are aiming to walk in different characters' rhythms, so it will be unsettling to your natural rhythm.
- A breaking rhythm in the line will disturb and re-focus you. As the heartbeat shifts, there is bound to be agitation. Check the content.

Is the character agitated? Is this a time of important transitions for him or her?

- If the iambic doesn't fit or is irregular, always take note of the content. Something is happening. Don't try to force the line into a regular beat if you feel it doesn't fit. As you beat the rhythm, it should be connected to the whole of your body, breath and voice. Try to feel it rather than analysing it. You might have to go over a line several times before this works for you.

- Play in the rhythm of the text without worrying too much if you are making sense. Walk it, dance it, skip it, throw a ball against a wall with it.

- Gradually you will feel the text's rhythm taking you over. Your rhythm is being transformed into the text's rhythm. You are beginning to be played. You can't describe this: just do it! The regular lines are emotionally freer and easier to think. The irregular ones are more fractured: thoughts and feelings constipated.

- When you sense the marriage between you and the text's rhythm, stop beating the iambic and go back to speaking the speech with sense. Change your point of concentration to make the words work, and try to put the iambic to the back of your mind. You will find that it stays in your body, emotions and voice, unconsciously enhancing meaning and feeling.

- Now pause. Suspend your thought but allow the feeling of the iambic still to pump away and remain present in the silence. Resume speaking after the pause, and you will pick up the energy again as you do so. In fact, the pause is not a dead silence but a filled and living one.

You don't have to hear the iambic consciously to be changed by it. Indeed, the actor who beats the verse out too rigidly will block its energy, exactly as the actor who doesn't use the rhythm at all will bore us, lose us and leave us cold.

If a whole company of actors speak with the iambic energy, they tell the story of the play with a shared drive and commitment. There may be pauses in scenes and between them, but the actors will always rejoin the underlying motor of the play and in doing so move both story and audience along. Participating in this shared energy is one of the most exciting experiences audience and actors can have in theatre.

Think by contrast how frustrating it is to play opposite an actor who doesn't use this energy. It's like throwing a ball at someone who refuses to throw it back – or does so only when you least expect it. Imagine a string quartet faced with the same problem and unable to play the music together; or a ballet where the dancers are out of step, the ballerinas dropped by their partners.

When you have understood and let this most fundamental rhythm into your body, you can choose many verse-speaking options. Underneath the text, the rhythm and pace of the heartbeat continue throughout the play, as throughout life, never stopping.

You can breathe and still hold this energy. You can pause and still hold it. You can think and still hold it. What you can't do is *stop*. Suspension is possible, but stopping is death.

Stop and you will deaden the rhythm and kill the energy; you will kill the verse and ultimately the play. You will know at once that you have stopped because you will pull off the verse, which might manifest itself in stopping the breath. Be aware of some of the common habits that might make you stop. It can happen if you:

- Speak the words so clearly that they stop the energy of the rhythm. You must be clear but able to move on through the word.
- Fall off a line or thought.
- Swallow a word or force energy by shouting or over-stressing it.
- Invest the line with too even a rhythm, flattening it and smoothing out the waves and disturbances.
- Block the rhythm in the throat behind the teeth or come to a grinding halt within yourself – an internal braking of thought or feeling.

Pauses and Irregularities of Rhythm

Rhythm is tied to meaning, and a guide to pace, character and situation. It incorporates stage directions and acting notes in the structure of the text.

Where a line is eleven syllables long, weakening the line end, it generally means that you are being moved quickly forward to the next line. It indicates urgency or a clumsiness of thought.

A strong break or caesura mid-line indicates a fragmentation of thought and feeling. The character might be uneasy or lacking in confidence.

A thought that starts mid-line interrupts flow, line and the sequence of thought. It usually indicates unease.

Half-finished or late-starting lines indicate pauses. In dialogue, characters will either pick up the incomplete line and finish it, or count the silent iambics before they speak. Like a conductor, the rhythm will cue the actor in.

As soon as you have experienced the iambic, you will begin to recognise when Shakespeare asks you to pause. Once you understand that the rule is to have ten syllables in a line, you will be alert to the exceptions. Examine these fragments of scenes with your knowledge of the iambic pentameter at the forefront of your mind.

> *Rosalind*:   Look, here comes the Duke.
> *Celia*: With his eyes full of anger.
> *Duke Frederick*: Mistress, dispatch you with your safest haste,
> And get you from our court.
> *Rosalind*:   Me, uncle?
> *Duke Frederick*:   You, cousin.
> Within these ten days if that thou beest found
> So near our public court as twenty miles,
> Thou diest for it.
> *Rosalind*:   I do beseech your Grace,

Let me the knowledge of my fault bear with me.
If with myself I hold intelligence,
Or have acquaintance with mine own desires;
If that I do not dream, or be not frantic –
As I do trust I am not – then, dear uncle,
Never so much as in a thought unborn,
Did I offend your Highness.
Duke Frederick: Thus do all traitors;
If their purgation did consist in words,
They are as innocent as grace itself.
Let it suffice thee that I trust thee not.

(As You Like It, I.iii)

What is to be found as you beat out and count the syllables here? There is no pause written into the exchange. As her uncle banishes her – a completely unexpected move for Rosalind – she stands up tenaciously for herself and doesn't back down. There is no pondering. She picks up the line and in this way defies him.

> *Duke Frederick*: And get you from our court.
> *Rosalind*:   Me, uncle?

But still she doesn't manage to finish the ten syllables – that is left to the Duke –

> *Duke Frederick*:   You, cousin.

– and perhaps in shock he can't neatly finish the ten syllables but seeps into an extra two. Thus in one twelve-syllable line there are three exchanges between two people without a pause.

Frederick in his next speech gathers some repose (although the stress falls out of iambic and emphasises 'ten days'); but again he doesn't finish the line off and Rosalind jumps in with 'I do beseech your Grace'. The next line is eleven syllables: 'If that I do not dream, or be not frantic'. She's losing the rhythm, tripping up in the next line. Next it's the Duke's turn to pick up the line, but he has to go into twelve syllables. Perhaps this is an indication that he is not used to being answered back – particularly by a girl.

There are no stage directions in this heated exchange – just lines that are irregular against the iambic and in the syllabic length. But it's very clear that the irregularities serve as directions for the actor, with the uneven rhythm underscoring an agitation, a floundering that communicates urgency, while the extra syllables propel the thought rapidly forward into the next line.

Next, look at this scene from *The Merchant of Venice*:

> *Portia*: A pound of that same merchant's flesh is thine.
> The court awards it and the law doth give it.
> *Shylock*: Most rightful judge!
> *Portia*: And you must cut this flesh from off his breast.
> The law allows it and the court awards it.
> *Shylock*: Most learned judge! A sentence! Come, prepare.
> *Portia*: Tarry a little; there is something else.
> This bond doth give thee here no jot of blood:
> The words expressly are 'a pound of flesh'.
> Take then thy bond, take thou thy pound of flesh;
> But, in the cutting it, if thou dost shed
> One drop of Christian blood, thy lands, and goods
> Are, by the laws of Venice, confiscate
> Unto the state of Venice.
> *Gratiano*: O upright judge! Mark, Jew. O learned judge!
> *Shylock*: Is that the law?
> *Portia*:   Thyself shalt see the act;
> For, as thou urgest justice, be assur'd
> Thou shalt have justice, more than thou desir'st.
> *Gratiano*: O learned judge! Mark, Jew. A learned judge!
> *Shylock*: I take this offer then: pay the bond thrice,
> And let the Christian go.
> *Bassiano*:   Here is the money.
> *Portia*: Soft!
> The Jew shall have all justice. Soft! No haste.
> He shall have nothing but the penalty.

(IV.i)

Beat this out and count the syllables. You will find pauses in the verse at three critical moments in the development of the scene.

The first is Shylock's 'Most rightful Judge!' Here there is a pause for four syllables, perhaps because Portia is still waiting for Shylock to continue her line by conceding. When he doesn't, she goes on to describe how the flesh is to be taken from Antonio's breast.

The second pause – of two syllables, after 'Unto the state of Venice'

– comes when she has dropped the bombshell that will at last save Antonio. Gratiano is the first to recover from the shock and react.

Portia orchestrates the third pause as Shylock is about to take the money, with 'Soft!' Here there is a long and pregnant silence, potentially a full nine syllables long. Wait, she says, and holds Shylock, the court and the audience in suspense before pursuing the law with the final penalty.

The iambic irregularities also occur at dramatically significant moments. The first two instances are Portia's lines, 'The court awards it and the law doth give it' and 'The law allows it and the court awards it.' While Portia's words seem to find the case in Shylock's favour, thereby ending it, these two eleven-syllable lines actually signal unfinished business because they are iambically unresolved.

Notice later how Shylock's rhythm falters: 'I take this offer then: pay the bond thrice'. He's lost his case and is trying to salvage something, asking Portia to go back to her initial offer of three times the value of the bond. His confidence and his triumph are gone.

You can spend hours examining the iambic and the line length. Each time there is an irregularity, the content will be highlighted and sense and intention made clearer. There are other kinds of irregularity too, which will help you act and gauge the temperature in a scene. For instance, it's worth looking at where in the line a thought changes gear. In evenly constructed, regular verse such changes usually happen at the start of a line. Breaks elsewhere often indicate a fragmentation of thought, feeling or action.

Compare the openings of *Love's Labour's Lost* and *The Merchant of Venice*:

> *King of Navarre*: Let fame, that all hunt after in their lives,
> Live register'd upon our brazen tombs,
> And then grace us in the disgrace of death;
> When, spite of cormorant devouring Time,
> Th' endeavour of this present breath may buy
> That honour which shall bate his scythe's keen edge,
> And make us heirs of all eternity.
> Therefore, brave conquerors – for so you are
> That war against your own affections
> And the huge army of the world's desires –
> Our late edict shall strongly stand in force:
> Navarre shall be the wonder of the world;

Our court shall be a little Academe,
Still and contemplative in living art.
You three, Berowne, Dumain, and Longaville,
Have sworn for three years' term to live with me
My fellow-scholars, and to keep those statutes
That are recorded in this schedule here.
Your oaths are pass'd; and now subscribe your names,
That his own hand may strike his honour down
That violates the smallest branch herein.
If you are arm'd to do as sworn to do,
Subscribe to your deep oaths, and keep it too.

(*Love's Labour's Lost*, I.i)

Feel the smoothness and flow of the verse's physical structure: it is full, easy and positive. The journey travelled within the verse is untroubled, and it opens a play that is itself a relatively gentle tale. *The Merchant of Venice*, by contrast, starts with troubled thoughts, an uneasy and disturbed flow:

Antonio: In sooth, I know not why I am so sad.
It wearies me; you say it wearies you;
But how I caught it, found it, or came by it,
What stuff 'tis made of, whereof it is born,
I am to learn;
And such a want-wit sadness makes of me
That I have much ado to know myself.

(I.i)

The strong mid-line caesura in 'It wearies me; you say it wearies you' and the pause after 'I am to learn' speak volumes. Even knowing nothing of the plot or the character, we can distinguish as much in the structure of the verse as in the meaning of the words the pain and confusion of Antonio's situation – just as we could feel the ease and confidence of the King of Navarre's. Look again at the trial scene in *The Merchant of Venice*: of twenty-four lines, ten are broken. Again, this fragmentation is an enormous clue for the actor. The relationship of form and content cannot be ignored.

Take next the harrowing scene in which Othello prepares to murder Desdemona – a scene of the most intense discord between lovers.

Othello: By heaven, I saw my handkerchief in's hand.
O perjur'd woman! thou dost stone my heart,
And mak'st me call what I intend to do
A murder, which I thought a sacrifice.
I saw the handkerchief.
Desdemona: He found it, then;
I never gave it him. Send for him hither;
Let him confess a truth.
Othello: He hath confess'd.
Desdemona: What, my lord?
Othello: That he hath – ud's death! – us'd thee.
Desdemona: How? unlawfully?
Othello: Ay.
Desdemona: He will not say so.
Othello: No, his mouth is stopp'd;
Honest Iago hath ta'en order for't.
Desdemona: O, my fear interprets! What, is he dead?
Othello: Had all his hairs been lives, my great revenge
Had stomach for them all.
Desdemona: Alas, he is betray'd, and I undone!
Othello: Out, strumpet! Weep'st thou for him to my face?
Desdemona: O, banish me, my lord, but kill me not!
Othello: Down, strumpet.
Desdemona: Kill me to-morrow; let me live to-night.
Othello: Nay, an you strive –
Desdemona: But half an hour!
Othello: Being done, there is no pause.
Desdemona: But while I say one prayer!
Othello: It is too late. [*smothers her.*]
Desdemona: O Lord, Lord, Lord!

                                                            (V.ii)

Even a simple glance at the shape of the text on the page reveals the lack of harmony. Irregular and broken lines and rhythms outnumber anything else – a husband murdering his innocent wife has thrown the verse into an agonised disorder. And as you go into closer detail, counting syllables, beating the iambic, observing the pauses and mid-line breaks, all the pain and distress in the scene are structurally revealed. It sears with discord. Regular, unbroken lines are the exceptions here, and when they occur their even flow suggests an impulse of hope shared by the character and the audience:

Desdemona: O, banish me, my Lord, but kill me not!

But the hope is dashed at once by the force of Othello's 'Damn strumpet', so by the time she makes her next appeal – 'Kill me tomorrow; let me live tonight' – both form and content are desperate, the iambic skipping and tripping over 'kill' and 'live'. To add to the chaos, note how many words are sharp and spiky – 'mak'st', 'perjur'd', 'confess'd', 'us'd', 'stopp'd', 'ta'en' and 'weep'st'.

For contrast with this structural and human disorder, consider now the harmonies of the first meeting between Romeo and Juliet:

> *Romeo [to Juliet]*: If I profane with my unworthiest hand
> This holy shrine, the gentle fine is this:
> My lips, two blushing pilgrims, ready stand
> To smooth that rough touch with a tender kiss.
> *Juliet*: Good pilgrim, you do wrong your hand too much,
> Which mannerly devotion shows in this;
> For saints have hands that pilgrims' hands do touch,
> And palm to palm is holy palmers' kiss.
> *Romeo*: Have not saints lips, and holy palmers too?
> *Juliet*: Ay, pilgrim, lips that they must use in pray'r.
> *Romeo*: O, then, dear saint, let lips do what hands do!
> They pray; grant thou, lest faith turn to despair.
> *Juliet*: Saints do not move, though grant for prayers' sake.
> *Romeo*: Then move not while my prayer's effect I take.
>
> (I.v)

They speak alternately, and in doing so develop a formal sonnet between them, binding them with line, rhythm and a rhyme scheme that that goes *abab, cdcd, efef, gg*.

Romeo speaks the first four-line thought. Juliet replies with a second. By the ninth line, as the sonnet form moves towards a conclusion, Romeo asks a one-line question.

Juliet answers. Romeo responds – with two lines; and when Juliet replies Romeo bonds himself with her by rhyming a line with hers. Then he kisses her! They become one through a brilliant harmony of form and content; and their shared enterprise in the elaboration of the form leads then to the bold action of love.

•

By now you should have begun to feel the puppet master pulling your acting strings. There's no rule, of course, that can't be broken, but it is a very good idea always to rehearse your text as conducted by Shakespeare at least once. Do so, and pace, pause, rhythm, break and texture will be revealed. You will have experienced the writer's intention before you impose your own.

The Line

The line is the next of the building blocks – the next given.

Each line has its own journey and energy, whether it's a regular iambic pentameter, or a different syllabic length or an irregular rhythm; fast-paced or slow-moving; broken by a pause or shared between characters. It's a block of syllables riding on the iambic energy, and a specific stage in a precisely calibrated journey of thought and emotion.

When spoken properly, the verse line sounds quite different from prose not only because of the iambic rhythm, but because there is a sustained vocal energy through the line. It starts with a kick and ends with a held focus, like a laser beam from beginning to end. This energy reflects the urgent heightened content that has been formally shaped into verse.

Today, unfortunately, many actors make verse sound like prose. They flatten it with casual speech habits – habits compounded by a tendency to stop at the end of a line regardless of whether the end of the thought has been reached. This is such a common failing that it is important to emphasise the distinction: a line is not the same as a thought. As we have seen, while a thought can start and finish in one line, it will more usually develop over several.

By confusing thought with line, the actor destroys both. The onward dynamic of the line becomes so interrupted that the audience loses its essential energy and sense. And every time the audience hears the line fall, it assumes the thought is over – which makes an eight-line thought impossible to follow.

Here is an analogy. Imagine an eight-line thought is a movement requiring eight stages to complete. It might be running up to vault over a horse and landing on your feet on the other side. It is obvious that if you stopped on the run-up or as your hands touched the horse – or even in mid-air – you wouldn't be able to perform the vault. In order to vault, you have to link and sustain a series of movements without stopping.

Similarly, the verse line needs to be physically sustained. You can pause and breathe within or at the end of one but you cannot stop, drop or droop. Your body, breath and voice must hold the line's energy so that any pause is a suspension, not a stop.

We already know that Shakespeare breaks rules. When he does, it's always for a reason. The perfect iambic pentameter line starts with an unstressed syllable and ends with a stressed. But when characters lose their flow and composure, the line will often start stressed and end unstressed. Likewise, it's not an accident if the line isn't ten syllables long or is broken half way through; or if a thought doesn't start at the beginning of a line and end at the end. Look for the reason why.

Look at the words that start and finish the lines. In a regular line, the first word moves you forward – like 'O', 'If', 'But', 'And', 'When', 'Then' or 'Therefore'. It kickstarts you into the speech. And the last word rounds the line off, with the sense of completion you get from nouns like 'world', 'nature', 'truth' or 'advice'. But if the opposite happens and a line starts with a more substantial word – 'Possess', 'Swear', 'Awake' – and ends with a 'but', a 'she' or an 'and', something important is being communicated to the actor.

Here's a simple line exercise:

- Take a verse speech – we will use one of Isabella's from *Measure for Measure*.
- Observe the first words of each line; just speak them out. Breathe and think the whole speech but only vocalise the first word.
- Do the same with the last words of each line.
- Then speak out the first word of each line followed by the last word.
- Now do the whole speech.
- If you launch yourself on the first word of a line and aim to hit the target on the last, you won't fall off the line.

> *Isabella*: To whom should I complain? Did I tell this,
> Who would believe me? O perilous mouths
> That bear in them one and the self-same tongue
> Either of condemnation or approof,
> Bidding the law make curtsy to their will;
> Hooking both right and wrong to th' appetite,
> To follow as it draws! I'll to my brother.
> Though he hath fall'n by prompture of the blood,

Yet hath he in him such a mind of honour
That, had he twenty heads to tender down
On twenty bloody blocks, he'd yield them up
Before his sister should her body stoop
To such abhorr'd pollution.
Then, Isabel, live chaste, and, brother, die:
More than our brother is our chastity.
I'll tell him yet of Angelo's request,
And fit his mind to death, for his soul's rest.

(II.iv)

Now let's look more closely at the first and last words in the speech:

First	Last
To	this
Who	mouths
That	tongue
Either	approof
Bidding	will
Hooking	appetite
To	brother
Though	blood
Yet	honour
That	down
On	up
Before	stoop
To	pollution
Then	die
More	chastity
I'll	request
And	rest

As long as you have spoken each word completely, touching each syllable and final consonant, you will have felt the kick of energy that starts the line and how it is harnessed on the last word.

It's worth analysing in detail just how this works in the act of speaking. Thus, 'To' throws you forward, and the *s* on 'this' hisses you into the second line, completing the thought mid-way on 'me'. 'O' is a sound that normally starts a line but here re-energises it, starting a new thought. The line ends on 'mouths'. *Ths* is difficult to say, so there is a minute pause as your mouth gets around the sounds and then has to make another *th* to start the third line: 'That'. 'Tongue' ends here, and the speaking of *gue* stops and holds you before you are propelled forward on 'Either'. Air escapes through the *f* on 'approof', but is immediately checked by the *b* of 'Bidding'. The power and substance of that word starting the line not only breaks the rhythm but blocks the energy. 'Will' ends this line, and as you dwell on *ll* you pause a fraction to recover before the next line starts with a substantial word but one that opens the breath on *h*. The *t* of 'appetite' stops and holds you, and this is reinforced by then having to speak another *t* – 'To' – as the next line begins.

'Brother' at the end of this one keeps you moving, but another *th* in 'Though' takes time to speak and accordingly defines the start of the next line. The *d* in 'blood' stops you, and *y* in 'Yet' unlocks your mouth to start the energy as you continue, and this propels you forward to 'honour', which doesn't stop you. The stop happens in the making of *th* in 'That' at the start of the next line. The end of 'down' holds you again, and now the next line has to be kicked off with 'On'. This fast-moving line is reined in by the *p* of 'up', and the reins are still in place on the *b* of 'Before' as you carry on. This reining pattern continues with the *p* of 'stoop', and again the *t* of 'To' as you enter the only foreshortened, seven-syllable line to 'such abhorr'd pollution'. Here the meaning and the horror of the act – sex with Angelo – are emphasised by the hidden pun on 'whore' as well as the physical challenge to the mouth of a phrase so weighty, ugly and foul that it makes you pause. 'Then' starts the next line, and moves you forward again to 'die', which is open but checked in by the *m* of 'More' immediately afterwards. 'Chastity' is open, and it is sustained through into the next line with 'I'll' until the *t* in 'request' interrupts the momentum. 'And' takes you forward again, but you are finally stopped on 'rest'.

You will already have realised that the line is another of Shakespeare's support systems, interwoven with word and rhythm in the creation of meaning. We haven't yet examined thought or rhyme, but note at this stage how most of the thoughts in the speech start mid-line – an indication of great unease – and that the rhyming couplets at the end of the speech further indicate the degree of Isabella's distress. She is having such difficulty resolving through rhyme that she needs two attempts to do it.

Another pleasing discovery is that the last words of a verse line create a collage of a character's concerns: *this, mouths, tongue, approof, appetite, brother, blood, honour, down, up, stoop, pollution, die, chastity, request, rest.*

This exercise provides another example of how Shakespeare builds the scaffolding of a line for you to speak: the beginning and the end. Once you realise this, the technique of 'line ending' that some actors and directors advocate becomes unnecessary. 'Line ending' is a method designed to help differentiate between spoken verse and prose by placing a small pause at the end each line. In fact, while it may be a useful technique for encouraging an initial respect for the verse, it also has important limitations. In the hands of an inexperienced or over-reliant actor it can not only dismantle the sense of a thought but entirely dismember the emotional flow of a speech.

Before leaving the line, let's do one more exercise to fill in the words between the beginning and end.

- Breathe and speak each word of the line separately. For instance: breathe – 'On' – breathe – 'twenty' – breathe – 'bloody' – breathe – 'blocks' – breathe – 'he'd' – breathe – 'yield' – breathe – 'them' – breathe – 'up'.
- If you manage to keep the breath low and the voice open, this simple exercise will connect you all to the words in the line.
- When you give each word oxygen, they will begin to settle in you.
- You should also begin to feel the forward thrust of the line. Each word will take you forward, step by step.
- By deliberately breaking up the line, you have blocked this thrust and the iambic, and you might feel the line's energy trying to escape through you.
- Now use the breath to build the line up word by word. Breathe – 'On' – breathe – 'On twenty' – breathe – 'On twenty bloody' – breathe – 'On twenty bloody blocks', etc.

As you build the line back up, you will begin to feel its energy and iambic – and feel them sustained through the whole line. Too often, actors commit themselves to half a line and then just mumble the other half, missing out on vital steps in the text's structure and meaning. This exercise helps address that loss. Shakespeare's characters need every word, line and thought to navigate through their testing times.

The Thought and the Structuring of Thoughts

Thought is a movement or journey within the brain. In this way, thought is physical – you can feel thoughts moving in you and you can sense them moving in others.

We know when a thought ends, when it starts, whether it's long or short. If there is a diversion along the way we feel that there has to be a return to the main road before the thought is complete.

Thoughts and the changes of gear within them are signposted by punctuation. A full stop, question mark or exclamation mark indicates the completion of a thought; other punctuation – commas, colons, semi-colons, etc. – marks the diversions, the turns and pauses within the thought.

Remember, though, that punctuation is a literary device to aid sense when we *read*. It needn't be heard when we speak. I emphasise this because all too often in Shakespeare, actors see a comma or a colon and stop thinking. They stop the physical journey of the thought. This impedes their making real sense of a speech and it throws confusion into the ears of the audience. The audience might be able to hear and under-stand every word, feel the drive of the iambic in the verse – but unless the actor is holding the energy of each thought, the audience won't know what's going on.

Holding that energy is all the more important because thoughts in Shakespeare don't exist in isolation from one another. Rather, they develop through structure and connection, linking with further thoughts, growing in intensity and excitement as they elaborate and resolve arguments, concerns and feelings. Each thought is tied to the next. Thought by thought, issues are opened up and out like a Russian doll. You have to open the first doll to get the next one out.

Thought links to thought just as scene to scene. This architecture of thought builds the story, moving the speaker and the audience forward through events. There is no time for stagnation: thought emerging through speech turns into action.

Thoughts have an inward momentum as well as a forward one. They move into their target, into the heart of a problem before they resolve it. They travel from the wide-lens perspective to the close-up, focusing and magnifying as they go. It's a sustained sharpness of attention that requires breath and support and a real intellectual fitness. Most of us aren't practised at speaking long, connected thoughts.

The brain is like a muscle: it needs work to nourish ideas of great moment and complexity.

Here is Hermione in the trial scene of *The Winter's Tale*. She is being tried by her husband, the king, for alleged adultery with his best friend.

> *Hermione:* The crown and comfort of my life, your favour,
> I do give lost, for I do feel it gone,
> But know not how it went; my second joy
> And first fruits of my body, from his presence
> I am barr'd, like one infectious; my third comfort,
> Starr'd most unluckily, is from my breast –
> The innocent milk in it most innocent mouth –
> Hal'd out to murder; myself on every post
> Proclaim'd a strumpet; with immodest hatred
> The child-bed privilege denied, which 'longs
> To women of all fashion; lastly, hurried
> Here to this place, i' th' open air, before
> I have got strength of limit.
>
> (III.ii)

Look for the full stop in this speech and you will realise that Hermione is speaking one twelve-and-a-half-line thought – a single journey.

Exercises

- Try pushing against a wall, and speak the thought. The push will help you maintain the connection of the thought. If you pull off because you've stopped thinking, you will feel it drop away physically through your body and your head. The push brings the energy of the thought into consciousness.
- Now move away from the wall and speak the thought with the conscious memory of the energy created by the push.

- You are feeling not only the physical energy of the thought, but the energy of Hermione's need to complete the thought.
- Now deliberately stop thinking and you will immediately feel the energy die in you and the text wane.
- Or break the thought at the end of each line and it will have the same result.
- There are turns and pauses on the way, but the internal energy of the thought never stops until 'limit'. As you speak it, you can pause and breathe but the engine must not stop. Sustain the thought and focus from 'The' to 'limit' – from beginning to end.
- Be conscious of this energy.

The energy of thought is a given. You and the audience will understand the text when you have this energy. When you don't, it will be harder for you both. For instance, some directors encourage actors in whom they're not entirely confident to speak a thought either on one breath – very difficult if it's fifteen lines long – or rapidly, which can be equally awkward for the audience. In fact, neither technique is needed if you can find and feel the physical energy contained in any penetrating thought – because a long thought is powered by the brain and has more emotional flow than a shorter one.

This will be evident if we return to Hermione, and put in place the exchange that precedes her long thought. Prosecuted by her own husband for treason and adultery, Hermione is her own defence counsel:

> *Leontes:* Look for no less than death.
> *Hermione:* Sir, spare your threats.
> The bug which you would fright me with I seek.
> To me can life be no commodity.

> (III.ii)

Hermione's first two thoughts are, in effect: don't bother to threaten me; I am not afraid of death because there is nothing worth living for. There then follows the long thought, which is in essence a list of all the cherished parts of her life that Leontes has taken away.

Part of the emotional reason for this long thought is the momentum of memory unleashed in Hermione at the thought of death. You can hear this memory surge in the speech of abandoned friends or betrayed lovers anywhere. And then she/he did that, and then.... and then...and then. The list perpetuates itself until the speaker has spilled it all out.

The other dramatic aspect of a thought as long as this is simply that it is hard to interrupt. Hermione is speaking about things that Leontes does not want to hear, so she doesn't give him a chance to intervene. It's just what any politician will tell you – if you are being interviewed by an aggressive journalist when you have something important to say and you don't want to be knocked off your point, make the point on a long thought.

To get feedback from this exercise, try it with a partner.

- Sit opposite your partner, close enough to be able to push against their hand if the exercise becomes too frustrating. The push against the hand will help you locate the sustaining energy of a thought. It will reconnect you if it drops.
- Take one long thought and speak it to your partner – you will take turns.
- If your partner knows you have dropped the thought or stopped it, they must send you back to the beginning. Within a few minutes you will feel the surge of energy required in holding a thought. Use the hand, and push if you don't feel it.

What will be evident to your partner in this exercise is how clear it is when you stop thinking. Similarly, your audience *knows* when you are not making sense. They might sit politely thinking it's their failure in not understanding Shakespeare, but in fact it is your responsibility.

- As you experiment, you can pause and breathe but still hold the thought and feel connected to it.
- You should now be able to hold a thought.

Walking the journey of a thought

The next stage is to go deeper into a long thought, which may have many changes of direction. I want you to feel physically that one thought can contain many turns and twists. It can contain one stage of the journey or five stages; and between each stage is a turn. In this exercise I'm asking you to place that turn into your body by walking it – for instance, 'To be – *turn* – or not to be – *turn* – that is the question – *turn*' and so on.

- Return to Hermione's twelve-and-a-half-line thought, and try walking the journey it takes. Keep physically centred, breathing and on voice.
- Start walking on the first word, and allow any pulse within the thought to change your direction and pace. The thought should change your walk, rather than your walk harnessing the text.
- You might be thrown forward rapidly; you might have to walk slowly. There could be many twists and turns in one line, or you might experience a huge arc of a thought moving in one smooth direction.
- Try to find as many turns as you can. You might have to walk this one thought several times and as the thought engages in the body, see if you can walk and turn on the text.
- You will begin to feel physically what is often described as 'being in the moment'. If you speak and turn simultaneously on a 'but' or an 'if', you are in the moment: the physical turn represents the turn in the brain on the word.

When I did this exercise with Hermione's speech, I discovered twenty-nine turns. To my surprise I also found myself moving forward and speaking with much more pace than before. I felt more emotional and released, and much closer to the texture of the thought.

Heightened text is vigorous in its ability to change on a single word. If you abandon yourself to the text and walk with it, not against it, you will realise that the turns are sharp and clear. The thinking isn't flabby: you are not on a journey that ambles or meanders. The verbal equivalent of ambling would be created by phrases such as 'well, perhaps; maybe'. You won't normally find such uncommitted dawdling in Shakespeare. His characters don't have time for it: they are alert, ready and trying to survive.

The thought is active, the language is active and the speaking is active. With this in mind, try walking the thought again and be diligent about turning on the words as you speak them – not before or after, but simultaneously.

- After each walk you should immediately return and speak the thought from a still position, but with the memory of the movements in your being. The breath, voice, head and heart will feel heightened. You will be breathing differently with the thought, the iambic and line, feel their forward energy more clearly, and be much more physically and emotionally engaged.

For variety, you can try some other exercises to find the turns in a thought.

- Sit in a circle of chairs and change seats at each turn.
- Take objects out of a bag – find a new object with each turn.

We have examined a single thought. Its contents, actions and complexities will have made you aware of how much is happening. But now things get richer and more interesting for the simple reason that no thought stands alone. Each links very clearly and directly to another, and with every link the speaking and the quest are intensified, moving the character closer to the heart of a debate. The thoughts build a structure. The first one opens up a debate, a concern, a question; then the following thoughts explore, clarify and deepen, looking for an answer, a resolve. The last thought moves towards a conclusion – even if that conclusion is the beginning of a new problem.

This sequential thinking is one of the great skills we have developed to survive and flourish: this leads to this; if I do this, this will be the result. You move forward as you explore the problem; you don't backtrack intellectually or emotionally. The procession of thoughts and connections intensifies the character, the scene and the play.

Still, actors tend to give up halfway through a scene, to de-energise as a speech progresses. This is the exact opposite of what the structure dictates. As you move forward through a speech, the thoughts invariably move towards greater focus and energy.

Exercises
- Look at a whole speech. Count the number of thoughts. Generally there will be between three and five. If more, the character might be unsure or emotionally hesitant. If less, they are very sure and emotionally charged.
- Observe where the thoughts start. Thoughts that begin mid-line are often a sign of unease or instability in the character's processes.
- Notice how long thoughts have more emotional flow, while shorter thoughts are relatively hard and tight.
- Speak the speech actively, linking thought to thought. Experience the power of the bridges and connections between each thought.
- You can do this sitting opposite a partner and gently pushing, hand to hand, to help you feel each thought connect and intensify.

- Now walk the whole speech, changing direction on each thought.
- When these turns are in your body, change directions within the thought as you did with Hermione's single long thought. Each stage and each turn will add more texture to the thoughts and the voice.
- You will notice how the structure moves a character towards a resolution. They rarely stand still in their thinking. They are always changing as they speak.

Try this with Lady Macbeth's first speech after she has read her husband's letter.

> *Lady Macbeth*: Glamis thou art, and Cawdor; and shalt be
> What thou art promis'd. Yet do I fear thy nature;
> It is too full o' th' milk of human kindness
> To catch the nearest way. Thou wouldst be great;
> Art not without ambition, but without
> The illness should attend it. What thou wouldst highly,
> That wouldst thou holily; wouldst not play false,
> And yet wouldst wrongly win.
> Thou'dst have, great Glamis, that which cries
> 'Thus thou must do' if thou have it;
> And that which rather thou dost fear to do
> Than wishest should be undone. Hie thee hither,
> That I may pour my spirits in thine ear,
> And chastise with the valour of my tongue
> All that impedes thee from the golden round
> Which fate and metaphysical aid doth seem
> To have thee crown'd withal.

> (I.v)

There are seven thoughts in seventeen lines: that's high-density thinking. Five of the thoughts start mid-line, an unease that speaks for itself. Two shortened lines – 'And yet wouldst wrongly win', and '"Thus thou must do" if thou have it' (six and eight syllables respectively) – create a hiatus of frustration at congested points of alliteration. Beat the iambic and you'll find nine irregular lines that trip you up, starting with the very first line on 'Glamis': further evidence of the character's agitation reflected in the structure.

All the physical evidence of the givens is ample proof of Lady Macbeth's mental state. Notice the friction as you speak many of the words. 'Wouldst' appears five times – in order to reach the *t* you really have to work. 'Thou'dst' and 'wishest' have the same effect. Rhythm and line structure are equally fraught. Look at the first two thoughts:

Glamis thou art, and Cawdor, and shalt be
What thou art promis'd. Yet do I fear thy nature;
It is too full o' th' milk of human kindness
To catch the nearest way.

The first line has nine syllables. It starts with a full weight on 'Glamis' and then gathers speed to 'and shalt be', which doesn't finish the line with any sense of completion but whisks you through into the next which has twelve syllables. The iambic wave underneath this line lifts up 'fear' and you then can feel the whole force of the word 'nature'. The third line also has twelve syllables. You are accelerated through 'full o' th' milk' and land on 'human kindness' before the fourth line picks you up with 'To catch'.

Macbeth is a play that deals with many forces within nature. Murder is unnatural and here in the ends of two lines the words 'nature' and 'human kindness' ring out with clarity from the commotion of Lady Macbeth's debate – a commotion which continues to dominate the structure of the thoughts. She is enormously frustrated with her husband. He could be king, but he doesn't like getting his hands dirty! Only she can resolve the issue: she realises that she needs to be beside him to strengthen him.

Now try *walking* the journey of the speech, physically changing direction every time you feel a turn in the thought. Try to turn as often as you feel the text shift. You might have to do it several times to get each change, but you will find that the first section of the speech has many turns. You are almost thrown around physically – a manifestation of the energy in Lady Macbeth's head and heart. But the moment you hit 'Hie thee hither...', you begin an easier journey with fewer turns and more directness. She has discovered a course of action; her head and heart can move on a more focused and straightforward path. It is as though she has been hacking her way through a forest and at last found a clear track on 'Hie thee hither'.

As you finish the walking exercise, the physical movement will have upset you, made you feel what Lady Macbeth is feeling, until she settles on her moment of purpose and resolve. You change alongside her, and reach a resolution. But sometimes a resolution is not reached within a speech – perhaps because a character is interrupted. We will stay with

Macbeth and see how Shakespeare constructs an unfinished soliloquy. Here, Macbeth is debating whether to kill Duncan. He is moving towards not doing so – but his wife interrupts him.

> *Macbeth*: If it were done when 'tis done, then 'twere well
> It were done quickly. If th' assassination
> Could trammel up the consequence, and catch,
> With his surcease, success; that but this blow
> Might be the be-all and the end-all here –
> But here upon this bank and shoal of time –
> We'd jump the life to come. But in these cases
> We still have judgment here, that we but teach
> Bloody instructions, which being taught return
> To plague th' inventor. This even-handed justice
> Commends th' ingredience of our poison'd chalice
> To our own lips. He's here in double trust:
> First, as I am his kinsman and his subject –
> Strong both against the deed; then, as his host,
> Who should against his murderer shut the door,
> Not bear the knife myself. Besides, this Duncan
> Hath borne his faculties so meek, hath been
> So clear in his great office, that his virtues
> Will plead like angels, trumpet-tongu'd, against
> The deep damnation of his taking-off;
> And pity, like a naked new-born babe,
> Striding the blast, or heaven's cherubin hors'd
> Upon the sightless couriers of the air,
> Shall blow the horrid deed in every eye,
> That tears shall drown the wind. I have no spur
> To prick the sides of my intent, but only
> Vaulting ambition, which o'er-leaps itself,
> And falls on th' other.
> [*Enter Lady Macbeth*]
> How now! What news?
>
> (I.vii)

First, walk the journey of the speech. There are seven thoughts in twenty-eight lines, six starting mid-line. Their energy and relentlessness take you to the edge. You might find that the physical structure of thoughts, words and lines makes you want to break into a run. The givens here work on you in the opposite way to those in Lady Macbeth's speech. There they created a tangled net of frustration, from which she cut free in her last thoughts. Here, Macbeth is swept along on an enormous swell of sound, rhythm and thought.

The first thought – 'If it were done when 'tis done, then 'twere well / It were done quickly' – has some control in it – the *t*'s and *d*'s in the first line, and the rhythm landing on 'done', 'done' and 'well', are an attempt to contain the surge of power in Macbeth. Remember, he has left the king at supper, an unusual breach of etiquette which will have made his heart beat faster and induced a sense of panic.

By the start of the second thought in the second line, the swell is increasing the pace and flow of the speech. This power is partially obtained by the open vowels that abound and dominate here: 'trammel', 'surcease', 'blow', 'be', 'be-all', 'all', 'here' (twice), 'shoal of time', 'life'. The very openness of these words pulls you along. After this thought, the next three thoughts contain a similar energy pattern.

Still Macbeth tries to keep himself and his imagination in check. Each thought starts with words and a rhythm that attempt to understand and capture his ideas and emotions. And each in due course bursts through the controlled run-up, taking Macbeth further and further out on a limb. So 'But in these cases' starts safely enough, but it continues:

> We still have judgement here, that we but teach
> Bloody instructions, which being taught return
> To plague th' inventor.

In meaning and form you can feel the gathering panic in the rhythm of 'that we but teach'. 'Bloody' starts the next line messily and brutally; 'instructions' tries to control it, but Macbeth is sent off again on the rhythm of 'which being taught return / To plague th' inventor.'

The next thought starts in a new attempt to control the full horror of this debate. 'This even-handed justice' has a clear containment in the rhythm to match the sense, and 'Commends' starts the next line powerfully – but not for long, as 'th' ingredients of our poison'd chalice / To our own lips' once more sets off the rhythmic urgency and panic.

The final effort to control and think rationally comes in the form of a list:

> He's here in double trust:
> First, as I am his kinsman and his subject –
> Strong both against the deed;

The control cannot last long. There is a gathering power beneath these lines which begins to break through on

> then, as his host,
> Who should against his murderer shut the door,
> Not bear the knife myself.

Next is the longest thought in the speech – 'Besides, this Duncan...': nine lines long, starting halfway through a line and finishing over halfway through another. As you walked this thought you will have felt its vast spaciousness. The room you were working in might have seemed too small to hold you and your imagination. The waves of the iambic might have made you feel you were trying to out-run an incoming unstoppable tide.

Macbeth seems to be moving rapidly to the conclusion that he shouldn't commit the murder; but he is cut off mid-line by the unexpected entrance of Lady Macbeth, and picks up again with 'How now! What news?' We can imagine that the audience at the first performance of Macbeth might have been as shocked as Macbeth by her appearance. Shakespeare is breaking a rule here. Thoughts are meant to reach a resolution in order to move on. Macbeth seems about to do so – and suddenly his wife prevents him.

The consequences are huge. Having considered his own actions in the perspective of a much larger debate about crime, punishment and cosmic law, Macbeth fails explicitly to conclude that he won't murder Duncan – and thus leaves himself exposed to manipulation by his wife. The bridge over the chasm is missing its final section – Macbeth has been left dangling within sight of the other side but unable to reach it. This incomplete architecture is the real tragedy of Macbeth. He kills Duncan knowing he shouldn't, that it is wrong and that 'tears will drown the wind'.

Thus there is a vital acting clue in the structure of a speech – or rather in the way it conforms or fails to conform to the classic structure of debate and resolution in the thought. The actor who doesn't recognise the structural norm, and feel where the work departs from it, will miss the clue.

Summary

Always learn a text thought by thought, not line by line.

Note the stages within the thought. Count the number of thoughts in a speech. Experience the bridges between thoughts and feel the forward motion in the speech.

When you don't understand a line or a section of a speech, go back to the beginning to unlock it stage by stage. If you can't find your direction in the middle of a structured piece of writing, you have to go back to the beginning of the road: the beginning of the speech. There is always a route to be followed – a road system – which will lead you to the meaning, and the givens are the map.

The Structure of Scenes

Just as thoughts move forward one to another, so a similar linking and bridging is found within and between scenes. Each scene links in some way to the next. This means that actors have a responsibility to start each scene with bridging energy. The connections between lines, thoughts, speeches and scenes are so crucial to the building of the whole that an actor who fails to energise just one line in a scene, fails to speak it clearly or make sense of it, can cause the entire house of cards to collapse. At the very least, other actors will have to supply extra energy to save the scene, if not the play.

Anyone who has worked on *Macbeth* knows that the play moves very quickly up to the murder of Duncan, the structure illustrating a whole nation sliding rapidly out of control. The action is slowed down only by the appearance of the Porter – who, incidentally, speaks the first prose in the play (apart from Macbeth's letter to his wife). The audience needs to have some relief, some laughter after the bloody and devastating scene between husband and wife immediately after the murder. But if the pace of the play lets up before the Porter appears, something essential is lost in the dramatic energy of the story.

The motor embedded in Shakespeare's scene structures is crucial. That is why experienced directors understand that the wrong placing of an interval can simply kill the potency of a production. For the same reason, actors need to run scenes and plays in rehearsal as soon as possible. It's not just that running scenes into each other helps expose weak links in telling the story, but also that the actors will be nurtured by tapping the structural energy Shakespeare provides. In the same way, actors should watch the rehearsal, especially any scenes preceding their own, in order to understand what they have to pick up and take further. Whatever happens, this knowledge must be firmly in place before the technical rehearsal: the technical always fragments the propelling structural energy, and it can take many public performances before it is found and released again.

Antithesis

The use of antithesis in Shakespeare is a common structural technique that works at the levels of both form and content – and, of course, the two are inextricably linked.

Viewed on a purely formal basis, the setting of opposites against each other was a popular Elizabethan device that satisfied in writing the pleasures of harmony. In terms of content, however, antithesis is also a very economic way of exploring complex thoughts and feelings. By swinging between extremes in one line, a character reveals the layers of experience that exists in any difficult decision or deep emotion – like 'I hate you, but I also love you'; or 'War is terrible, but peace is boring'; or 'You make me angry, but I find you attractive'. Antithesis refuses to make life simple or one-dimensional.

It's certainly true that many of our strongest feelings and thoughts can simultaneously provoke two opposite reactions within us. Antithesis explores that tension within the swing of a line or thought. Indeed, the ability to see both sides of an argument or an idea is something we're brought up to value: it's part of the reasoning process. Its absence can be frightening when we encounter another person who has no room for doubt in their thinking, or no sense of anybody else's feelings.

Hamlet has been educated to reason, to seek out opposites and see both sides of an argument.

> *Hamlet*:   What is a man,
> If his chief good and market of his time
> Be but to sleep and feed? A beast, no more!
> Sure he that made us with such large discourse,
> Looking before and after, gave us not
> That capability and godlike reason
> To fust in us unus'd.
>
> (IV.iv)

Indeed, he is so good at seeing both sides of an argument – so reasonable – that he is unable to take direct action until he realises that the impulse of revenge is incompatible with and cannot be tempered by reason.

> O, from this time forth
> My thoughts be bloody, or be nothing worth!
>
> (IV.iv)

When swings of thought and feeling like these are condensed in a verse line, the dramatic experience of both actor and audience can be considerably heightened by the compression of opposites. However, in practice the full power of antithesis is only realised in theatre when the actor is in the moment and on the exact meaning of the text. You cannot release both sides of an idea or emotion if you are ahead of or behind the words.

So, as you speak 'Roses have thorns and silver fountains mud' (Sonnet 35), you must experience the 'rose' before the 'thorn' and the 'silver fountain' before the 'mud'. In following this sequence you automatically discover the shock, the intellectual journey and emotional swing, that the antithesis reveals. If you are behind the text – because your breath system isn't free enough or your imagination not clear enough – the chances are that you will discover the rose but not the thorn. If you are ahead of the text, the thorn will be there but not the rose!

Some actors tend to generalise the emotional and intellectual journeys of their parts. This sketchiness is often linked to an inability to connect, moment by moment, to antithesis. There are similar problems for the actor who attaches primarily to one side of the antithesis or the other – the pleasant 'roses' and 'silver fountain', or the unpleasant 'thorns' and 'mud'. This one-sided approach entirely misses the point. Sonnet 35 is addressed to someone beautiful but corrupt. The complexity of the relationship is exposed in the tension between the two aspects of a single person. To serve the emotion of this relationship, you have to swing between the opposites and be on them as you swing.

Many of Shakespeare's speeches require the actor to recognise the intellectual power of antithesis. The actor who fails to see and explore it in the moment of speaking will flatten the complexity of thought and debate and fail to travel the journey of the speech.

> *Proteus*: Even as one heat another heat expels
> Or as one nail by strength drives out another,

So the remembrance of my former love
Is by a newer object quite forgotten.
Is it my mind or Valentinus' praise,
Her true perfection, or my false transgression,
That makes me reasonless to reason thus?

(*Two Gentlemen of Verona, II.iv*)

This is the beginning of a soliloquy delivered by Proteus after his best friend Valentine has shown him a picture of his love Silvia. Proteus has been completely smitten by Silvia even though he is supposed to be in love with another woman – Julia. A complex four-hander, worthy of tabloid headlines, is unfolding, and Proteus questions and debates the emotional realities of the situation through antithesis: 'remembrance' versus 'forgotten'; 'true perfection' versus 'false transgression'.

Later we will work on owning and experiencing every word in a text. The work will automatically reveal the antithesis in any text, but at this stage of exploring the givens, just be aware of the structural balancing that characterises so much of Shakespeare's writing. Sonnet 129 is typical in its account of lust – 'Enjoy'd no sooner but despised straight' and 'A bliss in proof, and prov'd, a very woe' – an appetite that reveals its opposite in being experienced.

In this speech from Romeo and Juliet, the main conflict is between love and hate – but the simple opposition is explored through antithesis in a variety of ways:

Romeo: What fray was here?
Yet tell me not, for I have heard it all.
Here's much to do with hate, but more with love.
Why then, O brawling love! O loving hate!
O anything, of nothing first create!
O heavy lightness! serious vanity!
Mis-shapen chaos of well-seeming forms!
Feather of lead, bright smoke, cold fire, sick health!
Still-waking sleep, that is not what it is!
This love feel I, that feel no love in this.
Dost thou not laugh?
Benvolio: No, coz, I rather weep.
Romeo: Good heart, at what?
Benvolio: At thy good heart's oppression.

(I.i)

'Anything...nothing'; 'heavy lightness'; 'mis-shapen chaos...well-seeming forms'; 'feather of lead, bright smoke, cold fire, sick health'; 'still-waking sleep'; and Benvolio gets in on the act and balances Romeo's 'laugh' with 'weep'. This excerpt illustrates how agile and alert you must be to catch all the swings – and how, as soon as you do so, you will release the energy in the conflict of heart and mind by setting 'the word itself / Against the word' (*Richard II*).

Shakespeare also uses antithesis to help his characters explore one another through dialogue. The exchanges rely on the keenest of attention: characters bonding by listening intently to one another, and picking up each other's language – even if they don't like the result.

> *Richard*: Lady, you know no rules of charity,
> Which renders good for bad, blessings for curses.
> *Anne*: Villain, thou knowest nor law of God nor man:
> No beast so fierce but knows some touch of pity.
> *Richard*: But I know none, and therefore am no beast.
> *Anne*: O wonderful, when devils tell the truth!
> *Richard*: More wonderful when angels are so angry.
> [...]
> *Richard*: Fairer than tongue can name thee, let me have
> Some patient leisure to excuse myself.
> *Anne:* Fouler than heart can think thee, thou canst make
> No excuse current but to hang thyself.
>
> (*Richard III*, I.ii)

In fact, this whole altercation between Richard and Anne is based around antithesis. Anne matches Richard by finding the opposite of his words, which he in turn reverses back on her in a spirit of escalation. She links herself to him by following his 'fairer' with her 'fouler', and he spars with equal skill, matching her 'devils' with his 'angels'. The most important thing, though, is that she has joined the verbal tussle with him and engaged over meaning – which is precisely what he uses to woo her. They are joined through the operation of antithesis: opposites attract.

Antithesis works across lines and thoughts, as much in prose speeches as in verse. While prose lacks the obvious structural principles of verse – line and rhythm – an underlying framework of opposites is often present. This structure once revealed will support the speaker and help focus the feelings and ideas contained in the speech. Take an example from *The Merchant of Venice*. Here Launcelot Gobbo is debating whether to run away from Shylock. That would be a severely punishable offence so the comedy of the speech is acutely heightened by the danger of the consequences.

> *Launcelot*: Certainly my conscience will serve me to run from this Jew my master. The fiend is at mine elbow and tempts me, saying to me 'Gobbo, Launcelot Gobbo, good Launcelot' or 'good Gobbo' or 'good Launcelot Gobbo, use your legs, take the start, run away'. My conscience says 'No; take heed, honest Launcelot, take heed, honest Gobbo' or, as aforesaid, 'honest Launcelot Gobbo, do not run; scorn running with thy heels'. Well, the most courageous fiend bids me pack. 'Via!' says the fiend; 'away!' says the fiend. 'For the heavens, rouse up a brave mind' says the fiend 'and run.' Well, my conscience, hanging about the neck of my heart, says very wisely to me 'My honest friend Launcelot, being an honest man's son' or rather 'an honest woman's son'; for indeed my father did something smack, something grow to, he had a kind of taste – well, my conscience says 'Launcelot, budge not'. 'Budge' says the fiend. 'Budge not' says my conscience. 'Conscience,' say I, 'you counsel well.' 'Fiend,' say I, 'you counsel well.' To be rul'd by my conscience, I should stay with the Jew my master, who – God bless the mark! – is a kind of devil; and, to run away from the Jew, I should be ruled by the fiend, who – saving your reverence! – is the devil himself. Certainly the Jew is the very devil incarnation; and, in my conscience, my conscience is but a kind of hard conscience to offer to counsel me to stay with the Jew. The fiend gives the more friendly counsel. I will run, fiend; my heels are at your commandment; I will run.
>
> (II.ii)

Here the opposite forces of good and bad are made vividly concrete. One is represented by the personification of Launcelot's conscience while the other is a fiend; and both are counselling him – tugging and swinging him from one side of the debate to the other.

Finally, antithesis extends as an organising principle beyond individual speeches, exchanges and even scenes. It represents the underlying structure of the plays themselves. *King Lear* is infused with concepts of all versus nothing and natural versus unnatural; *Measure for Measure* is about the balance between lust and restraint; *Romeo and Juliet* that between love and hate. Stay alert to antithesis at all levels of Shakespeare's work, alive to its energy and true to its tension, and you will discover a compression of form and content that goes to the heart of his complexity and genius.

Rhyme

The next of the givens is rhyme. Until now, we have been dealing mostly with blank verse. When Shakespeare uses rhyme, he does so deliberately. The actor needs to observe and respond accordingly.

Rhyme satisfies. It can be delightful or sinister; light-hearted or profound; it can order our thoughts and emotions, and round them off with a rewarding sense of fulfilment. It creates rhythm and heightens expectation; and on a practical level, it can aid memory and, if your voice is free, lighten your vocal tone. The completion of a rhyme is like the aural version of a child's toy where bricks slide effortlessly into their right holes – round into round, square into square. When this aural consonance is coupled with the completion of a thought or feeling, it creates only greater satisfaction.

Equally, rhyme can be used in counterpoint to the content. The disturbance this creates is extremely effective: our ears are unsettled, the meaning gains texture and odd – often sinister – tensions are established. Here is Pericles reading a riddle:

> I am no viper, yet I feed
> On mother's flesh which did me breed.
> I sought a husband, in which labour
> I found that kindness in a father.
> He's father, son, and husband mild;
> I mother, wife, and yet his child.
> How they may be, and yet in two.
> As you will live, resolve it you.

> (*Pericles, Prince of Tyre*, I.i)

The regular rhyme here feels safe and secure. When you realise, however, that the riddle describes the incest of the King of Antioch and his daughter, you start to appreciate the powerful tension between the innocent form and the aberrant content. The form is there to conceal the nature of the intimate relationship, to dupe our ears with its childlike quality. Without the rhyme, we might crack the language and the incestuous secret more quickly, and it is this very neatness of form that so shocks us when the content is fully understood.

Good rhyming works subliminally in our ears, pulling us along on an invisible thread through the lines it twins together. Less skilful rhyme can feel clumsy and annoying to the ear – yet used deliberately it too can serve a dramatic purpose, telling us something about the situation or the character who uses it. Similarly, any movement from blank verse into rhyme or vice versa operates as a dramatic signal to which you must be alert.

Different patterns of rhyme work, of course, in different ways. The *rhyming couplet* consists of a pair of rhyming lines, like King Henry's from *Henry V*:

> His jest will savour but of shallow wit,
> When thousands weep more than did laugh at it.
>
> (I.ii)

A *quatrain*, by contrast, is a group of four lines with a rhyming pattern. Shakespeare often uses an *abab* pattern – the first line rhyming with the third, and the second with the fourth – as well as other variations.

Both quatrain and couplet can be full iambic pentameters or take a shorter line. The rhymes are heard more clearly in the shorter lines because they appear more quickly, lending a playful, less sophisticated feel to the verse. Speak and compare Henry's rhyming couplet, a ten-syllable line, with Pericles' riddle where the line is eight syllables long:

> I am no viper, yet I feed
> On mother's flesh which did me breed.

The rhyme feels much more vivid and potent in the shorter line.

Here is an excerpt from the beginning of *Love's Labour's Lost*. Rhyming couplets and quatrains are used together in iambic pentameter lines.

> *Berowne*: Why, all delights are vain; but that most vain
> Which, with pain purchas'd, doth inherit pain,

As painfully to pore upon a book
To seek the light of truth; while truth the while
Doth falsely blind the eyesight of his look.
Light, seeking light, doth light of light beguile;
So, ere you find where light in darkness lies,
Your light grows dark by losing of your eyes.
Study me how to please the eye indeed,
By fixing it upon a fairer eye;
Who dazzling so, that eye shall be his heed,
And give him light that it was blinded by.
Study is like the heaven's glorious sun,
That will not be deep-search'd with saucy looks;
Small have continual plodders ever won,
Save base authority from others' books.
These earthly godfathers of heaven's lights
That give a name to every fixed star
Have no more profit of their shining nights
That those that walk and wot not what they are.
Too much to know is to know nought but fame;
And every godfather can give a name.
King: How well he's read, to reason against reading!
Dumain: Proceeded well, to stop all good proceeding!
Longaville: He weeds the corn, and still lets grow the weeding.
Berowne: The spring is near, when green geese are a-breeding.
Dumain: How follows that?
Berowne: Fit in his place and time.
Dumain: In reason nothing.
Berowne: Something then in rhyme.

(I.i)

Berowne is contesting the King of Navarre's notion of three years' study. The light-hearted feel of the rhyme perhaps serves to disguise the challenge. It would feel much more serious to confront a king in blank verse. His speech contains a feast of rhymes:

    a rhyming couplet *a a*
    a quatrain *b c b c*
    a rhyming couplet *d d*
    a quatrain *e f e f*
    a quatrain *g h g h*
    a quatrain *i j i j*
    a rhyming couplet *k k*

At first glance the sequence might seem complex and rigid, but take a closer look. Each change of sequence is harnessed to a change of thought or a change of gear within the thought, and heightens both drama and sense. And when reason finally deserts the dialogue after the extravagance of 'reading', 'proceeding', 'weeding' and 'a-breeding', Berowne observes wittily that only rhyme now holds it together – fitting in its time and place.

Berowne is showing off. These young men are sparring through language and rhyme. In the same way, some of my students spend breaks between classes rapping, testing each others' skills until one of them manages the final bravura finish.

Rhyme is bravura speech. It doesn't need thumping out, but it has an energy and quality of display that you must convey. Like any given, it is there to help you understand character and situation. Berowne uses rhyme, among other techniques, to show off. He speaks with bravado. He's clever and he knows it. The rhyme is a way of preening through language.

The King of Navarre knows what Berowne is doing: 'How well he's read to reason against reading'. Not only is Berowne well-informed, but his style is equally cultivated. The King doesn't attempt to rhyme here with Berowne. Maybe in his position he doesn't feel the pressure to compete.

It is the other young men who pick up the rhyming challenge. Dumain rhymes with the king, and Longville with Dumain. They have decided to compete with Berowne, and criticise his ideas, extending the king's rhyme and elaborating on the antithetical figure he established. Dumain's 'Proceeded well, to stop all good proceeding' – speaking well to stop their three-year period of study – could end the debate but Longaville wants in on the act and the attack on Berowne as well: 'He weeds the corn, and still lets grow the weeding'. There's a concealed insult here to Berowne's intellect: he may weed the corn but not sufficiently well to stop weeds growing. In other words, his reasoning is impaired.

But Berowne is not to be outdone. The rhyme is obvious, but like Dumain we can't immediately follow his train of thought: 'green geese a-breeding'. Actually, it's a kind of tease or riddle. Green geese – young, inexperienced geese who make a lot of noise honking – are breeding; they are breeding rhymes. And that's just what these young, testosterone-filled men are doing, so that there is almost no sense by the end of this exchange except the pleasure challenge of rhyme, as Berowne makes clear in his own final ingenious couplet. Sparring wittily in rhyme gives them a safe and harnessed outlet for their competitive energy. Challenges can be made through the delights of form without coming to actual physical blows.

Here the rhyme and rhythm are light and easy, almost frivolous, as befits the story. The main body of *Love's Labour's Lost* is a romp: youth exploring love and the games of love. Shakespeare uses many devices, theatrical and verbal, to create this carefree world – until the closing scenes, when death casts a shadow across the lives of the lovers and responsibility initiates them all into adulthood. In that moment the language has to shift and be appropriate to sorrow. As Berowne observes, 'Honest plain words best pierce the ear of grief'. Accordingly, the last parts of the play are mostly conducted in blank verse.

It is now that Rosaline, whom Berowne loves, challenges the worth of his skilful way with language. All the ladies ask their loves to wait a year and a day before their courtship continues – this is to give the Princess of France time to mourn her father's death. Rosaline adds an extra challenge for Berowne, who is known as someone who can wound with words. To test if his wit is of any real value, he must visit the hospitals and asylums to see if he can bring laughter to those in pain. Berowne accepts the challenge but he can't resist a final flourish with a rhyming couplet.

> *Rosaline*: Oft have I heard of you, my Lord Berowne,
> Before I saw you; and the world's large tongue
> Proclaims you for a man replete with mocks,
> Full of comparisons and wounding flouts,
> Which you on all estates will execute
> That lie within the mercy of your wit.
> To weed this wormwood from your fruitful brain,
> And therewithal to win me, if you please,
> Without the which I am not to be won,
> You shall this twelvemonth term from day to day
> Visit the speechless sick, and still converse
> With groaning wretches; and your task shall be,
> With all the fierce endeavour of your wit,
> To enforce the pained impotent to smile.
> *Berowne*: To move wild laughter in the throat of death?
> It cannot be; it is impossible;
> Mirth cannot move a soul in agony.
> *Rosaline*: Why, that's the way to choke a gibing spirit,

Whose influence is begot of that loose grace
Which shallow laughing hearers give to fools.
A jest's prosperity lies in the ear
Of him that hears it, never in the tongue
Of him that makes it; then, if sickly ears,
Deaf'd with the clamours of their own dear groans,
Will hear your idle scorns, continue then,
And I will have you and that fault withal.
But if they will not, throw away that spirit,
And I shall find you empty of that fault,
Right joyful of your reformation.
Berowne: A twelvemonth? Well, befall what will befall,
I'll jest a twelvemonth in an hospital.

(V.ii)

You will notice both the sensuousness of the blank verse here, and the heavier weight of the rhythm through the pace of Rosaline's iambic. The lovers' world has changed, and with it their language and their spoken forms. Berowne's closing couplet is like a last youthful fling at the merriment of happier, more indulgent times.

A switch in verse form between blank and rhyming often signals a change in character, a maturing. In *A Midsummer Night's Dream*, for instance, the lovers speak in rhyme before they enter the wood. After their night there – which serves as a form of initiation – they emerge speaking blank verse: they have begun to grow up. Indeed, it's instructive to examine more closely the ways in which rhyme and blank verse alternate throughout the *Dream*, and to see what it tells us about both character and situation.

The play opens in blank verse, spoken by the older lovers – Duke Theseus and Hippolyta, the Queen of the Amazons. This is not young love in the way we saw in *Love's Labour's Lost*: not a frivolous flirtation to be expressed through rhyming couplets. The wooing of Hippolyta has been a serious affair, as Theseus reminds us: 'Hippolyta, I woo'd thee with my sword, / And won thy love doing thee injuries'.

The conversation is interrupted by Egeus, who enters with his daughter Hermia and two young men, Demetrius and Lysander. There's a problem. Egeus wants Hermia to marry Demetrius, but she is in love with Lysander. In line with Athenian law, Egeus demands his daughter's death if she insists on disobeying him. Theseus asks Hermia to consider her fate: marry Demetrius, or face either death or a nun's life. The whole serious and important discussion is conducted in blank verse.

Now the stage empties, leaving Hermia and Lysander alone. Initially they continue in blank verse, lamenting their crossed love. Then Lysander offers a solution: they can leave Athens together, forever. This is the moment that rhyme makes its entrance, introduced by Hermia who picks up from Lysander's blank verse and then launches into couplets on a line about simplicity – a suitable moment, as the form does indeed 'knitteth well together':

> *Hermia:* My good Lysander!
> I swear to thee by Cupid's strongest bow,
> By his best arrow, with the golden head,
> By the simplicity of Venus' doves,
> By that which knitteth souls and prospers loves,
> And by that fire which burn'd the Carthage Queen,
> When the false Troyan under sail was seen,
> By all the vows that ever men have broke,
> In number more than ever women spoke,
> In that same place thou hast appointed me,
> To-morrow truly will I meet with thee.
>
> (I.i)

The couplets bring an entirely different energy to the troubled exchanges in blank verse. They come as a relief to the ear, lightening the atmosphere and introducing a compelling urgency to the scene now that elopement offers a way out. Rhyme is the vehicle of hope; perhaps it also signals the private language the young lovers use together – their intimate code, not meant for adult or public ears.

Lysander's reply – 'Keep promise, love. Look, here comes Helena' – doesn't have a chance to continue the rhyming because Helena's arrival breaks the intimacy. Hermia similarly chooses not to rhyme with Lysander as she greets her friend: 'God speed fair Helena! Whither away?' Instead it is Helena who picks up the rhyming pattern with 'Call you me fair? That fair again unsay', rhyming 'unsay' with Hermia's 'away'.

This has real dramatic possibilities. Helena is bonding with Hermia through rhyme, re-establishing her relationship with her friend and perhaps at the same time excluding Lysander. It's something most of us will be familiar with if we've had the experience of hearing our partners speaking to their friends and feeling left out by the bonding devices in their language. Old friends have their special codes and references as they communicate.

Let's pick up immediately in the rhyming couplets that Helena uses:

> *Helena*: Call you me fair? That fair again unsay.
> Demetrius loves your fair. O happy fair!
> Your eyes are lode-stars and your tongue's sweet air
> More tuneable than lark to shepherd's ear,
> When wheat is green, when hawthorn buds appear.
> Sickness is catching; O, were favour so,
> Yours would I catch, fair Hermia, ere I go!
> My ear should catch your voice, my eye your eye,
> My tongue should catch your tongue's sweet melody.
> Were the world mine, Demetrius being bated,
> The rest I'd give to be to you translated.
> O, teach me how you look, and with what art
> You sway the motion of Demetrius' heart!

This is a girl talking to the best friend who has drawn Demetrius – Helena's ex-boyfriend – into loving her. Although the form sounds innocent, the content is complex and potentially explosive. The energy and ease of the rhyme hide a painful topic. Helena must need the rhyme as a device, a way of confronting Hermia without ending in a fight – that's for later in the play. Any actress playing Helena has to feel all the passion of a wronged young woman and make Hermia understand her part in the pain. The rhyme acts as a safety net that enables them to discuss a dangerous subject without falling apart. Although Lysander is present, Helena and her rhymes have pushed him to one side. Painful emotional conversations between girls are not normally conducted in the presence of a man.

Hermia, when she responds, doesn't pick up on Helena's rhymes. It is Helena who does the rhyming, perhaps in an attempt to stay close enough to her friend to discuss the betrayal of friendship.

> *Hermia*: I frown upon him, yet he loves me still.
> *Helena*: O that your frowns would teach my smiles such skill!
> *Hermia*: I give him curses, yet he gives me love.
> *Helena*: O that my prayers could such affection move!
> *Hermia*: The more I hate, the more he follows me.
> *Helena*: The more I love, the more he hateth me.

Hermia: His folly, Helena, is no fault of mine.
Helena: None, but your beauty; would that fault were mine!

Helena's attempts to continue rhyming begin to falter as she resorts to repetition of end words – 'me' and 'mine' – rather than true rhyme. The strain in her heart is beginning to show in the form.

In an act of compassion and empathy, Hermia's next speech takes up Helena's rhyming couplets. She starts this shift with the actual reassurance of 'Take comfort':

> *Hermia*: Take comfort: he no more shall see my face;
> Lysander and myself will fly this place.
> Before the time I did Lysander see,
> Seem'd Athens as a paradise to me.
> O, then, what graces in my life do dwell,
> That he hath turn'd a heaven unto a hell!

At this point Lysander moves into couplets, joining with Hermia and Helena's as he describes the plan to flee Athens. In effect he is signalling the disintegration of the girls' friendship while speaking to Helena in her language. We haven't yet heard Helena speak blank verse in the play; maybe this is Lysander's way of reaching out to Hermia's best friend.

> *Lysander*: Helen, to you our minds we will unfold:
> To-morrow night, when Phoebe doth behold
> Her silver visage in the wat'ry glass,
> Decking with liquid pearl the bladed grass,
> A time that lovers' flights doth still conceal,
> Through Athens' gates have we devis'd to steal.

Hermia carries on in couplets to Helena and then says goodbye forever:

> Farewell, sweet playfellow; pray thou for us,
> And good luck grant thee thy Demetrius!

– before returning to Lysander:

Keep word, Lysander; we must starve our sight
From lovers' food till morrow deep midnight.

Lysander too continues the couplets. He is so good at them that he can break the line and still hold the form as he bids farewell to both girls:

Lysander: I will, my Hermia; Helena adieu, [*Exit Hermia*]
As you on him, Demetrius dote on you!

Helena is left alone on stage and now speaks the first soliloquy of the play in couplets.

Helena: How happy some o'er other some can be!
Through Athens I am thought as fair as she.
But what of that? Demetrius thinks not so;
He will not know what all but he do know.
And as he errs, doting on Hermia's eyes,
So I, admiring of his qualities.
Things base and vile, holding no quantity,
Love can transpose to form and dignity.
Love looks not with the eyes, but with the mind;
And therefore is wing'd Cupid painted blind.
Nor hath Love's mind of any judgment taste;
Wings and no eyes figure unheedy haste;
And therefore is Love said to be a child,
Because in choice he is so oft beguil'd.
As waggish boys in game themselves forswear,
So the boy Love is perjur'd everywhere;
For ere Demetrius look'd on Hermia's eyne,
He hail'd down oaths that he was only mine;
And when this hail some heat from Hermia felt,
So he dissolv'd, and show'rs of oaths did melt.
I will go tell him of fair Hermia's flight;
Then to the wood will he to-morrow night
Pursue her; and for this intelligence
If I have thanks, it is a dear expense.
But herein mean I to enrich my pain,
To have his sight thither and back again.

Such a long speech in rhyming couplets can be rather intimidating for the actor. The rhyme could either dominate the meaning or be completely lost in the attempt to sound 'real' and unaffected. It is a very fine tightrope to walk: neither to deny the support of the form, nor to be swamped by it.

Exercise

- First, use the thought exercise on page 114 to hold the meaning in the speech. Use the line breaks to give the speech texture. Although the couplets drive you forward, it's not a smooth passage. Notice how the iambic falters – 'And as he errs, doting on Hermia's eyes, / So I, admiring of his qualities'. Helena is distressed and the couplet manages to contain but not soothe her.
- Now invest in the rhyme. Spring from the first word to the last in each line, speaking only those words aloud: 'How, be, though, she, but, so, he, know'. The first word springs you forward and out of the preceding rhyme, although you can still feel it vividly.
- Return to speaking the whole speech: you will feel that you are beginning to balance the form with the content.
- Notice how the rhyming is not arbitrary but helps to complete thoughts. The first line of the couplet sets up the thought and the meaning is brought home in the second line and its rhyme. Even if the thought moves through several couplets, each one has some form of completion.

When we next meet Lysander and Hermia in another part of the wood, they are still conversing in rhyme. Lysander starts with an *abab* quatrain, and Hermia introduces couplets which Lysander then picks up:

> *Lysander:* Fair love, you faint with wand'ring in the wood;
> And, to speak troth, I have forgot our way;
> We'll rest us, Hermia, if you think it good,
> And tarry for the comfort of the day.
> *Hermia:* Be it so, Lysander: find you out a bed,
> For I upon this bank will rest my head.
> *Lysander:* One turf shall serve as pillow for us both;
> One heart, one bed, two bosoms, and one troth.
> *Hermia:* Nay, good Lysander; for my sake, my dear,
> Lie further off yet; do not lie so near.

Lysander: O, take the sense, sweet, of my innocence!
Love takes the meaning in love's conference.
I mean that my heart unto yours is knit,
So that but one heart we can make of it;
Two bosoms interchained with an oath,
So then two bosoms and a single troth.
Then by your side no bed-room me deny,
For lying so, Hermia, I do not lie.
Hermia: Lysander riddles very prettily.
Now much beshrew my manners and my pride,
If Hermia meant to say Lysander lied!
But, gentle friend, for love and courtesy
Lie further off, in human modesty;
Such separation as may well be said
Becomes a virtuous bachelor and a maid,
So far be distant; and good night, sweet friend.
Thy love ne'er alter till thy sweet life end!
Lysander: Amen, amen, to that fair prayer say I;
And then end life when I end loyalty!
Here is my bed; sleep give thee all his rest!
Hermia: With half that wish the wisher's eyes be press'd!
[*They sleep.*]

(II.ii)

Notice again how the rhymes support the thoughts and complete them. Indeed, Lysander and Hermia are so closely intertwined that they twice share couplets here.

The next time we meet Helena she is with Demetrius. They speak blank verse together – there's nothing frivolous in this relationship. No games exist between them any more. His infidelity has cast a shadow on their speech. However, as they wander further into the wood they too start to converse in couplets, perhaps in a remnant of their old relationship. Unconsciously the rhymes begin to bind them even if what Demetrius says is far from pleasant:

Helena: Stay, though thou kill me, sweet Demetrius.
Demetrius: I charge thee, hence, and do not haunt me thus.
Helena: O, wilt thou darkling leave me? Do not so.
Demetrius: Stay on thy peril; I alone will go.

(II.ii)

Here it is Demetrius who completes the rhyme. He is closer to Helena than he thinks, even as he abandons her. After another soliloquy in couplets Helena finds and wakens Lysander – who, drugged, falls in love with the first thing he sees, and immediately responds in rhyme.

> *Helena*: Lysander, if you live, good sir, awake.
> *Lysander*: [*Waking*] And run through fire I will for thy sweet sake.

The rest of the lovers' scenes in the wood are in couplets apart from one *abab* quatrain Lysander uses to woo Helena:

> *Lysander*: Why should you think that I should woo in scorn?
> Scorn and derision never come in tears.
> Look when I vow, I weep; and vows so born,
> In their nativity all truth appears.
>
> (II.ii)

It's the same form he used to tell Hermia that he was lost in the wood. Perhaps the *abab* quatrain is what Lysander employs to explain his weaknesses. It's not as relentless as the iambic, but it's not as serious as blank verse; it's a form that puts Lysander somewhere midway between youth and maturity.

The couplets continue until the painful moment when Helena concludes that the others – even, shockingly, Hermia – have joined in a plot to mock her. On a broken line she moves into blank verse mid-speech and they all follow her as the scene begins to turn ugly – so ugly that the men might end up fighting to the death. The game of love is suddenly frighteningly serious and the change in form is appropriate – remember Berowne's 'Honest plain words best pierce the ear of grief'.

> *Helena*: Lo, she is one of this confederacy!
> Now I perceive they have conjoin'd all three
> To fashion this false sport in spite of me.
> Injurious Hermia! most ungrateful maid!
> Have you conspir'd, have you with these contriv'd,
> To bait me with this foul derision?
> Is all the counsel that we two have shar'd,
> The sisters' vows, the hours that we have spent,
> When we have chid the hasty-footed time
> For parting us – O, is all forgot?
>
> (III.ii)

The shift into blank verse occurs poignantly on the line 'Injurious Hermia! Most ungrateful maid!' – the moment Helena faces the treachery of her best friend, siding with men.

Thus Shakespeare makes specific points and conscious choices in his use of rhyme. The switch to blank verse is almost complete, apart from the bravado of Lysander's challenge to Demetrius –

> *Demetrius*: I say I love thee more than he can do.
> *Lysander*: If then say so, withdraw, and prove it too.

– and the moment when Helena runs from Hermia and Hermia responds in amazement, her third desperate rhyme (and indeed the fourth, hidden in 'amaz'd') a wrenching indicator of bafflement and the desire not to lose her friend:

> *Helena*: I will not trust you, I,
> Nor longer stay in your curst company.
> Your hands than mine are quicker for a fray,
> My legs are longer though, to run away.
> *Hermia*: I am amaz'd and know not what to say.

Rhyme returns more consistently in the last section in the wood, when Puck has to undo all his mistakes. He manipulates Lysander and Demetrius by rhyming with them and makes them slip out of the more serious blank verse. Rhyme defuses the situation, and as Puck draws the lovers together, making them sleep in a bunch, they all fall back into it – the young men in couplets and both the women in *abab* quatrains followed by a rhyming couplet.

> *Lysander*: Where art thou, proud Demetrius? Speak thou now.
> *Puck*: Here, villain, drawn and ready. Where art thou?
> *Lysander*: I will be with thee straight.
> *Puck*:   Follow me, then,
> To plainer ground.
> [*Exit Lysander as following the voice.*]
> *Enter Demetrius.*
> *Demetrius*:   Lysander, speak again.
> Thou runaway, thou coward, art thou fled?
> Speak! In some bush? Where dost thou hide thy head?
> *Puck*: Thou coward, art thou bragging to the stars,

Telling the bushes that thou look'st for wars,
And wilt not come? Come, recreant, come, thou child;
I'll whip thee with a rod. He is defil'd
That draws a sword on thee.
Demetrius: Yea, art thou there?
Puck: Follow my voice; we'll try no manhood here.
[*Exeunt.*]

(III.ii)

So the hypnotic, calming lightness of the rhyming form envelops the
lovers in an embrace that permits repose, recuperation and the restora-
tion of some degree of order. The next morning, on being awakened by
the Duke, they will finish their journey in the play in blank verse.

Puck, of course, is the main manipulator in this scene. In the play as
a whole he speaks almost entirely in rhyme, of varying line lengths. Even
to Oberon, his powerful master, he only uses blank verse when he has
an important task like finding the sleeping herb, or when he must seem
serious in order to avoid scolding –

> *Puck*: Believe me, King of Shadows, I mistook.
> Did not you tell me I should know the man
> By the Athenian garments he had on?

(III.ii)

Puck can't risk rhyming when the stakes are high, but as soon as he
knows that there's fun to be had with humans, he's back in rhyme. He
doesn't value ordinary mortals enough to give them the respect of blank
verse. The only exception is the time he comes across the mechanicals
rehearsing in the wood, an unexpected discovery that seems to shake
him out of his customary rhyming:

> *Puck*: What hempen home-spuns have we swagg'ring here,
> So near the cradle of the fairy queen?
> What! a play toward: I'll be an auditor;
> An actor too perhaps, if I see cause.

(III.i)

The play within the play reveals further changes in form, for while the
mechanicals speak in prose, they act in rhyme. Their play is mostly in
iambic pentameters, some rhyming in couplets, others *abab* quatrains.

Either the mechanicals are unconsciously reflecting the lovers' form, or they have learnt that important events are chronicled in verse whose most obvious definition is rhyme. The problem is that they're not very good at it. Shakespeare – or rather, Quince, the carpenter of the play – has given them some rather clunky verse:

> *Bottom*: The raging rocks
> And shivering shocks
> Shall break the locks
> Of prison gates;
> And Phibbus' car
> Shall shine from far,
> And make and mar
> The foolish Fates.
>
> (I.ii)

The *aaabcccb* scheme in the very short four-syllable lines may be an ambitious technical achievement for the amateur poet, but its result is to expose the absurd dominance of rhyme over content in poor Bottom's speech. It is also true, in broader human terms, to the fact that we often resort to rhyme as the first step in heightening our utterances – the sentimental but heartfelt written tributes that mourn the deaths of loved ones are ample evidence of this.

Like the other key characters in the play, Oberon and Titania also switch forms. They can speak blank verse but sometimes choose not to, and they use a mixture of line lengths with the rhyming couplet. When they argue, fuelled by jealousy, they do so in blank verse – except towards the end of one scene in which Titania has made two attempts in blank verse to appease Oberon, which he seems to ignore.

> *Oberon*: How long within this wood intend you stay?
> *Titania*: Perchance, till after Theseus' wedding day.
>
> (II.i)

The switch to rhyme has a mocking tone which Titania immediately stops, returning to blank verse for one final appeal for peace with Oberon.

> *Titania*: If you will patiently dance in our round,
> And see our moonlight revels, go with us;

If not, shun me, and I will spare your haunts.

Oberon replies in blank verse, still wanting the boy that Titania has. This blockage sends Titania spinning into a rhyming couplet.

> *Oberon:* Give me that boy, and I will go with thee
> *Titania:* Not for thy fairy kingdom. Fairies, away!
> We shall chide downright if I longer stay.

With Titania gone, Oberon plots his revenge in blank verse: a serious business. He begins to rhyme only when Puck returns with the flower – indeed, this is the first time we have heard Oberon speak in rhyming couplets. The ease of the form might be a reflection of the ease entering his troubled spirit after the lengthy quarrel with his wife: he now has a tool to get his own way.

The next time we meet Titania she is back in blank verse as she prepares to sleep and arranges the duties of her fairies. After the spell is placed on her, she awakes and falls in love with Bottom. Her first three exchanges with him are in blank verse, while Bottom stays relentlessly in prose. Perhaps in compromise, Titania now moves into rhyming couplets for the rest of the scene except for the last five lines which have an *ababb* scheme:

> *Titania:* Come, wait upon him; lead him to my bower.
> The moon methinks, looks with a wat'ry eye;
> And when she weeps, weeps every little flower,
> Lamenting some enforced chastity.
> Tie up my love's tongue, bring him silently.

(III.i)

There's an uneasy order and sadness in these lines, which sets them apart from the fun and irreverence of the rest of the scene.

Later, with Bottom in her bower, Titania continues in rhyme with another *abab* quatrain.

> *Titania:* Come, sit thee down upon this flow'ry bed,
> While I thy amiable cheeks do coy,
> And stick musk-roses in thy sleek smooth head,
> And kiss thy fair large ears, my gentle joy.

(IV.i)

Bottom refuses to respond in kind – he's having none of this verse business, let alone rhyme. He'll do it in Quince's play, but otherwise he sticks to prose. Titania's compromise is to drop the rhyme but stay in blank verse. Perhaps prose is too far below her royal person.

It is now Oberon's turn to mend his mischief. He has spent the night since receiving the magic flower in rhyming couplets of varying line lengths, many of them created by Puck who is trying to make light of his own mistakes and please his master. Oberon starts this scene with Titania and Puck in blank verse as he realises the pity he feels for Titania in the love for Bottom – 'This hateful imperfection of her eyes' – he has helped create.

Rhyming starts with the spell to release her and as Titania comes to, she begins to rhyme with Oberon – a sign of their reuniting. It's inconsistent at first; she's recovering from a powerful drug. At the end, though, she speaks for the first time in seven-syllable lines, finally bonding with Oberon in form.

> *Oberon*: But first I will release the Fairy Queen.
> [*Touching her eyes.*]
> Be as thou wast wont to be;
> See as thou was wont to see.
> Dian's bud o'er Cupid's flower
> Hath such force and blessed power.
> Now, my Titania; wake you, my sweet queen.
> *Titania*: My Oberon! What visions have I seen!
> Methought I was enamour'd of an ass.
> *Oberon*: There lies your love.
> *Titania*:   How came these things to pass?
> O, how mine eyes do loathe his visage now!
> *Oberon*: Silence awhile. Robin, take off this head.
> Titania, music call; and strike more dead
> Than common sleep of all these five the sense.
> *Titania*: Music, ho, music, such as charmeth sleep!
> *Puck*: Now when thou wak'st with thine own fool's eyes peep.
> *Oberon*: Sound, music. Come, my Queen, take hands with me,
> [*Music*]
> And rock the ground whereon these sleepers be.
> Now thou and I are new in amity,
> And will to-morrow midnight solemnly
> Dance in Duke Theseus' house triumphantly,
> And bless it to all fair prosperity.

There shall the pairs of faithful lovers be
Wedded, with Theseus, all in jollity.
Puck: Fairy King, attend and mark;
I do hear the morning lark.
Oberon: Then my Queen, in silence sad,
Trip we after night's shade.
We the globe can compass soon,
Swifter than the wandering moon.
Titania: Come, my lord; and in our flight,
Tell me how it came this night
That I sleeping here was found
With these mortals on the ground.

(IV.i)

We have seen how rhyme in Shakespeare helps to characterise, to forge relationships – or break them – and to indicate the temperature of a scene. But it has a range of other uses. For a start, it's easier to learn because by marking the end of a line it gives the actor something to aim for and sound against.

Rhyme aids not only learning but also accuracy and precision. This makes it ideal for spells, which have to be phrased accurately if they are to work:

Puck: On the ground
Sleep sound;
I'll apply
To your eye,
Gentle lover, remedy.

(III.ii)

Or, from *Macbeth*:

1st Witch: Round about the cauldron go;
In the poison'd entrails throw.
Toad that under cold stone
Days and nights has thirty-one,
Swelt'red venom sleeping got
Boil thou first i' th' charmed pot.
All: Double, double toil and trouble;
Fire burn, and cauldron bubble.

(IV.i)

Just by speaking these two spells with their short lines and regular rhymes, you will feel the pace and directness in the form. You will also observe how rhyme, normally associated with a lightness of touch or mood, can conceal a dark purpose. This is a very important aspect of rhyme in Shakespeare: what seems to be trivial is in fact often of highly charged significance. Thus while song lyrics in the plays are frequently overlooked, their message can be at the very heart of a scene. Properly attended to, the rhyme creates a pithiness which highlights any important message in the song.

In *The Merchant of Venice*, for instance, Bassanio must choose between gold, silver and lead caskets to find Portia's picture. It is hidden in the lead casket, and this song is sung as he makes his choice:

> Tell me where is fancy bred,
> Or in the heart or in the head,
> How begot, how nourished?
> Reply, reply.
> It is engend'red in the eyes,
> With gazing fed; and fancy dies
> In the cradle where it lies.
> Let us all ring fancy's knell:
> I'll begin it – Ding, dong, bell.
> *All*: Ding, dong, bell.

> (III.ii)

Portia's other suitors didn't have the aid of a song containing subliminal messages for them. If Bassanio listens to the lyrics he will be helped in his choice: the first three lines all rhyme with 'lead'.

The message of the song can be found in the lyrics, but it is of course emphasised by the rhymes. Another example is this from *The Tempest*, sung by Ariel on the verge of freedom from Prospero:

> *Ariel*: Where the bee sucks, there suck I;
> In a cowslip's bell I lie;
> There I couch when owls do cry.
> On the bat's back I do fly
> After summer merrily.
> Merrily, merrily shall I live now
> Under the blossom that hangs on the bough.

> (V.i)

We hear in this lyric not only Ariel's gathering joy in being free, but also how he will live, how he lived before Sycorax encased him in the tree. It's a memory reinforced by the rhyme scheme which begins *aaaa* – 'I', 'lie', 'cry', 'fly' – followed by the half-rhyme of 'merrily', then *bb* with 'now' and 'bough'. In this easy scheme, 'merrily' stands out, its importance underlined by the repetitions. There is an intoxication in playing with the word, in its meaning and its rhyming with itself – almost with its novelty. Ariel will be merry for the first time in many years, free at last, as the rhyming takes us, to live now under the blossom.

The fact that rhyme can disguise meaning also has a political dimension. It can be very useful in tricky situations. Clowns and fools in Shakespeare are anarchic figures who frequently exploit the apparent innocence of harmless-sounding rhymes to get away with voicing unpalatable truths to their masters.

The Fool in *King Lear* knows the depths of his master's folly in banishing Cordelia and splitting the realm between Goneril and Regan. The problem is in telling him, as Lear, like many powerful leaders, does not want to hear the truth. 'Take heed, sirrah: the whip,' he warns at the Fool's first attempt. It is a testament to the Fool's love for his master that he continues trying to alert Lear, at the risk of real trouble. But by constantly juggling styles, switching between prose, rhyme and song, he manages to change the tone and feel of his message, getting it across while avoiding giving dangerous offence.

> *Fool:* Dost thou know the difference, my boy,
> between a bitter bitter fool and a sweet one?
> *Lear:* No, lad; teach me.
> *Fool:* That lord that counsell'd thee
> To give away thy land,
> Come place him here by me –
> Do thou for him stand.
> The sweet and bitter fool
> Will presently appear;
> The one in motley here,
> The other found out there.
> *Lear:* Dost thou call me fool, boy?
> *Fool:* All thy other titles thou has given away; that thou wast born with. [...] Thou hadst little wit in thy bald crown when thou gav'st thy golden one away. If I speak like myself in this, let him be whipp'd that first finds it so.

[*Sings*] Fools had ne'er less grace in a year;
For wise men are grown foppish,
And know not how their wits to wear,
Their manners are so apish.
Lear: When were you wont to be so full of songs, sirrah?
Fool: I have us'd it, nuncle, e'er since thou mad'st thy daughters thy
mothers;

(I.iv)

The Fool stays nimble on his feet, swapping styles with skill and humour, sailing close to the wind while staying out of trouble. In every case the meaning is both heightened and disguised by the form he chooses, which sounds frivolous while carrying serious content.

Throughout history, politically subversive or awkward messages have been contained in simple rhyme forms. Most children's nursery rhymes have their roots in political satire or criticism, in saying the unsayable. The form is particularly useful when you are dealing with an absolute ruler who can seal your fate with a nod of the head. Its very 'silliness' makes it difficult to take seriously enough to prosecute in the courts. This is what the Fool is counting on. Rhyme enables a freedom of speech that would not otherwise be possible or safe.

To a certain extent, then, rhyme is also the voice of the outsider or the one in danger. Consider Edgar in *King Lear*. The legitimate son of the Duke of Gloucester, he has been duped by his illegitimate brother Edmund into going into hiding. He disguises himself as a Bedlam beggar – a mad, deranged outsider – with an altered speech pattern that includes rhyme. Until then, he has spoken only prose and blank verse.

We meet him in disguise for the first time on the heath as he bursts out of the hovel, speaking in rhyme.

Edgar: Away! the foul fiend follows me!
Through the sharp hawthorn blows the cold wind.
Hum! go to thy cold bed and warm thee.

(III.iv)

Throughout the scene, Edgar utters pithy madness, mostly in prose, but at key moments, he slips into nursery rhymes. These both contain his distress, and offer some relief for us all in the heart-rending moments of Lear's disintegration. The form is so strict that at least it offers a degree of comfort, security and direction.

Edgar: Child Rowland to the dark tower came,
His word was still. 'Fie, foh, and fum,
I smell the blood of a British man'.

Even when the verses don't make immediate sense, the rhymes alert our ears and make us pay attention. We are wooed to try and crack their code. But above all there's a solace in the rhymes with which Edgar, as Mad Tom, tries both to keep himself going and to heal the distressed Lear in the painful midst of chaos.

Be thy mouth or black or white,
Tooth that poisons if it bite;
Mastiff, greyhound, mongrel grim,
Hound or spaniel, brach or lym,
Or bobtail tike or trundle tail –
Tom will make them weep or wail;
For, with throwing thus my head,
Dogs leapt the hatch, and all are fled.

(III.vi)

At the end of this scene, Edgar is left alone and speaks a soliloquy in iambic pentameter rhyming couplets:

Edgar: When we our betters see bearing our woes,
We scarcely think our miseries our foes.
Who alone suffers suffers most i' th' mind,
Leaving free things and happy shows behind;
But then the mind much sufferance doth o'erskip
When grief hath mates, and bearing fellowship.
How light and portable my pain seems now,
When that which makes me bend makes the King bow –
He childed as I father'd! Tom, away!
Mark the high noises; and thyself bewray,
When false opinion, whose wrong thoughts defile thee,
In thy just proof repeals and reconciles thee.
What will hap more to-night, safe 'scape the King!
Lurk, lurk.

Here Edgar discovers, in the light of the king's agony, that no one has a monopoly on suffering. He speaks himself through his distress, using rhyme to chart his way, until the couplets begin to break down with the impure repetition of 'thee' and then the speech is back to blank verse.

Edgar has become himself again. You can hear a different voice in 'What will hap more tonight, safe 'scape the King. / Lurk, lurk'.

Edgar's next soliloquy is in blank verse. Straight afterwards, his father enters with his eyes put out. Edgar knows he must return to his mad disguise and language. There is a poignant struggle between his two voices:

> *Edgar*: Poor Tom's a-cold. [*Aside*] I cannot daub it further.
> *Gloucester:* Come hither, fellow.
> *Edgar*: [*Aside*] And yet I must. – Bless
> thy sweet eyes, they bleed.
>
> (IV.i)

Although he no longer rhymes in this scene, he answers Gloucester's blank verse in prose.

By the time they reach Dover, however, Edgar has joined with his father in blank verse. Gloucester notices this: it's not just a change of accent but a change in form. Edgar even scans and finishes Gloucester's lines. 'Methinks y'are better spoken,' as his father observes:

> *Gloucester*: When shall I come to th' top of that same hill?
> *Edgar*: You do climb up it now; look how we labour.
> *Gloucester:* Methinks the ground is even.
> *Edgar*:   Horrible steep.
> Hark, do you hear the sea?
> *Gloucester*:   No, truly.
> *Edgar*: Why then, your other senses grow imperfect
> By your eyes' anguish.
> *Gloucester*:   So may it be indeed.
> Methinks thy voice is alter'd, and thou speak'st
> In better phrase and matter than thou didst.
> *Edgar*: Y'are much deceiv'd: in nothing am I chang'd
> But in my garments.
> *Gloucester*:   Methinks y'are better spoken.
>
> (IV.vi)

Edgar uses no more rhymes in the play until the final couplets. As the full horror of the tragedy unfolds, his language becomes fuller and he stays in mature blank verse. When he was not Edgar, he rhymed; as he finds himself, he doesn't. The switch in form supports the change in character.

Let's look at another character who speaks in different forms: this time, prose and song. Autolycus in *The Winter's Tale* is a low thief. He has been hounded out of the court for stealing, and now leeches off the goodwill of an honest, hardworking rural community. These people are not as streetwise as him: he uses his courtly flair and verbal skills to steal their hard-earned wages while mocking them – 'What a fool honesty is'.

Autolycus speaks prose except when he's singing. We watch him sell trinkets to the shepherds: he's good at it. Most successful salesmen are good communicators, as are all confidence tricksters. It's not that the shepherds are stupid to be taken in but that Autolycus is so skilled at counterfeiting – most charmingly so when he sings.

We tend to trust those who burst into song even if we know them to be villains. Their mean-spiritedness is somehow more forgiveable if they sing – especially if they sing jolly, rhyming songs, like Autolycus when we meet him:

> *Autolycus*: When daffodils begin to peer,
> With heigh! The doxy over the dale,
> Why, then comes in the sweet o' the year,
> For the red blood reigns in the winter's pale.
> The white sheet bleaching on the hedge,
> With heigh! The sweet birds, O, how they sing!
> Doth set my pugging tooth on edge,
> For a quart of ale is a dish for a king.
> The lark, that tirra-lirra chants,
> With heigh! with heigh! the thrush and the jay,
> Are summer songs for me and my aunts,
> While we lie tumbling in the hay.

(IV.iii)

It's not that Autolycus is being dishonest with us. He admits that he wants to steal – 'pugging tooth on edge' – but in the pleasure of the tune and the lyric his admission is sweetened and we begin to like him. The words themselves are not innocent but the rhyming makes them seems so. Song is how Autolycus woos the world, harnessing violence in rhyme and melody.

I once helped to organise a concert in a top-security prison in which the inmates performed various dramatic scenes for their fellows. The audience was pretty rowdy and the whole thing was on the edge of chaos as the prison officers struggled to keep control. Suddenly on stage, grabbing the microphone, appeared a terrifying-looking prisoner I had never seen before. The whole room fell silent. This man was feared by all – I later found out that he almost ran the prison. In a gruff voice he said, 'Shut up, I'm going to sing for you.' You could have heard a pin drop. Then in a beautiful tenor he sang 'Scarlet ribbons for her hair', a simple rhyming ballad. The hall was transfixed. The singer and the song controlled the near-riot and at the same time, as he sang, we all fell slightly in love with the hardest man in the gaol. He was a modern Autolycus.

In Shakespeare too we can see how song and rhyme are employed to give us respite and yet simultaneously heighten a scene. In *Othello*, for instance, Desdemona sings the beautiful 'Willow song'. The placing of this simple rhyming lament is hugely effective. Othello has just struck Desdemona and sent her to bed. She is traumatised; so are we. We also know that he is planning to murder her; that she is innocent; and that Iago has plotted it all. The beauty of the song itself is a balm to our ears, but there are also important clues in the story of the girl which, if Desdemona could find them, might save her:

> *Desdemona*: I call'd my love false love;
> But what said he then?
>   Sing willow, willow, willow;
> If I court moe women, you'll couch with moe men – .
>
> (IV.iii)

The song is a conduit into the centre of Desdemona's trauma and contains the clue to Othello's rage: 'false love', 'couch with moe men'. If only she could use the lyric to crack the source of his anger she might be able to save herself.

Likewise in *Hamlet*, Ophelia, in her madness and distress, moves into song and rhyme. Again the regular forms try to contain and soothe her disordered mind, and in their subject matter we hear the themes that are breaking her heart – her father's death and Hamlet's betrayal.

> *Ophelia*: He is dead and gone, lady,
> He is dead and gone;
> At his head a grass-green turf,
> At his heels a stone.
>
> (IV.v)

In states of emotional and psychological anguish, we will often find consolation in songs that seem to fit our situation. They bring reassuring order and insight, shaping and extending our experience, and focussing our thoughts in healing ways.

For similar reasons, Shakespeare often uses rhyming couplets at the end of a long debate in blank verse to signal a resolution. The ease and completion of the form perfectly matches the intellectual satisfaction of conclusion. After a conflict in blank verse, the rhyme is a relief to speak and hear – like the relief of closure or realising what to do next. So these couplets are there to be spoken and experienced with a sense of freedom and flair. You shouldn't apologise for them.

> *Richard*: Shine out, fair sun, till I have bought a glass,
> That I may see my shadow as I pass.
> > (*Richard III*, I.ii)

> *Viola*: O Time, thou must untangle this, not I:
> It is too hard a knot for me t'untie!
> > (*Twelfth Night*, II.ii)

> *Queen Margaret*: Off with the crown and with the crown his head;
> And, whilst we breathe, take time to do him dead.
> > (*Henry VI Part III*, I.iv)

> *Berowne*: Well I will love, write, sigh, pray, sue and groan:
> Some men must love my lady, and some Joan.
> > (*Love's Labour's Lost*, III.i)

Each of these rhyming couplets concludes a rich and densely explored problem.

Richard, Duke of Gloucester, has just won Lady Anne and in his amazement begins to believe he might be attractive – so much so that he asks the sun to shine in order that he can view his own shadow.

Viola, who has been disguised as a man, has tried to discover why she has been given a ring. She has realised that Olivia has fallen in love with her in her disguise, which hugely complicates Viola's relationship with her master, Duke Orsino. Viola loves Orsino, he loves Olivia and now Olivia loves her. It's too complex and dangerous for Viola to solve: time must sort it out.

Queen Margaret has captured her great enemy. Before executing him, she wants to see him break, so she tortures him with the death of his youngest son. He fails to satisfy her, so she concludes by ordering the removal of his crown and his head. The couplet not only signals York's death but, within its rhyme, reduces it to a trivial event.

Berowne has struggled against falling in love. This couplet declares that he can resist no longer, but reduces the practices of courtly love in the play to an everyday level: 'groan' and 'Joan' do not smack of high romance. Berowne is a realist in love.

Couplets that conclude blank verse, however, are not always simple. Where the character finds it hard to reach a conclusion, the first line is often broken, fracturing the couplet. Just as the solution is less apparent and more unsettling than in smooth couplets, so the mid-line break disturbs the resolve and makes the texture choppy.

> *Ophelia*: Blasted with ecstasy. O woe is me
> T' have seen what I have seen, see what I see!
>
> (*Hamlet*, III.i)

> *Hamlet*: More relative than this. The play's the thing
> Wherein I'll catch the conscience of the King.
>
> (II.ii)

It's not just speeches and scenes in blank verse that conclude with the dispatch of a couplet: the same is true of the plays themselves. Indeed, only four of Shakespeare's plays end without a hint of rhyme: *Two Gentlemen of Verona*, *The Winter's Tale*, *Much Ado About Nothing* and *Henry VI Part I*. Two end in rhyme but then have a prose epilogue – *As You Like It* and *Henry IV Part II*. Four almost end in rhyme. There are brief commands after the last rhyming couplets in *Coriolanus* ('Assist'), *Timon of Athens* ('Let our drums strike') and *Hamlet* ('Go, bid the soldiers shoot'); and *Love's Labour's Lost* ends in a song followed by two prose comments. It is as though Shakespeare is reminding us that, although the play is over, life goes on.

The rest of the plays end in a rhyming couplet, marking the final completion of the journey. Sometimes it is a happy ending. Sometimes, it is so difficult, unsure and painful that one couplet will not serve. At the end of *King Lear*, for instance, the ruling class has been wiped out. Lear is dead; all three daughters are dead; Edmund is dead; and so – offstage – is Gloucester. Who will govern? How can this realm survive? The Duke of Albany names Kent and Edgar as rulers. Four couplets end this play.

Albany: Bear them from hence. Our present business.
Is general woe. Friends of my soul, you twain
Rule, in this realm and the gor'd state sustain.
Kent: I have a journey, sir, shortly to go;
My master calls me, I must not say no.
Edgar: The weight of this sad time we must obey;
Speak what we feel, act what we ought to say.
The oldest hath borne most; we that are young,
Shall never see so much, nor live so long.

(V.iii)

We have witnessed in this play the collapse of an entire social order, and a host of personal tragedies in consequence. It is given to rhyme to express, through its measured form, the sober hope that structure can return and with it the rebuilding of harmony and government. These are more than blank verse could achieve, for rhymes complete and resolve ideas and troubles differently and more thoroughly than blank verse. In essence, they can simplify an idea – they have a fundamentally light and child-like quality that heightens directness. Just as clowns and fools can speak profound or dangerous truths in rhyme, so too the form helps contain the turmoil of heart and mind. It is, in the English tradition of theatre, ultimately for comedy and optimism, not for tragedy and despair. Rhymes amuse and delight the ears of English audiences; their internal twinkle signals pace, flow and completion; and they are – like all the givens – there for a reason.

Prose

Prose in Shakespeare is one of the least examined aspects in rehearsal, though it is as important as verse. The most common advice given by directors is simply to 'Speak it quickly'. It's true that a degree of speed can release a vernacular rhythm in the actor, but it hardly helps with finding an anchor in the real structure and therefore the purpose of the speech. In fact, although prose lacks the obvious verse scaffolding of the iambic rhythm and line endings, it is nonetheless just as carefully structured, and its use by a character or as part of a scene always represents a deliberate choice whose implications need to be fully understood. Don't believe that because it seems less formal it can be less clearly spoken or energised, or is less important in the story of the play.

The first way into a prose speech is via its thought structures. If you rely on them, working from thought to thought, you will find they observe the same structures as verse. While the lack of line or regular beat can make prose seem initially less dynamic than verse, approaching it through the thought exercise will quickly engage you with the particular energy, the vernacular rhythm of the character.

As you pursue the thoughts, you will find it useful to know of some of the main devices of classical rhetoric. The young William, 'creeping like snail unwillingly to school', would have been drilled in these from an early age and they can be seen at the heart of all his speeches, prose and verse alike. Three are particularly important for the development of an argument and the choice of language: invention, disposition and style.

Invention means the gathering together of all relevant subject matter to assist in the full exploration of a problem or debate: the making of an catalogue or inventory of ideas and themes. Disposition involves organising the material for maximum effect in oratory, ensuring that thoughts and ideas move forward progressively towards a conclusion. Such organisation is especially important in oral argument, because when we listen we have to understand the logic immediately: we can't control the speaker and go back over what has been said as we can with the written word. Finally, style requires that the choice of language is appropriate to the occasion and the subject. In other words, don't use trivial phrases to describe profound events or tell inappropriate jokes in the wrong forum (as the best man usually does at a wedding). Another aspect of style is that the language should suit the speaker. You can see the importance of this when people use language they feel is appropriate but don't fully own. Political speechwriters frequently get this wrong, producing texts that politicians can't deliver effectively because the speeches contain words they wouldn't use. The converse of this, of course, is that language style is an aspect of character – as Shakespeare very well understood.

Let's see these devices at work in a speech from *The Tempest*:

> *Trinculo*: Here's neither bush nor shrub to bear off any weather at all, and another storm brewing; I hear it sing i' th' wind. Yond some black cloud, yond huge one, looks like a foul bombard that would shed his liquor. If it should thunder as it did before, I know not where to hide my head. Yond same cloud cannot choose but fall by pailfuls. What have we here? a man or a fish? dead or alive? A fish: he smells like a fish; a very ancient and fish-like smell; a kind of not-of-the-newest Poor-John. A strange fish! Were I in England now, as once I was, and had but this fish painted, not a holiday fool there but would give a piece of silver. There would this monster make a man; any strange beast there makes a man; when they will not give a doit to relieve a lame beggar, they will lay out ten to see a dead Indian. Legg'd like a man, and his fins like arms! Warm, o' my troth! I do now let loose my opinion; hold it no longer: this is no fish, but an islander, that hath lately suffered by a thunderbolt. [*Thunder*] Alas, the storm is come again! My best way is to creep under his gaberdine; there is no other shelter hereabout. Misery acquaints a man with strange bedfellows. I will here shroud till the dregs of the storm be past.
>
> (II.ii)

Note first that, though it's not verse, the thoughts are structured to find a resolve just as in so many verse soliloquies. Trinculo has a problem – where to find shelter in the storm – and the thoughts journey towards his hiding beneath Caliban's gaberdine. So the thought structures offer the first way into the speech. The next aid is rhetoric.

In the mode of invention, Trinculo gathers the relevant evidence together. Looking for shelter, his eye and mind focus on all the significant aspects of his environment. There is no bush or shrub. He hears the wind. He sees the clouds. Then he discovers Caliban and gathers all the relevant physical information he can about his find: the smell, the look, the touch of this 'strange beast'. Finally, as the storm starts again, he gathers more information, which leads him to shelter with the 'beast' under the 'gaberdine'.

As for disposition, Trinculo arranges his thoughts in a most straightforward way until he discovers Caliban. Then we have three questions: 'What have we here? A man or a fish? Dead or alive?' In his attempt to answer these questions, he moves in orderly sequence from Caliban's smell to England, and back to Caliban's leg, arm and physical warmth. At last, having organised the evidence and sorted his thoughts in apparently logical order, he draws his conclusion: 'I do now let loose my opinion; hold it no longer: this is no fish, but an islander, that hath lately suffered by a thunderbolt.'

The third element of rhetoric is style, and of course Trinculo's perfectly suits his character. He will spend a great part of this play drunk, but before we ever see him so his language is already drenched in alcohol. 'Bombard' is a leather drinking bottle; 'liquor', 'dregs' – these words reek of booze.

Although his speech has all the flavour of an informal vernacular, it is a delightful discovery to find that Trinculo uses the organising devices of classical rhetoric. Professor Higgins in Shaw's *Pygmalion* was equally delighted to find similar devices in the dustman, Doolittle. Similarly, London taxi drivers are famed for their use of rhetoric. It is not surprising that Shakespeare sought it out at all levels of society, and that tracing these three threads in his prose speeches will further anchor the insights gained by following the thought structure.

Trinculo speaks only prose – indeed it seems unlikely that he could speak anything else – but the shift between verse and prose, where it occurs, always signals a potent change of energy and intensity and demands many theatrical choices involving character, formality and setting. The essential question for the actor is, 'Does my character use both verse and prose?' If the answer is 'yes', then when and why do they shift from one to the other? On the other hand, if they speak only prose, is it a matter of choice, or is it because they are – like Trinculo – too uneducated to speak verse?

Take Caliban, generally considered a base character, who in the scene before Trinculo's soliloquy speaks verse that stumbles and becomes uneven when he sees Trinculo approaching. His verse is powerful and fluent for the violent cursing against Prospero, but collapses as Trinculo enters, signalling a milder and more conversational tone. It lowers the temperature of the scene, as Caliban falls out of cursing into actually falling flat on his face.

> *Caliban*: All the infections that the sun sucks up
> From bogs, fens, flats, on Prosper fall, and make him
> By inch-meal a disease! His spirits hear me,
> And yet I needs must curse. But they'll nor pinch,
> Fright me with urchin-shows, pitch me i' th' mire,
> Nor lead me, like a firebrand, in the dark
> Out of my way, unless he bid 'em; but
> For every trifle are they set upon me;
> Sometime like apes that mow and chatter at me,
> And after bite me; then like hedgehogs which
> Lie tumbling in my barefoot way, and mount
> Their pricks at my footfall; sometime am I
> All wound with adders, who with cloven tongues
> Do hiss me into madness.
> [*Enter Trinculo*]
>   Lo, no, lo!
> Here comes a spirit of his, to torment me
> For bringing wood in slowly. I'll fall flat;
> Perchance he will not mind me.

Falstaff demonstrates in another way the significance of switching between prose and verse. We meet him in *The Merry Wives of Windsor*, which is mostly written in prose and is sometimes called Shakespeare's 'middle-class' play. Verse here is used in particular circumstances. It's spoken by the romantic lover Fenton, and by Mistress Page when she recounts an old tale; and it's used as well for the ritualised taunting of Falstaff. In other words, it's a fairly formal code – but Sir John Falstaff, the only titled person in the play, resists speaking it even when other characters address him in verse. Falstaff speaks and does what he wants. As a higher-class person, he dictates forms and levels of formality.

As Falstaff journeys through *Henry IV Parts I* and *II*, he speaks only prose except for two lines of verse at the end when he makes an appeal to the new King Henry V – his one-time playmate. This is an excellent illustration of the power of verse and how it is reserved for the high and important moments in life.

The young Prince Hal, by contrast, moves constantly between the two forms. He's in prose in the tavern with Falstaff and his cronies, but resorts to verse as he grows increasingly aware of the changes he needs to make in his life. Still, his ease in prose is an important indication of his ability to speak with his subjects: he has learnt how to speak with a common touch and ultimately because he knows how to converse with his men, he is able all the more effectively to rally them.

Prose is effectively a character choice in Shakespeare: only those who have no need or ear for conversation have no choice about it. Any character interested in language, argument and story-telling will play with form, be it prose or verse, moving between the informality to the heightened speech of the other. Thus it's absurd when Phoebe in *As You Like It* is played as an uneducated rural idiot: she speaks good verse throughout the play, as does her lover, the shepherd Silvius. The older shepherd also speaks some verse. Shakespeare, a rural boy himself, knows that you can find good speakers with a bardic flair for form and language in the countryside!

Audrey is the one rural character who speaks only prose, as does the clown Touchstone – though Touchstone shows that he can improvise in rhyme when he mocks Orlando's verses. Touchstone's insistence on prose feels deliberately subversive and anarchic. Whoever he talks to, including his so-called betters, he stubbornly remains in prose – but it's completely infused with wit, rhetoric and a clear understanding of the ways of the court. He is the only person in the play to satisfy the intelligence of Jaques.

> *Duke Senior*: By my faith, he is very swift and sententious.
> *Touchstone*: According to the fool's bolt, sir, and such dulcet diseases.
> *Jaques*: But, for the seventh cause: how did you find the quarrel on the seventh cause?
> *Touchstone*: Upon a lie seven times removed – bear your body more seeming, Audrey – as thus, sir. I did dislike the cut of a certain courtier's beard; he sent me word, if I said his beard was not cut well, he was in the mind it was. This is call'd the Retort Courteous. If I sent him word again it was not well cut, he would send me word he cut it to please himself. This is call'd the Quip Modest. If again it

was not well cut, he disabled my judgment. This is call'd the Reply Churlish. If again it was not well cut, he would answer I spake not true. This is call'd the Reproof Valiant. If again it was not well cut, he would say I lie. This is call'd the Countercheck Quarrelsome. And so to the Lie Circumstantial and the Lie Direct.

(V.iv)

With his brilliant grasp of all the finer flourishes of rhetoric, it's clear that Touchstone could easily converse in verse if only he chose to – and that understanding why he doesn't is essential for the actor interpreting his character. Where there is a choice, it is a reflection of the character's soul.

So Iago in *Othello* speaks verse only when it is absolutely necessary to his betters and the audience. He feels at ease in prose with Roderigo but lacks Touchstone's tenacious ability and wit to stay in it with his superiors. Switching forms enables him to deceive: too relaxed in prose, and he might display the evil in his soul.

Macbeth, by contrast, is a play with very little prose. Lady Macbeth reads a prose letter from her husband, and the porter speaks a comic prose speech in a section that serves to lance the horror of the scene immediately before it – the agonised meeting between husband and wife in the aftermath of Duncan's murder.

The only other prose is when Lady Macbeth revisits the horror as she sleepwalks. In her distraction and despair, she speaks in prose although the events themselves took place in a verse scene. She would normally speak in verse: the lack of form, the perturbation in the prose, reflects the loss of control she's feeling in her nightmare:

> *Lady Macbeth*: Out, damned spot! out, I say! One, two; why then 'tis time to do't. Hell is murky. Fie, my lord, fie! a soldier, and afear'd? What need we fear who knows it, when none can call our pow'r to account? Yet who would have thought the old man to have had so much blood in him?

(V.i)

As Lady Macbeth speaks, she is observed by her gentlewoman and the doctor. They too start the scene in prose: a sign perhaps of intimacy and trust. They have been watching for two nights now, and it must have been a hard decision for the gentlewoman to get a witness to her mistress' self-exposure. By the end of the scene – which is harrowing for them both – the doctor heightens the mood by moving into verse, and the gentlewoman concludes by finishing his incomplete verse line. They are united by the verse, as well as by the dreadful sight and knowledge they share.

> *Lady Macbeth*: To bed, to bed; there's knocking at the gate. Come, come, come, come, give me your hand. What's done cannot be undone. To bed, to bed, to bed. [*Exit.*]
> *Doctor*: Will she go now to bed?
> *Gentlewoman*: Directly.
> *Doctor*: Foul whisp'rings are abroad. Unnatural deeds
> Do breed unnatural troubles; infected minds
> To their deaf pillows will discharge their secrets.
> More needs she the divine than the physician.
> God, God forgive us all. Look after her;
> Remove from her the means of all annoyance,
> And still keep eyes upon her. So, good night.
> My mind she has mated, and amaz'd my sight.
> I think, but dare not speak.
> *Gentlewoman*:   Good night, good doctor.
> [*Exeunt.*]

                                                    (V.i)

Just as changes between prose and verse are of great significance for what they tell us about individual characters, so the contrast between the two forms is also part of the structural dynamic of the plays as a whole. The shifts provide acting clues, highlight changes of intensity within scenes, and reflect in structure different kinds of content.

We can see this clearly at the start of *King Lear*. The play begins in prose with Kent and Gloucester informally discussing the division of the kingdom. Lear enters and the speeches switch into verse. The final part of the first scene, between Goneril and Regan, reverts to prose as they plan discussing a very different division of the state.

The scenes are mirrors of one another. In the first, we witness a father dealing with his daughters and the daughters dealing with each other. In the second we have the relationship between a father and his sons, and the sons with each other. In each, verse and prose alternate: in the first, the destruction of a kingdom and a daughter is told in verse; in the second, the planned manipulation is told in prose. The parallels help mesh the play's themes together, and the shifts in form play with our ears and sense of energy almost subliminally to reinforce them.

Sometimes, form speaks almost louder than words. It's arguable that in *Julius Caesar* Brutus makes the political mistake of his life when he addresses the Roman crowds in prose. We know he can speak fine blank verse so it's a conscious choice. He misjudges the mood of the people and, by being too informal about Caesar's assassination, condemns himself:

> *Brutus*: Romans, countrymen, and lovers! Hear me for my cause, and be silent, that you may hear. Believe me for mine honour, and have respect to mine honour, that you may believe. Censure me in your wisdom, and awake your senses, that you may the better judge.
> (III.ii)

Mark Antony, on the other hand, speaking after Brutus, addresses the citizens in verse.

> *Antony*: Friends, Romans, countrymen, lend me your ears;
> I come to bury Caesar, not to praise him.
> The evil that men do lives after them;
> The good is oft interred with their bones;
> So let it be with Caesar.

Both speeches have all the anchoring devices of rhetoric, but the verse adds an extra energy and appeal that wins the crowd. It heightens the debate and in doing so engages their allegiance – and thereby changes the course of history.

Irony

Ironic language conveys the opposite of its apparent literal meaning.

Many speakers manage to imply an opposite meaning through tone. This is sarcasm rather than irony. Sarcasm – meaning, in the Greek, the tearing of flesh – is a low form of ridicule because it has no concrete reality in the word itself. It's a sneer in the voice which creates an impenetrable paradox. Sarcasm is ultimately unambiguous and closes debate, while irony keeps all possibilities open. Irony lies in the word and its context, which means that the person who hears it can penetrate the paradox of meaning through the language; and because it is more than tone of voice it conveys a deeper set of meanings than mere vocal colour. In order for it to operate, both speaker and listener have to fire on two engines simultaneously. Irony requires wit, intelligence and an ability to see beyond the obvious.

Irony creates a paradox. It does so according to context, so that the apparent message is unsettled by the possibility of alternative ones. It can be very subversive: it means you can say many things at once, and those you say them to can't be quite sure which you mean.

In *Richard III* we have the absurd spectacle of Richard begging Queen Elizabeth to help him woo her daughter so he can marry his niece. The monstrosity of this request grows as we know he has killed her brothers, her uncles and her aunt (Richard's last wife Anne). When Elizabeth realises what he is proposing, she responds ironically:

> *Queen Elizabeth*: How canst thou woo her?
> *King Richard*:   That would I learn of you,
> As one being best acquainted with her humour.
> *Queen Elizabeth*: And wilt thou learn of me?
> *King Richard*:   Madam, with all my heart.
> *Queen Elizabeth*: Send to her, by the man that slew her brothers,

A pair of bleeding hearts; thereon engrave
'Edward' and 'York'. Then haply will she weep;
Therefore present to her – as sometime Margaret
Did to thy father, steep'd in Rutland's blood –
A handkerchief; which, say to her, did drain
The purple sap from her sweet brother's body,
And bid her wipe her weeping eyes withal.
If this inducement move her not to love,
Send her a letter of thy noble deeds;
Tell her thou mad'st away her uncle Clarence,
Her uncle Rivers; ay, and for her sake
Mad'st quick conveyance with her good aunt Anne.
King Richard: You mock me, madam; this is not the way
To win your daugher.

(IV.iv)

Richard is intelligent enough to know when he is being spun around with irony. The motives and context for Elizabeth's response are important to understand. She is profoundly shocked – as any mother would be – when she realises that Richard wants to marry her daughter. She could have chosen to react with direct fury, but the play has shown that violent argument with Richard doesn't work – he relishes head-on attacks. Irony, here, is more powerful. It momentarily confuses him, stops him in his tracks and enables her to say dangerous words in disguise. It is an appropriate tool for her to use in the defence of her daughter.

As you begin to identify the use of irony, you will find that its rhythm is light and pleasant: gentle waves rippling over dark shadows. Don't confuse it, however, with subtext. You have to embrace the literal message to plumb the deeper one. In other words, you have to be able to express simultaneously the actual meaning and the spin.

Those characters who use irony are generally of high intelligence, and they resort to its indirection when 'straight talking' hasn't worked or is inappropriate. It is a device often used where what is being said is so fraught with peril that it can only be witnessed aloud by in disguise. Where the partners in debate are equal and want to listen and transform, they don't need it, but it's fair play when the listener has more power than the speaker. Used against someone weaker or less clever, it is either an abuse of power or passes unnoticed – but in the right hands, it can unseat a bully.

Similarly, the most skilled bowlers or pitchers in any ball game know how to disguise a lethal delivery with spin. It takes more guile and intelligence than brute strength, but it can always penetrate. In this sense, irony is a fearsome, linguistic delivery – though as with ball games, you have to know how to throw the ball straight before you can spin it. Thus, it is essential to understand what the direct delivery of a speech would be in order to comprehend irony. Failure to do so will flatten the speech and reduce its power.

Irony is reliant on context and character. As in antithesis, where opposites are explored by placing a word against a word, so we understand when a speech is ironic according to who says it and in what situation. We are alerted to it when a thought is placed in a context that cannot support its literal meaning, or when it is incompatible with what we know of a character's 'true self'. Irony is a kind of mask that helps meaning penetrate in disguise. You will recognise its presence when what is apparently being said is inconsistent with what you know of the character's preoccupations and values in the context.

Let's examine a section from *The Winter's Tale*. Paulina is a very forceful and outspoken lady. She is direct and expects to get her way. She is the only member of the court who actively takes on Leontes and calls his crimes to account. When she first confronts him with his daughter in her arms, she has no need of irony as she has not yet discovered how lost in jealousy he is. By the time of the trial she has to tackle him quite differently:

> *Paulina*: That thou betray'd'st Polixenes, 'twas nothing;
> That did but show thee, of a fool, inconstant,
> And damnable ingrateful. Nor was't much
> Thou wouldst have poison'd good Camillo's honour,
> To have him kill a king – poor trespasses,
> More monstrous standing by;
>
> (III.ii)

We know that Paulina doesn't really believe "twas nothing": it would be ridiculous to play the speech earnestly, and would make her seem heartless and stupid. So why does she resort to irony? The answer is simply that she can't afford to be direct if she wants to get through to Leontes and expose his tyrannies. Using irony, she is much less likely to be stopped. It will confuse his ear enough for her to finish the catalogue of his cruelties, which will end with her announcing the death of the Queen.

When she comes to this Paulina reverts to her true self without any hint of irony. She says what's on her mind and in heart without any twists, and the contrast with the earlier lines further highlights the horror of the death of the virtuous Queen.

> – the Queen, the Queen
> The sweet'st, dear'st creature's dead, and vengeance for 't,
> Not dropp'd down yet.

Irony is useful when the playing field is not flat: with it you can outwit a more powerful person. So Henry V's public humiliation as he realises that the 'treasure' the Dauphin of France has sent him is tennis balls means it's clear that his gratitude is ironic. The Dauphin has mocked him and he has to save face or weep – 'We are glad the Dauphin is so pleasant with us; / His present and your pains we thank you for.'

Of course he doesn't want to thank the Dauphin – he's furious. Anyone who has ever opened a present in public only to find that it's a mockery, knows only too well the pain and distress Henry must be feeling. If he showed his distress, he would be perceived as weak and the Dauphin would have won. Irony disguises his real feelings and simultaneously raises the stakes between the two men. A direct response might be more honest but it would have less potential power. In this moment the battle lines are drawn; Henry will go to war to appease his real pain.

Irony is not employed when direct and equal dialogue is possible. It does not occur in 'the marriage of true minds' because it coats true meaning with a protective layer. At unequal moments, where naked truth is not possible or makes you vulnerable, irony is safer. Thus Hamlet cannot risk expressing exactly what he feels and thinks after his mother's marriage to his uncle. No one else at court seems to think their relationship is wrong, so he resorts to punning and irony.

> *King*: But now, my cousin Hamlet, and my son –
> *Hamlet*: [*Aside*] A little more than kin, and less than kind.
> *King*: How is it that the clouds still hang on you?
> *Hamlet*: Not so, my lord; I am too much in the sun.
> *Queen*: Good Hamlet, cast thy nighted colour off,
> And let thine eye look like a friend on Denmark.
> Do not for ever with thy vailed lids
> Seek for thy noble father in the dust.
> Thow know'st 'tis common – all that lives must die,

Passing through nature to eternity.
Hamlet: Ay, madam, it is common.

(I.ii)

It is impossible for Hamlet to be straightforward. He is politically gagged and emotionally confused. Something very wrong has happened to his whole world and no one seems to be remarking on it. There's no straightforward debate, so he has to comment on the situation ironically. Interestingly the King is either deaf to Hamlet's irony – is he not intelligent enough? – or chooses not to notice it. Nevertheless, it enables Hamlet to be extremely impudent, to slice into a more powerful person with some chance of surviving because irony always leaves an exit route. He calls his mother 'common' – but because he is picking up her reference to death being common, the irony conceals the insult.

Language is a sparring weapon and irony is one tool in the armoury. It doesn't go for the frontal assault but finds openings in any clash of intellect where a direct attack is unwise or impossible. It is the stone in David's sling that can slay the giant Goliath.

The anarchic and mocking dimension of irony, coupled with the need to disguise true feelings, manifests itself vocally with a light and even playful tone. It doesn't have the bite of sarcasm or the earnestness of a straight delivery. In order to play it well, you have to be a practised communicator with confidence in your intelligence and wit: you have to be prepared to play with modes of communication. This can sometimes make it hard for less experienced actors to do it well, let alone identify it.

If what your character is saying cannot be true but is not a direct lie, think irony.

I remember a rehearsal of the *Dream* where the director was infuriated by a young, earnest actor playing Demetrius. The particular problem was a mocking line about the quality of acting in the play within the play – which is a terribly written tragic love story constantly interrupted by the men in the audience:

> *Wall*: This loam, this rough-cast, and this stone, doth show
> That I am that same wall; the truth is so;
> And this the cranny is, right and sinister,
> Through which the fearful lovers are to whisper.
> *Theseus*: Would you desire lime and hair to speak better?
> *Demetrius*: It is the wittiest partition that ever I heard discourse, my lord.

(V.i)

The actor couldn't realise this last line. He sounded intense and dull. 'Play, play,' yelled the director. The result was a biting, sarcastic delivery. 'No, no! Is that how you play? I pity your girlfriend.' (He was one of those directors who mock). Later I found the frustrated young man outside the rehearsal room and asked whether he believed that Demetrius found the Wall's speech witty. 'No,' he answered; 'that's why I played it sarcastically.'

'What does partition mean?'

Pause. 'I suppose it means a wall.'

'Has Demetrius ever heard a wall speak before?'

Another pause. 'No,' he answered carefully. 'So it isn't true and is true at the same time.'

Sarcasm reduces the line to one energy – contempt – but irony releases another layer of truth which the speaker has to be aware of, and this awareness is what keeps both the debate and the voice open. Demetrius is playing with the Duke off the performance of the Wall. They know that it's bad text and they are having fun with that knowledge. It's an unspoken secret they are sharing between them.

'But how do I do it?' the unhappy actor lamented. 'I understand, but I can't do it.' The tea break was over, the scene was to be run. I told him that the director Ron Eyre once described irony as a wine gum stuck behind your back teeth. You keep it there to suck on whenever you want: a secret language power to be used when open chewing of words – or gums – is not allowed. Somehow it worked, and the actor received the praise of his director. 'Wine gums,' he teased as he passed me after the run. Then he stopped. 'Demetrius is being very mean to those actors, rather like the director was to me.'

It was an important discovery. The men in this last scene are using a shared knowledge to mock Bottom and his fellows – a knowledge that the actors don't have. It is unfair, unequal and consequently a misuse of power. Happily, the mechanicals seem unaware of it. They don't know that a game is being played out around them.

Puns

Punning is another game: a word game, in which one word releases two and occasionally three meanings simultaneously.

Like irony, a pun can be appreciated in the read form of text but is given huge potency when it marries with the voice and sound. Language games reach their full potential when spoken.

Puns and other word games are central to the way the British use language. Most advertising campaigns, for instance, contain either puns or other hidden teasing linguistic conundrums. They delight and intrigue us, they engage and complicate thought and feeling; they have a generative, active, living energy, not just an academic or theoretical one.

A pun can be used just for fun, or to riddle a darker meaning within its double sense for attack or defence. As a device, it has enormous power and economy: it's a word that is always more than it seems.

> *Richard*: Now is the winter of our discontent
> Made glorious summer by this sun of York;
>
> (*Richard III*, I.i)

Sun and son: Prince Edward is the son of the Duke of York, who in rising to the throne is the sun that dispels the winter of war and brings in the summer of peace. The power is compacted around the pun. As with irony, context is important. We know that Richard is consciously punning because of the presence of 'winter', 'discontent', 'summer' and 'York'. The pun fuses all these words together and in doing so detonates intellectual and emotional resonances in these two lines. The texture of the iambic rhythm falls on 'sun' to heighten our experience of the word even more.

A pun can also hide a darker or bawdier meaning beneath an innocent one, as here in *The Taming of the Shrew*:

Petruchio: Who knows not where a wasp does wear his sting?
In his tail.
Katherina: In his tongue.
Petruchio: Whose tongue?
Katherina: Yours, if you talk of tales; and so farewell.
Petruchio: What, with my tongue in your tail? Nay, come again,
Good Kate; I am a gentleman.

(II.i)

It is Kate who turns 'tail' into 'tale' by putting the pun in context with 'talk'. Petruchio responds and continues her theme of 'talk' and 'tales' by adding 'tongue', but because 'tale' has already been 'tail' the picture of his tongue in Kate's tail resonates in our ears and imaginations, considerably reinforced by the alliteration of *t*'s, which puts the tongue directly to work. It's as bawdy as you can get but the play in the pun makes it clever too, and the double meaning gives the imagination an escape hatch if you don't want actually to go to the physical picture it paints. Wit just civilises Petruchio's suggestion – though he knows he's gone too far as he has to reassure Kate that he is a gentleman.

Speaking at cross-purposes with puns is one of the ways Petruchio tames Kate. It works by intriguing and confusing her at once. Punning plays for time: the fraction of a second before the listener grasps the double meaning. And the speaker if called to order, of course, can always cite the more innocent meaning of the word in defence.

When two people pick up puns and play with them, they become bonded to each other. It signifies attachment and complicity in the game. You place yourself together in the arena and are no longer innocent of the other's intentions. At this moment you challenge, flirt and aim to display equal power: by playing the game, you are making contact with both head and heart.

It could be a symptom of sexual attraction – or just the inability to resist a linguistic challenge:

Petruchio: Good Kate; I am a gentleman.
Katherina: That I'll try.
[*She strikes him.*]
Petruchio: I swear I'll cuff you, if you strike again.
Katherina: So may you lose your arms.
If you strike me, you are no gentleman;
And if no gentleman, why then no arms.

> *Petruchio*: A herald, Kate? O, put me in thy books!
> *Katherina*: What is your crest – a coxcomb?
> *Petruchio*: A combless cock, so Kate will be my hen.
> *Katherina*: No cock of mine: you crow too like a craven.

Kate hits Petruchio. For a moment the verbal battle becomes an actual physical attack. Petruchio warns her that he'll hit back. This leads Kate to challenge his assertion that he is a gentleman. Gentlemen don't hit women, though they do have coats of arms that signify their status. Both meanings explode in 'arms': arms to hit her with, and the arms of a gentleman.

Petruchio plays with her as a herald who would announce his status. She suggests his crest would be represented by a coxcomb – an idiot. Remember a crest is not only the symbol of a gentleman but also the tuft of feathers on a bird's head. Petruchio runs with 'crest' and 'comb' and deepens through punning his sexual assault on Kate by introducing a 'cock'. A cock has a crest and Kate will be the cock's hen.

It's as rude as you can imagine and simultaneously as innocent as a nursery rhyme. Kate doesn't back off, but continues in full knowledge with a further link created by the *c* alliteration. She started the sound off, he picks it up and she stays with it. Kate's playing!

Puns can marry our conscious and unconscious together, but they are not always so light-hearted. Consider Angelo's soliloquy in *Measure for Measure*, where he finds himself tormented by desire for Isabella:

> *Angelo*: What's this, what's this? Is this her fault or mine?
> The tempter or the tempted, who sins most?
> Ha!
> Not she: nor doth she tempt: but it is I
> That, lying by the violet in the sun,
> Do as the carrion does, not as the flow'r,
> Corrupt with virtuous season. Can it be
> That modesty may more betray our sense
> Than woman's lightness? Having waste ground enough,
> Shall we desire to raze the sanctuary
> And pitch our evils there?
>
> (II.ii)

With 'lying by the violet' Angelo signifies two kinds of lying – deceiving himself and Isabella, and lying down for sex. Then 'Shall we desire to raze the sanctuary', where 'raze' means both to lay waste and to raise – to destroy Isabella's chastity with his erection. Angelo puns throughout the play as he tries to wrestle with and understand the conflict between his puritan exterior and his newly awakened sexual interior.

Sometimes an actor will decide that one meaning in the pun is known by Angelo but the other remains in his unconscious; that language is exposing his heart's secrets. But you can only make this choice if you fully understand the potential of both meanings.

A pun can be for the audience's benefit. The character is unaware of the pun but the audience knows more than the character. For instance, we know that Angelo desires Isabella and that he is playing a part:

> *Isabella*: Nay, call us ten times frail;
> For we are soft as our complexions are,
> And credulous to false prints.
>
> (II.iv)

We know as she says 'false prints' that she has also called Angelo a 'false prince'. At this point in the scene, she is unaware that he is a false prince morally speaking, but she does know that he is only a deputy. The pun could be a conscious challenge – or perhaps it's her unconscious warning of his depraved intentions.

You hear puns when you are ready to. 'Hear', 'here'; 'no', 'know': as soon as a pun explodes in the mouth, immediate complications are released. The emotional and intellectual line within the scene begins to spin.

To appreciate a pun fully you have to speak it out aloud and know the context. When it is a conscious pun, it is generally to tease, mock and confound someone – even yourself. The more direct the scene, however, the less the characters play this way. There is always a place for wit, word games and irony but for true and direct connections between people, Shakespeare requires them to speak without riddles. If you really need to convey an important and heartfelt point, you don't play games or use paradox – both options are too risky.

Language Games

Hamlet uses every form of language available to him. He is extremely skilled at expressing himself. As his life is complicated through the discovery of his father's murder, he has to use all his language skills to disguise his true intentions and is only straightforward with the audience – whom he trusts – and Horatio. All the other characters in the play, who he believes are betraying him, suffer the barb of his wit.

> *Hamlet*: Lady, shall I lie in your lap?
> *Ophelia*: No, my lord.
> *Hamlet*: I mean my head upon your lap.
> *Ophelia*: Ay, my lord.
> *Hamlet*: Do you think I meant country matters?
> *Ophelia*: I think nothing, my lord.
> *Hamlet*: That's a fair thought to lie between maids' legs.
> *Ophelia*: What is, my lord?
> *Hamlet*: Nothing.
> *Ophelia*: You are merry, my lord.
>
> (III.ii)

It's hard to imagine that, before the start of the play, Hamlet would have been so crude with Ophelia as to pun on 'lie' and 'country', particularly in public. Her shock emphasises how out of character it seems to her. The exchange is a one-way street. Ophelia, unlike Kate, is not playing. She is confused.

The first exchange we see between Hamlet and Ophelia is by contrast straightforward – almost clumsy:

> *Ophelia*: How does your honour for this many a day?
> *Hamlet*: I humbly thank you; well, well, well.
>
> (III.i)

Only when she hurts him by returning his gifts does he resort to punning, mocking and irony.

All Hamlet's enemies – Polonius, the King, the Queen, Rosencrantz and Guildenstern – are on the receiving end of his wit, and none is capable of competing with him.

> *Queen*: What have I done that thou dar'st wag thy tongue
> In noise so rude against me?
>
> (III.iv)

This unhappy remonstration comes after Hamlet has battered her with innuendo, irony and insinuation. His mother is completely unsettled, unsure of her footing. It's not just that Hamlet has been shouting at her: 'noise' also indicates how ruthless and overwhelming has been the language from his wagging tongue. Hamlet's verbal skills confuse his enemies and safeguard his secret. Indeed, they are so confusing that Hamlet achieves the desired effect of seeming mad.

Only Horatio, his one true friend, receives Hamlet's clear and honest affection, uncluttered by innuendo, irony or puns.

> *Hamlet*: Horatio, thou are e'en as just a man
> As e'er my conversation cop'd withal.
> *Horatio*: O my dear lord!
> *Hamlet*:   Nay, do not think I flatter;
> For what advancement may I hope from thee,
> That no revenue has but thy good spirits
> To feed and clothe thee? Why should the poor be flatter'd?
> No, let the candied tongue lick absurd pomp,
> And crook the pregnant hinges of the knee
> Where thrift may follow fawning.
>
> (III.ii)

Hamlet's is an extreme example, but the ability to play with language is an important social skill in all sorts of situation. If you haven't got it, you face humiliation – like Sir Andrew Aguecheek in *Twelfth Night*:

> *Sir Andrew*: Sir Toby Belch! How now, Sir Toby Belch!
> *Sir Toby*: Sweet Sir Andrew!
> *Sir Andrew*: Bless you, fair shrew.
> *Maria*: And you too, sir.
> *Sir Toby*: Accost, Sir Andrew, accost.

Sir Andrew: What's that?

Sir Toby: My niece's chambermaid.

Sir Andrew: Good Mistress Accost, I desire better acquaintance.

Maria: My name is Mary, sir.

Sir Andrew: Good Mistress Mary Accost –

Sir Toby: You mistake, knight. 'Accost' is front her, board her, woo her, assail her.

Sir Andrew: By my troth, I would not undertake her in this company. Is that the meaning of 'accost'?

(I.iii)

Sir Andrew's literal-mindedness is a social embarrassment and, as the scene develops, Maria, a low-status servant, runs rings around the bemused knight.

Equally, however, there are times when language games are inappropriate and the situation demands a direct and powerful poetic use of language. Thus Mercutio in *Romeo and Juliet*, who never seems able to open his mouth without some pun, mock or stream of irony escaping, is eventually doomed by his taunting of Tybalt.

Tybalt: Follow me close, for I will speak to them. Gentlemen, good den; a word with one of you.

Mercutio: And but one word with one of us? Couple it with something; make it a word and a blow.

Tybalt: You shall find me apt enough to that, sir, an you will give me occasion.

Mercutio: Could you not take some occasion without giving?

Tybalt: Mercutio, thou consortest with Romeo.

Mercutio: Consort! What, dost thou make us minstrels? An thou make minstrels of us, look to hear nothing but discords. Here's my fiddlestick; here's that shall make you dance. Zounds, consort!

(III.i)

Mercutio is playing with fire here. He is playing with language with someone not equally armed to compete through words. Tybalt is either unable or unwilling to vent his anger through language alone, and the result is fatal. Thus do many bar fights start, when verbal insults break down or one combatant is unable to spar through language and resorts instead to physical attack.

We saw earlier how Berowne is asked by Rosaline to stop his endless witticisms. At certain moments in life, games are inappropriate. We might enjoy flirting with language games but at some point we all yearn for simple, uncomplicated lines of contact. The well-rounded communicator may not be able to perform equally well in every kind of language, but they will certainly know which forms are appropriate at which moments.

As Edgar says in the last lines of *King Lear*:

> The weight of this sad time we must obey;
> Speak what we feel, not what we ought to say.
> The oldest hath borne most; we that are young
> Shall never see so much nor live so long.

Repetition

Repetition is one of the oldest and most powerful poetic devices, and Shakespeare uses it in a variety of ways. Repetition of ideas, images and themes: his plays are woven through these threads. For the actor, however, it can pose problems, especially when words or phrases are repeated side by side.

Remember that the givens move you constantly forwards, the words acting like stepping stones – each word a step forward. Where there is repetition in a line, therefore, it probably indicates that the character is momentarily overwhelmed. Because each stage and word of the character's journey is a new pulse to be experienced, the words must be owned and expressed differently even though they are the same. So in *Richard III*, the second 'set down' of Lady Anne's 'Set down, set down' has to be played differently from the first.

The actor who skids over all or part of this repetition will miss a dramatic moment and texture in the line. Here, the request she makes to the men carrying Henry IV's body is so unusual – to put a body down in the street – that she has to repeat it. This sort of understanding has to be developed to make the repetition relevant and effective. Thus, Angelo's 'What's this? What's this?' in *Measure for Measure* are the words of an apparently unemotional, unsexual puritan who's been actively persecuting licentious young men, and suddenly finds himself sexually tempted by a novice nun. The shock to his system and his entire moral universe is so profound that he has to ask the question twice.

The sorts of disturbance represented by repetition are fully evident in Hamlet's 'O, that this too too solid flesh would melt' soliloquy:

> *Hamlet:* O, that this too too solid flesh would melt,
> Thaw, and resolve itself into a dew!
> Or that the Everlasting had not fix'd

His canon 'gainst self-slaughter! O God! God!
How weary, stale, flat, and unprofitable,
Seem to me all the uses of this world!
Fie on't! Ah, fie! 'tis an unweeded garden,
That grows to seed; things rank and gross in nature
Possess it merely. That it should come to this!
But two months dead! Nay, not so much, not two.
So excellent a king that was to this
Hyperion to a satyr; so loving to my mother,
That he might not beteem the winds of heaven
Visit her face too roughly. Heaven and earth!
Must I remember? Why, she would hang on him
As if increase of appetite had grown
By what it fed on; and yet, within a month –
Let me not think on't. Frailty, thy name is woman! –
A little month, or ere those shoes were old
With which she followed my poor father's body,
Like Niobe, all tears – why she, even she –
O God! a beast that wants discourse of reason
Would have mourn'd longer – married with my uncle.
My father's brother; but no more like my father
Than I to Hercules. Within a month,
Ere yet the salt of most unrighteous tears
Had left the flushing in her galled eyes,
She married. O, most wicked speed, to post
With such dexterity to incestuous sheets!
It is not, nor it cannot come to good.
But break, my heart, for I must hold my tongue.

(I.ii)

The naturally articulate prince is struggling throughout this whole speech – 'Oh God! God!'; 'Fie on't! Ah, fie'; 'Within a month / A little month'; 'Why she, even she'; 'Within a month'. The amount of repetition highlights the difficulty and lack of flow. Accepting his mother's betrayal, marriage and sexual behaviour is a tortuous process. The repetition is like chipping away at a block of stone that eventually reveals the heart of his pain – his mother in bed with his uncle: then Hamlet's heart breaks. That it should so seems inevitable given the degree of struggle shown not just by the repetitions, but also by the fractured nature of the iambic and the broken thoughts in the speech.

Remember that this is Hamlet's first soliloquy. The audience meets someone struggling to speak. It is only later in the play that we realise how naturally fluent and articulate he is. But on the evidence of this speech, he is an almost stuttering communicator, unable to gather his thoughts coherently. That is the measure of his distress: his natural eloquence has been shattered.

The Story

The story is another given: a line or set of lines that guide you through a play. Because Shakespeare's language is so rich, his situations so heightened and the plays themselves sometimes so familiar, we can forget to tell the simple stories. Instead, actors can get swamped by the poetry and drown in the emotion. The story can help us here: it is the ball of string that leads through the dense maze of form and language.

Shakespeare's stories may be complex but all their details are clearly and specifically present in the text if you look for them. In some less explicitly plotted plays, actors have to fill in the gaps – not so in Shakespeare. All the important steps in the story are there.

The actor who doesn't follow these steps will get lost and lose the audience or, by failing to go through the stages of the plot, will inadvertantly signal the end of the play. This is a common consequence of allowing over-familiarity to override attention. For instance, many actresses play Juliet in her first scene as if her final tragedy is already known. This is not only confusing but emotionally exhausting. What a relief to realise that Juliet is merely being called by her nurse to meet her mother – who tells her that she is to attend a party given that night by her father, and to view Paris as a possible husband. The scene starts normally enough and is quickly heightened because Juliet realises she is being groomed for marriage and womanhood – but she is not expecting to die.

If it's important not to anticipate the end of the play at the beginning, it's equally vital to pay attention to the very specific story details in the text. Thus in this first scene there are many facts to be discovered: Juliet's age, for instance; the exact date of her birthday; that Lammas Eve is the 29th of August; Lady Capulet's age (twenty-six); the name of the nurse's daughter – Susan; that Susan died. There was an earthquake eleven years ago. The nurse's husband is dead. The Capulets were away in Mantua at the time of the earthquake – all this in the first scene, all rooted in the language and all important in the complete story of the play.

Playwrights are essentially practical thinkers and their storylines are well constructed. The facts of a play must work. In the storyline of *Hamlet*, it is important to understand that the audience knows of the ghost before Hamlet. In his first soliloquy he is distressed, but he hasn't had any supernatural information about his father's murder. All he knows is that his father is dead and that his mother has rapidly married his uncle. He asked permission to return to university but that request has been denied. He is to remain at court. It is, at this stage, all very straightforward – and yet I have sat through innumerable rehearsals when these basic facts weren't understood, and both actor and director were hitting problems because they didn't know the story.

What Happens Next?

You should go through the whole play, line by line, entrances and exits, scene by scene asking 'what happens next?' It's a wonderful exercise to do with a whole company as it will make the storyline crystal clear. You will be astonished by the number of plot points and story details embedded in the text.

The idea for this exercise comes from an experience I had teaching actors in Lithuania. We were working the first Isabella and Angelo scene in *Measure for Measure*. I didn't realise it, but the play had previously been banned by the Russians so the actors had never seen or read it before. At the end of the scene one of them asked, 'What happens next?' I told them about the next stage of the story but that only led to another 'What happens next?' The questions gathered momentum and I had to tell them, in detail, the whole plot of the play.

They were so enthralled that it made me realise completely afresh how great a storyteller Shakespeare was. Later I got my students to try the exercise with other plays, and each time we discovered an equally exciting story that had to some degree been smothered by the weight of assumptions and familiarity.

It's worth remembering here the classical structure of thought we looked at earlier, where each idea and scene links to the one before and each unit of thought moves the actor and the audience forwards. This applies equally to the storyline. If we don't understand and convey the story elements in the first scene of a play, then the rest becomes impossible to follow. Once a given is in place, the story can move ahead without any reference back; if we miss it, it will remain at least partially lost for the rest of the play.

A good example is the opening scene of *A Midsummer Night's Dream*. There's a wealth of detail in it that's necessary to understand what follows. At a basic level, for instance, the second scene, in which the mechanicals discuss the play they will perform for the Duke and Hippolyta on their wedding day, relies on an exchange early in the first where Theseus dispatches Philostrate to ensure that the Athenian youth celebrate the marriage. Likewise, unless we hear Egeus demand Hermia's death for refusing to marry Demetrius, we can't appreciate the acute dilemma faced by the lovers; and we must hear and understand Lysander's remarks about Helena and her love for Demetrius in order fully to grasp extent of her recent betrayal and public humiliation.

As you ask 'what happens next?' – and you can put the question repeatedly – you will discover other specific and essential givens. Take the opening thirty-five lines of prose in *King Lear*, where concrete, particular storylines are placed that affect the audience's understanding of Lear, Edmund and Cornwall.

> *Kent*: I thought the King had more affected the Duke of Albany than Cornwall.
> *Gloucester*: It did always seem so to us; but no, in the division of the kingdom, it appears not which of the Dukes he values most; for equalities are so weigh'd that curiosity in neither can make choice of either's moiety.
> *Kent*: Is not this your son, my lord?
> *Gloucester*: His breeding, sir, hath been at my charge. I have so often blush'd to acknowledge him that I am now braz'd to it.
> *Kent*: I cannot conceive you.
> *Gloucester*: Sir, this young fellow's mother could; whereupon she grew round-womb'd, and had indeed, sir, a son for her cradle ere she had a husband for her bed. Do you smell a fault?
> *Kent*: I cannot wish the fault undone, the issue of it being so proper.
> *Gloucester*: But I have a son, sir, by order of law, some year elder than this, who yet is no dearer in my account. Though this knave came something saucily to the world before he was sent for, yet

was his mother fair; there was good sport at his making, and the whoreson must be acknowledged. – Do you know this noble gentleman, Edmund?

Edmund: No, my lord.

Gloucester: My Lord of Kent. Remember him hereafter as my honourable friend.

Edmund: My services to your lordship.

Kent: I must love you, and sue to know you better.

Edmund: Sir, I shall study deserving.

Gloucester: He hath been out nine years, and away he shall again.

(I.i)

Three characters: the Dukes of Gloucester and Kent, and Edmund. We learn that Kent thought the King favoured Albany above Cornwall. This is relevant for the actors playing these parts. After all, Albany stays faithful to Lear and Cornwall doesn't, so perhaps Lear's judgement about them before the play, as witnessed by Kent, was right.

From Gloucester we learn that the kingdom has already been divided equally. If this is true, then Lear's sudden decision to test his daughters in the following moments of the scene is really dramatic and shocking to the whole assembly. Kent then asks whether Edmund is Gloucester's son. This tells us that Edmund has not met Kent before and is therefore a newcomer at the court. Now Gloucester admits that he believes Edmund to be his illegitimate son and has paid for his upkeep. There was good sport at his making, he says, and then we hear his name: Edmund. What's very apparent in the language is that while Gloucester speaks crudely about Edmund's mother, Kent remains perfectly gracious. (A director might well decide that Edmund should overhear this exchange – which would certainly colour his relationship with his father.)

Finally we hear that Edmund has been away for nine years and will be leaving again. Does Edmund know of the plan to send him away from the court? This question, based on the storyline, is pivotal to the way Edmund is played.

The givens of the plot weave a tapestry. Without this firmly in place, it's impossible for actor or audience to venture deeper into the emotional and imaginative journey of the play. Keep asking 'what happens next?' It will help establish the basic ground on which you and your character walk.

Location

Always check location. Is the action set in the country? In a wood? A street? A tent?

Setting is a given. Although for the purposes of the production it is possible to alter the location, it is essential not to lose the dramatic relevance of the given. So often a scene is transferred to fit a designer's concept without fully exploring why Shakespeare has chosen the particular setting. Location almost always adds to the action in some way, and carelessly changing it can make the actor's task much harder. Some alternatives can have the same quality and energy as Shakespeare's setting, but inappropriate ones can confound the play.

In *The Winter's Tale*, Hermione's trial takes place in the open air, presumably so that more people can see her humiliated. The given – and its dramatic function – might be satisfied by showing the trial on television instead, while a closed courtroom setting would be likely to reduce the scene's impact.

In *Julius Caesar*, Cassius talks to Brutus in the street about treason. Anyone who has lived in a society where there is no freedom of speech knows that you don't speak treason indoors where you could be overheard or be accused of holding a secret meetng.

Lady Anne in *Richard III* mourns Henry VI in a street in the City of London. It's an odd place to do so: is it a political act to witness her father-in-law's death in public? Such questions must be examined: the given cannot be ignored.

In *Richard II* the gardeners feel safe in their garden – they wouldn't speak about Richard's fall in a place that didn't feel secure. The garden is their space: people tend to gossip in settings that feel familiar and unthreatening. They don't expect the queen to be there, so it is a double surprise that she is and has heard their views on the state. The location at once releases the gardeners, and produces a dramatic shock for them.

In *King John* Constance enters a tent filled with men on a battlefield – not a place many women go. Her distress takes her to a place she is barred from, and both corsets her grief and gives it vent.

In *King Lear*, Lear and his knights run riot in Goneril's house. Lear doesn't wreck his own palace, but hers. By contrast, Gloucester's eyes are taken out in his own home – in his drawing-room, the last place he might have suspected danger. If you are walking down an alleyway, you are at least alert and in a state of readiness. Gloucester might have been safer anywhere but home. As his torture begins he says, 'You are my guests' and then later 'I am your host'.

Likewise, in *Macbeth* Duncan says, as he approaches his host's house, 'This castle hath a pleasant seat; the air / Nimbly and sweetly recommends itself / Unto our gentle senses.' Duncan feels safe with the castle's aura. Not suspecting that the rules of hospitality are about to be overthrown, his sound sleep aids Macbeth's bloody murder.

Location is key too in *Antony and Cleopatra*. Like the political conflict, the emotional dynamics are heightened as the settings swing between Alexandria and Rome. Separation is bad enough but distance and slow lines of communication frustrate lovers even more. Cleopatra, after her parting from Antony, tries to fill the empty hours with music and games. On the arrival of a messenger from Italy, she is overjoyed –

> Cleopatra: O! from Italy?
> Cram then thy fruitful tidings in mine ears,
> That long time have been barren.
>
>   (II.iv)

Her happiness is soon smashed as she hears the news of Antony's marriage. The distance between their worlds makes the pain more unbearable, the gap more unbridgeable, in love as in politics.

Romeo experiences a similar anguish when he is banished from Verona and Juliet. Mantua is a long way from Verona, and this distance becomes horribly important when the letters from Friar Lawrence explaining that Juliet is not dead are delayed. If the letters had arrived, both the lovers would have lived. As it is, distance got in the way.

Never underestimate or disregard location: as one of the givens in the play; it is there for a purpose.

Stage Directions, Props, Entrances and Exits

Trust them. They are all written into the text. Whole scenes can fail if a director or actor doesn't take note of them. They include entrances, exits and props.

Good playwrights are pragmatic. Part of their craft is to get actors on and off stage, give them the right prop and tell them what to do and when to do it. When King Lear says 'Give me the map there', he needs a map before he can continue. Until Phoebe looks at Rosalind, Rosalind can't ask 'Why what means this? Why do you look on me?'

The timing of the directions is precise, clear and on the text, as this scene from *Two Gentlemen of Verona* shows.

> *Julia*: This babble shall not henceforth trouble me.
> Here is a coil with protestation!
> [*Tears the letter*]
> Go, get you gone; and let the papers lie.
> You would be fing'ring them, to anger me.
> *Lucetta*: She makes it strange; but she would be best pleas'd
> To be so ang'red with another letter. [*Exit*]
> *Julia*: Nay, would I were so ang'red with the same!
> O hateful hands, to tear such loving words!
> Injurious wasps, to feed on such sweet honey
> And kill the bees that yield it with your stings!
> I'll kiss each several paper for amends.
> Look, here is writ 'kind Julia'.
>
> (I.ii)

You cannot begin to tackle this speech until you have the letter. There aren't many props in Shakespeare but the ones he mentions are crucial. There is no way to make the speech work unless you tear the letter after 'Here is a coil with protestation'. Julia has to be kissing or about to kiss the paper in order to see her name written; and so it continues through the rest of the speech.

Exits and entrances are equally clearly defined. By failing to follow them accurately you can distract the audience or layer the scene inappropriately. I once saw a production of *Macbeth* where the servant came in during Lady Macbeth's letter scene and it seemed that he could overhear her views on her husband. The text makes it clear that he actually enters after her speech, and that she reacts immediately with 'What is your tidings?' The servant's early entrance not only cluttered the last section of Lady Macbeth's speech but deflated the urgency of his message that 'The King comes here tonight.'

Later in this same production the same actor was commanded by Macbeth 'get thee to bed'. The stage direction then is *Exit Servant*, followed by Macbeth's awestruck 'Is this a dagger which I see before me?' It was undoubtedly Shakespeare's intention that Macbeth should be alone. Unfortunately, however, the servant hadn't left the stage: he was hovering, completely cooling Macbeth's moment and failing to obey his master's – and his author's – orders.

Respect the evidence of the text. In *Romeo and Juliet* both lovers make it absolutely clear that Romeo won't and doesn't dance. Sue Lefton, the Royal Shakespeare Company's Head of Movement, often has battles with directors who nonetheless want Romeo to dance. Sue says she cannot make a dance work if Romeo is involved. Shakespeare knows what he is doing. Experiment and change if you will but at least ensure you try it his way at some time during the process. Only when you've found the path can you really afford to disregard it.

Soliloquy

An actor alone on stage speaking: until recently that meant the actor was addressing the audience. The connection between actor and audience would have been more potent in earlier days, but now stage lights have become so strong that the actor can't see the people he's speaking to. If a play is done in daylight or under weaker lighting – as it would have been in Shakespeare's day – it is hard *not* to talk to the audience.

Soliloquy has the dramatic effect of making the audience complicit with the character, for good or ill. It means we know more about what is going on than other people in the play. By addressing us, the character engages us in the story and perhaps even in a moral debate. If we know what Iago is doing, why don't we shout out and stop him?

Through soliloquy, characters invite the audience inside their heads, to witness their motives. Soliloquy is only written for characters who have no one else to speak to. The audience is their only friend and confidante. They test their ideas with us through soliloquy; and as soon as they have found out what to do they cease speaking to us. Once they have friends within the play we are no longer needed.

Thus Hamlet establishes a relationship with us but as soon as he decides on a course of action – 'my thoughts be bloody or be nothing worth' – he breaks it off. He doesn't need us anymore. It can make the audience feel surprisingly lonely.

In the *Dream*, Helena is alone from the start. She makes the first connection to us in the play. Hermia on the other hand only turns to soliloquy when she has been abandoned by her lover and is suddenly alone; then she needs us and speaks accordingly.

Some characters don't have soliloquies at all. King Lear addresses the elements in 'Blow wind' but never the audience, and in any case he is with the Fool at that point. It is the outcasts in the play who have the soliloquies – Edmund, Edgar, Kent and the Fool.

Part 3 The Imaginative

'It is requir'd
You do awake your faith.'

(The Winter's Tale, V.iii)

'And as imagination bodies forth
The form of things unknown, the poet's pen
Turns them, shapes, and gives to airy nothing
A local habitation and a name.'

(A Midsummer Night's Dream, V.i)

The Imaginative Exploration of the Text

We are now ready to embark on the work that will make your interpretation of a play unique by freeing your emotional connection to the word and to characterisation in language. This section builds on the foundation of the givens. It will take you into a deeper exploration of words and images, and animate the language with specific, felt, imaginative experience. While the givens create a structure of language that moves you forward through thought and story, the imaginative work will connect you emotionally to the text, excavating the 'vertical' power of words.

The casual, unmemorable episodes of life do not need to be recorded in emotionally profound and specific language, but the sorts of event that Shakespeare describes do. His plays witness the most memorable experiences, that will forever affect those involved – events the characters will remember on their deathbeds. The language he uses is appropriate to the importance of these moments and etches them in the body, heart, mind and spirit. To experience this unity in our being we must use our imagination to connect to the language with meaning and precision, and make it our own.

Such ownership will enable us to hear and feel character. When we are heightened it is harder to censor and disguise our true feelings and view of the world. We are all more likely to say what we mean in a heated argument, when we are tested (and Shakespeare tests most of his characters) or just in moments of sheer irritation. Then aspects of our selves are exposed by how and what we speak.

Thus Cleopatra behaves badly towards an innocent messenger who has the unfortunate task of telling her Antony has married.

> *Cleopatra*: The most infectious pestilence upon thee!
> *Messenger*: Good madam, patience.

> *Cleopatra:*   What say you? Hence,
> Horrible villain! or I'll spurn thine eyes
> Like balls before me; I'll unhair thy head;
> Thou shalt be whipp'd with wire and stew'd in brine,
> Smarting to ling'ring pickle.
>
>   (II.v)

In this moment, Cleopatra's violence is revealed. Charmian, her close companion, has to intervene: 'Good madam, keep yourself within yourself / The man is innocent.' It's a wonderfully concrete image – keep yourself within yourself – but the language has exposed the truth.

The Duke of Kent acts in a similar way at the beginning of *King Lear*. He is the only one in the scene to defend Cordelia. At the moment Lear calls Cordelia his 'sometime daughter' Kent intervenes.

> *Kent:* Good my liege –
> *Lear*: Peace, Kent!
> Come not between the dragon and his wrath.
>
>   (I.i)

Even despite Lear's vivid warning, Kent stands by Cordelia and faces the consequences of his words when he is banished. He is a fine and courageous man and throughout the play the character revealed in this initial test is confirmed.

Just as we reveal what we are when we speak in a heightened state, so as we transform through experience and life, our choice of language changes with us. Revisiting our old diaries, poems or letters will usually prove embarrassing – at least – because of the inevitable shift in voice and language between our younger and older selves. The different words we use chart and witness our progress through life.

In Shakespeare that transformation, when it occurs, is marked either in new ways of speech or in unaccustomed silence. The impassioned and loquacious Isabella in *Measure for Measure*, for instance, is silent at the end of the play. The Duke suggests they marry but she never replies, leaving the scales portrayed in the title in balance. The Isabella we've known is strangely lost for words.

In *Othello* on the other hand Iago gives them up deliberately. The man who has spun words around everyone else in the play elects silence at the end. He pulls a further perverse triumph from the disaster of being discovered by never deciding more to speak, either in remorse or explanation of his actions: 'Demand me nothing; what you know you know. / From this time forth I never will speak word.'

This is quite the opposite of Edmund in *King Lear*, who on hearing Edgar's description of their father's death, says 'This speech of yours hath mov'd me, / And shall perchance do good'. It's as startling an about-turn in its way as Iago's; and in part it's because Edgar's own language has transformed completely in the course of his trials. The last time Edmund heard Edgar speak was when he had been easy to manipulate – Edmund sent him scampering off with only Edgar's 'I am sure on't, not a word' spoken in his own defence. But by the end of the play Edgar's language is capable of commanding all.

As a general rule language becomes simpler and more direct as characters transform. It is as though speech reflects the amount of clutter surrounding a person: the more in touch people are with themselves and their surroundings, the more direct and simple the language.

Lear is an obvious example. His speech at the beginning of the play is grand and then angry, violent and even obscene. By the end, having come through madness to self-realisation, it's as sad and simple as can be. He's even saying 'please' and 'thank you':

> Never, never, never, never, never.
> Pray you undo this button. Thank you, sir.
> Do you see this? Look on her. Look, her lips.
> Look there, look there!
>
> (V.iii)

Language fully owned not only reflects a character's transformation: it has itself the power to transform. There is a summoning power in words: it is sometimes dangerous to say what we mean because it will occur. Powerful words and ideas create the thing itself. Ask with clarity and passion, and you will receive. Hence the power of curses, like Aaron's in *Titus Andronicus*:

> *Aaron*: If there be devils, would I were a devil,
> To live and burn in everlasting fire,
> So I might have your company in hell,
> But to torment you with my bitter tongue!
> *Lucius*: Sirs, stop his mouth, and let him speak no more.
>
> (V.i)

The power of his words must be stopped – and in this play the word 'tongue' has a resonant, concrete reality. Lavinia had hers cut out and her hands chopped off after she was raped. 'Tongue' resonates throughout *Titus* as a tangible reminder of the power of words.

Lady Macbeth summons her husband –

> Hie thee hither,
> That I may pour my spirits in thine ear
> And chastise with the valour of my tongue
> All that impedes thee from the golden round,
> Which fate and metaphysical aid doth seem
> To have thee crown'd withal.

(I.v)

– and at once a servant enters with the news of the king's visit. The 'seem' becomes a reality. Her tongue will not only chase away her husband's inhibitions about murder, but will immediately summon up supernatural aid: 'Come you spirits'.

Examples of the summoning power of words are numerous in Shakespeare, and the message is clear. Words reveal us and transform our surroundings as we speak them. Fully owned, their power is enormous: take care of them because they change both you and the world.

But this power can only be experienced by attaching yourself to every word and allowing it to move you appropriately to its meaning. Making the connection requires courage as Shakespeare asks you to examine through language the matters most of us try to not think about – the shadows we would choose not to observe in ourselves and the world – but you will be helped by the work you have already done on the givens. With their scaffolding in place it is possible to investigate the power of Shakespeare's writing without feeling that it will knock you off course.

Some young actors worry during the work on the givens about feeling corseted, too heavily constrained by the writer's forms. They feel that their interpretation of a part doesn't fit the givens and that their creativity is being curbed. In fact, of course, your creativity should never reduce a text to what you think or want it to mean but should instead strive towards inhabiting the world of the play and the character as created in the language. Finding what is in the language, even at the level of the givens where form equals content, is always more exciting and helpful than distorting a text into something feels safe, familiar and limited to your own experience. Yet still, any playwright needs your voice and imagination to breathe life into their words – and that's where you come into the picture, with your unique imaginative response to language filling every thought and movement with colour and passion.

The Aims

- To use your imagination to explore the text in such a way that you own every word you speak.
- To make each thought sound as if it is the first and only time it has lived in you and been spoken by you; and that each word is the only word that will serve it.
- To see and experience every image as you speak it, not before or after.
- To feel imaginatively the depth and weight of each word – the cost of each word.
- To experience the particular meaning of each image, noun and verb.
- To allow these words to transform you imaginatively.
- To ensure precision with every word and thought.
- Through these to own the text from your point of view.
- Then to own the text from the character's point of view.

The Reasons

Release the emotional texture of the word and the cost of its speaking, and you will heighten the language and its context by experiencing every moment, making the language real, vibrant and exact in its place. If you do not do this and fulfil only the givens, you will communicate primarily the form and the thoughts in the text. You will probably tell the story – the surface of the work – but not the heart or the passion within it. You will not communicate the play's real soul or its world. You will be skidding across the surface of the text; you will sound clear but bland. The imaginative work connects you to the vertical power of the text. As you step on each word, it comes alive through you and changes your being.

We are what we speak. The language we choose to use is a reflection of our inner selves. It comes from our centre; what we say and how we say it is a map to our inner world. And so until you own every word from the character's world, you cannot characterise. Until you experience the concrete nature of the language, you cannot present a different world from your own – a philosophy, a belief system and a social structure – either to yourself or to an audience.

The Work

You may temporarily lose the work on the givens as you dig into these imaginative exercises. They take time and can be demanding, so you will go through a phase when you are not in the moment, not following the physical structures of the iambic, thought, line and so on. But provided the givens are in place you will re-engage them in due course.

In the work on the givens you will have been shocked sometimes by the power of structure. Now you must prepare to be shocked by the power of words as you come to explore them in all their particular, specific meaning. These exercises are designed to strengthen your 'language muscle' – to make it less flabby and to ensure the circulation of words in your bloodstream. So in what follows try constantly to heighten your reactions to any word or phrase – leave behind the realm of 'sort of', 'kinda', 'quite', and get clear and committed.

Eventually you will have to access dense language quickly so that you can connect to a word and yet still serve the forward thrust of the givens. To be able to perform this juggling act effortlessly is essential in speaking any heightened text. You will need to mean what you say as you say it, and simultaneously move forward with the thought and the givens.

In exploring the power of Shakespeare's language and your connection to it, three basic principles need to be understood.

Shakespeare is always concrete and specific in his choice of words. In heightened states we experience events clearly and precisely, not in a generalized haze or a fog. When Hamlet says 'To be or not to be' it means something very different to 'to live' or 'to exist'. You must face up to the full weight of being and not being, not some paraphrase or loose version. It is an enormous and fearful concept, but that is what Hamlet is going through and what Shakespeare asks his actors to find courage to confront.

Claudio in *Measure for Measure*, facing death the next day, says 'Ay, but to die, and go we know not where.' A real and intimate connection to that line is terrifying. It's worse than the certainty of going either to heaven or hell – it's an absolute uncertainty on which the rest of the speech relies. To add even more to this, Claudio is speaking to his novice sister who believes in heaven – a security and consolation he entirely lacks.

Lady Percy in *Henry IV Part II* speaks to her father-in-law about his failure to support his son – her husband – in battle, leading to his death:

> When your own Percy, when my heart's dear Harry
> Threw many a northward look to see his father
> Bring up his powers;
>
> (II.iii)

Look how precise she is – she names the son 'Percy' to his father, and then goes further and calls him by her heart's name, Harry. She was there on the battlefield and saw him turn to look for help: a son looking northward for his father to appear. The memory of those glances has to be experienced and owned as you speak them; it has to be that specific.

Shakespeare uses language to give concrete reality to potentially abstract ideas and feelings. These include images ('my heart is like a cleft apple') and metaphors where language transfers you into the thing itself ('in the evening of my life I sailed into a room and fell in love').

When passions become vast and life difficult, we can no longer rely on casual language – we have to move into poetic figures of speech to express the full reality of our experience. Indeed, the greater the experience, the starker and clearer the image. Shakespeare's poetic language does not embellish: it works to create more reality and fix conflict and emotion. And as his characters are tossed around and fall deeper into their joys or losses, the more they need this type of language – like Macbeth, who talks of 'pity, like a naked new-born babe / Striding the blast'.

Macbeth fully understands how foul is the murder he and his wife are plotting; any imaginative connection to this line requires the actor to see a new-born baby and confront what it is to place that baby outside in the cold. We know that Macbeth must know, for later in the scene Lady Macbeth says 'I have given suck and know / How tender 'tis to love the babe that milks me'. So they have had children, and Macbeth has seen new-born babes. The image must be as real to the actor as it is to the character.

Shakespeare understood that as enormous feelings pass through us, our world fragments and reorders itself. We see and experience things differently, more intensely. Parts of our beings leave us, change. Everyday places and objects take on characteristics expressive of love or grief or fear, and huge emotions are made not abstract but tangible. He explores these intense moments through image and metaphor, and as you trust and explore these devices in all their reality you will discover the precise experience of your character.

> *Constance*: Grief fills the room up of my absent child,
> Lies in his bed, walks up and down with me,
> Puts on his pretty looks, repeats his words,
> Remembers me of all his gracious parts,
> Stuffs out his vacant garments with his form;
> Then have I reason to be fond of grief.
>
> (*King John,* III.iv)

Play this, imagining grief as a real person who walks into your room, and turning into your lost child: by connecting and anchoring yourself in the poetic language you will intensify your acting and release the emotional cost of the play without having to push or emote. You will be present in the moment of the speech, and communicate to the audience its exact emotional gravity.

In Shakespeare you are what you speak. By anchoring yourself in the text, you will discover a character's interests and their attitude to others and the world. Here is Ophelia's soliloquy after her distressing scene with Hamlet in which he has been extremely cruel:

> *Ophelia*: O, what a noble mind is here o'er-thrown!
> The courtier's, soldier's, scholar's, eye, tongue, sword;
> Th' expectancy and rose of the fair state,
> The glass of fashion and the mould of form,
> Th' observ'd of all observers – quite, quite down!
> And I, of ladies most deject and wretched,
> That suck'd the honey of his music vows,
> Now see that noble and most sovereign reason,
> Like sweet bells jangled, out of time and harsh;
> That unmatch'd form and feature of blown youth
> Blasted with ecstasy. O, woe is me
> T' have seen what I have seen, see what I see!
>
> (III.i)

She is very upset but in spite of this she speaks of Hamlet first. Her concern is with him before she talks about her own wretchedness. Other, perhaps more selfish people would speak about themselves first or be less generous about Hamlet.

The Duke of Gloucester in *King Lear* has an equally distressing journey to make in his relationship with his sons. Remember how in the first scene he talked insensitively to Kent in front of Edmund about his son's conception – 'there was good sport at his making, and the where's son must be acknowledged'. This insensitivity may be of a piece with Gloucester's reaction later in the play when he goes out to help the distraught Lear in the storm. He addresses the disguised Kent, believing him to be a stranger:

> *Gloucester*: Thou sayest the King grows mad; I'll tell thee friend,
> I am almost mad myself. I had a son
> Now outlaw'd from my blood; he sought my life,
> But lately, very late. I lov'd him, friend –
> No father his son dearer. True to tell thee,
> The grief hath craz'd my wits.
>
> (III.iv)

In the presence of the King's grief, Gloucester has to speak about his own. It is almost as if he is competing for the pain 'stakes' – just as we have all experienced times in our own lives when a so-called friend has tried to upstage our pain with theirs. It will take some greater loss of self before either Lear or Gloucester, both of whom have in some way abused their children, can accept their responsibilities and receive forgiveness from their wronged offspring.

The way characters address their servants also tells us a great deal about them. So Lady Anne, after an emotional outpouring over the body of her father-in-law, takes time to reassure the men carrying the coffin that at their destination they will be able to rest: 'as you are weary of the weight / Rest you.' Other characters are less thoughtful or generous to their servants. In *Lear*, when Regan's husband Cornwall orders Kent, who is disguised as a servant, to be put in the stocks 'till noon', she says 'Till noon. Till night, my lord and all night too.' It's a meanness consistent in her character: she wants Gloucester hanged, and when he is bound on Cornwall's 'Bind him I say', she adds 'Hard, hard'.

Finally, the language reveals much about what really interests a character. So Antigonus in *The Winter's Tale* constantly refers to horses: they obviously feature strongly in his life and imagination, as in his language: 'I'll keep my stables where / I lodge my wife'; 'I'll geld them all'; 'The whole dungy earth'; 'Where she will take the rein I let her run / But she'll not stumble'.

Our vocabulary and speech structures reflect our interests and pre-occupations. Observing closely how people speak in Shakespeare gives the clearest indication of how they see and what they are in the world.

Anchoring the Text

- It is essential that you are warmed up with a free, low breath, a ready support system and an open voice with no vocal constrictions.
- You can lie on your back, knees up with your feet on the floor; or sit well rooted – not slumped; or stand centred and ready.
- Speak a speech, and as you do so imagine every word as completely as you can. Keep breathing (it is tempting to stop as this exercise can become emotional) and keep an open throat, jaw and voice (the exercise can begin to choke you).
- Don't speak a word or phrase without some experience of what it really means. This will take time.
- Breathe and wait until images form and attach themselves to all the words and phrases. Search out a deep connection to every word.
- You will begin to feel the presence of the people and the objects in the world of the text.
- The verbs will find movement within and without you.
- The adverbs will heighten and specify the movement.
- The adjectives will give texture and importance.
- The metaphors and similes will live.
- Every image will be seen, heard, smelled, touched or tasted.

This will be your first in-depth encounter with the text. Use it initially to try and find what the language actually contains – what you can connect to imaginatively and what you can't, what you really understand and what you don't. What you should have discovered is a different experience in your reading of a text. You are probably already familiar with most of the words intellectually, but now you should have begun to feel them penetrate more deeply into your breath, your body and your heart – to know them by heart. Shakespeare's language is sensual.

You will have blown the dust off a world and experienced it on the pulse. Don't worry if there are sections you can't imagine or understand. This merely exposes those holes that need more work to fill – perhaps by looking up a word, or researching an object in a museum. But you can do this exercise repeatedly, and each time you will experience the language differently and more profoundly. New connections will constantly be made. You will feel more anchored because you will begin to own the text from your experience of the world; and at the same time, as you face and speak words that you would normally never use, you will start organically to characterise. As soon as you speak alien words, you are no longer yourself.

Now go back and voice the text with all the givens in place, allowing the energy of the text to pass through you. You will be amazed at what remains of the earlier work and how much richer the speaking has become. For now the language is seeping into your blood, changing the tone of your voice and the breath needed to support it.

Most importantly, discover how concrete the writing is. Of course, there are complex intellectual ideas but it is the specifics of the text that fix you in the moment and open up the channel in your being of vertical connection to language. The givens will thrust you forwards, and the specifics open you up.

Let's try the exercise with a speech from *All's Well That Ends Well*. After the death of her father (a doctor), Helena is brought up by the Countess of Rousillon. She falls in love with the Countess's son, Bertram. When he goes to the French Court, she follows. She has her father's skills and agrees to cure the King of France of a troublesome ailment on the proviso that she can choose any of the court as a husband. On the king's recovery, she chooses Bertram, who is forced to marry her but in disgust runs from the court to war without consummating the marriage. Helena is left with his letter of rejection, and has to face the consequences of her actions:

> *Helena*: 'Till I have no wife, I have nothing in France.'
> Nothing in France until he has no wife!
> Thou shalt have none, Rousillon, none in France;
> Then hast thou all again. Poor lord! Is't I
> That chase thee from thy country, and expose
> Those tender limbs of thine to the event
> Of the none-sparing war? And is it I
> That drive thee from the sportive court, where thou
> Wast shot at with fair eyes, to be the mark

Of smoky muskets? O you leaden messengers,
That ride upon the violent speed of fire,
Fly with false aim; move the still-piecing air,
That sings with piercing; do not touch my lord.
Whoever shoots at him, I set him there;
Whoever charges on his forward breast,
I am the caitiff that do hold him to't;
And though I kill him not, I am the cause
His death was so effected.

(III.ii)

The ownership exercise generates unique personal responses in each individual, but I think it's useful to remark on some of the concrete realities of Helena's journey in this speech.

It starts with a quotation from Bertram's letter. The power of his words, which include the enormously resonant 'Nothing', is revisited by and settles in Helena through her own words. In every line there are concrete objects and details. Wife, France: Helena is Bertram's wife; France is a place. Nothing is no *thing*. She uses his formal title – 'poor Lord', 'Rousillon' – instead of his name. Experience the power of the verb 'chase' and the reality of 'thy country', the vulnerability of 'expose' and the true horror of 'the none-sparing war'. Instead of reacting violently against him for his humiliating rejection, she pities him. Notice how she specifies his body parts: 'tender limbs', 'forward breast'. The full horror of war is experienced in the detail of a loved one being mangled.

War is as much an entity as the court: Helena has seen eyes 'shoot' at Bertram, and now it will be lead shot fired from smoky muskets – 'upon the violent speed of fire'. That explosive burst of flame is a precise image of the reality: you can see it in paintings that show musketeers in battles, just as 'sings with piercing' is true to the actual sound that accompanies the musket ball's flight. The air on a battlefield does sing. The noise, smoke and death that Helena evokes are part of the very texture of Bertram's danger, and her emotional experience. So each line is filled with detail and each detail has a specificity that needs to be trusted and engaged with.

You should work on any speech for at least half an hour before the next stage of the exercise. It will rapidly become apparent that the language and images grow more readily available with each working of the text as your imaginative responses grow stronger and more flexible.

Owning the Text from the Character's Experience

This next stage is one that many actors never take. They can be very happy owning the world and words of Shakespeare from their own experience, but never venture further than that. This inability to move towards the character's world is what some directors call 'the reduction of the text'. It's something that would not be tolerated in modern plays, where the audience knows about the world depicted and any lack of truth would be immediately exposed.

Imagine an actor playing you in two hundred years' time. Your passions might include, for instance, your Harley Davison, Greenpeace, Bud beer, your nine-year-old daughter, a new lover and a pair of Birkenstocks. Taken individually and together, they would say a great deal about you. The actor playing you might be able to connect imaginatively to your nine-year old daughter and new lover – but the rest would have to be researched. If the actor didn't so, your ghost would feel cheated. Your passions would be generalised, made shallow: there would not be much truth involved.

It will take all your imagination and empathy, and perhaps a great deal of research, to enter your character's world. It is a spiritual, emotional, historical, social and philosophical journey that requires courage and a ruthless check on any censoring. Now is the moment you have to suspend moral judgements as your character says things you might find abhorrent. You will have to risk being disliked by the audience.

For instance, if you are playing Antonio in *The Merchant of Venice*, you cannot soft-pedal, in an attempt to win the audience's favour, his response to Shylock's

'Fair sir, you spit on me on Wednesday last;
You spurn'd me such a day; another time

You call'd me dog; and for these courtesies
I'll lend you this much moneys'.

(I.iii)

Antonio's reply is straightforward and blunt:

I am as like to call thee so again,
To spit on thee again, to spurn thee too.

You mustn't try to dilute the reality of this spitting and spurning. That's who Antonio is. Shakespeare writes fully rounded characters with all their prejudices and failings. It's what makes them real people.

Pay attention to detail and you will also reveal the more likeable or vulnerable side of those characters often depicted as one-dimensional villains. In *Henry VI Part II* Queen Margaret, for example, has her reasons for being enraged and dangerous: she has been humiliated in the English Court by the Duchess of Gloucester.

Margaret: She vaunted 'mongst her minions t'other day
The very train of her worst wearing gown
Was better worth than all my father's lands,
Till Suffolk gave two dukedoms for his daughter.

(I.iii)

Anyone who has been stung by the scorn of others knows how it much it can hurt – and how the pain can breed hatred. Here the detail of the mockery – wealth and clothes – is wonderfully precise and telling; as is 'She sweeps it through the court with troops of ladies'. We might not approve of Margaret's eventual behaviour, but this kind of specific observation helps us understand it and her.

Likewise, Iago has a revealing moment in his second soliloquy.

Iago: I do suspect the lusty Moor
Hath leap'd into my seat; the thought whereof
Doth like a poisonous mineral gnaw my inwards;

(II.i)

Again, we cannot condone Iago's action – but the pain of suspected infidelity may help explain it, especially when it is so vividly expressed in the detail of the gnawing 'inwards' and the visualisation of someone leaping into his wife's 'seat'.

This is the most exciting and rewarding work in acting. It might not feel safe but it's the work that keeps actors engaged, and those who work on this level are always rich human beings. It takes compassion to see and understand beyond yourself; it is, therefore, a life's work.

You are going to repeat the exercise you have just done, but this time begin to move towards owning the text from the character's point of view. You will see the world through another's eyes and senses; experience his or her interests, obsessions and passions.

Before vocalising, think through the speech and make a mental note of where you might have difficulties understanding the character's relationship to a word or a phrase. It could be a word like 'God': the character is probably a believer, but you might not be. You might not believe in ghosts and spirits – but you will have to enter your character's belief. You will have a problem playing Hamlet if you can't let go of your own disbelief in them.

Equally, there might be images that need research, customs to be investigated and concepts to be made clear. Honour, for instance: how easy it is to ignore the powerful reality of that word, or justice. These are not dead concepts. Even now the world can go to war to protect them. You must find precisely what they mean for your character in his or her world.

Sometimes this will require a deeper understanding of the history of a relationship, word or situation. From simply looking up certain words to get exact meanings, you might eventually be led to explore history, political theory, social manners of the court, Christian beliefs, pagan beliefs. You might have to visit museums, art galleries, even the zoo! Women might have to drop their current views of womanhood, and men their idea of what a man is. Every piece of this thrilling work is an opening of the actor's imaginative landscape.

The mental journey through the speech will heighten your awareness of where and how you might need to work your imagination. Now go through and vocalise the text when you have some view of it. At the end, make a list of any words, thoughts or beliefs you still can't connect to or fully understand. The pleasant surprise is likely to be that there are many more areas you have engaged with from a new perspective.

Now comes in the wonderful human commodity – imagination. You have to use your imagination and knowledge of the character to move towards their life and existence. We will try it with a speech of Lady Percy's from *Henry IV Part II*.

> *Lady Percy*: O, yet, for God's sake, go not to these wars!
> The time was, father, that you broke your word,
> When you were more endear'd to it than now;
> When your own Percy, when my heart's dear Harry,
> Threw many a northward look to see his father
> Bring up his powers; but he did long in vain.
> Who then persuaded you to stay at home?
> There were two honours lost, yours and your son's.
> For yours, the God of heaven brighten it!
> For his, it stuck upon him as the sun
> In the grey vault of heaven; and by his light
> Did all the chivalry of England move
> To do brave acts. He was indeed the glass
> Wherein the noble youth did dress themselves.
> He had no legs that practis'd not his gait;
> And speaking thick, which nature made his blemish,
> Became the accents of the valiant;
> For those that could speak low and tardily
> Would turn their own perfection to abuse
> To seem like him: so that in speech, in gait,
> In diet, in affections of delight,
> In military rules, humours of blood,
> He was the mark and glass, copy and book,
> That fashion'd others. And him – O wondrous him!
> O miracle of men! – him did you leave –
> Second to none, unseconded by you –
> To look upon the hideous god of war
> In disadvantage, to abide a field
> Where nothing but the sound of Hotspur's name
> Did seem defensible. So you left him.
> Never, O never, do his ghost the wrong
> To hold your honour more precise and nice
> With others than with him! Let them alone.
> The Marshal and the Archbishop are strong.
> Had my sweet Harry had but half their numbers,
> To-day might I, hanging on Hotspur's neck,
> Have talk'd of Monmouth's grave.
>
> (II.iii)

Read through this speech, using all the givens to understand it. Certain words and phrases resonate from any point of view: 'wars', 'father', 'broke your word', 'he did long in vain', 'sons', 'brave acts', 'did dress themselves', 'legs that practis'd not his gait', 'accents', 'in speech, in gait, in diet', 'fashion', 'miracle of men'. But if you connect only to these, and only from your own perspective, you will generalise Lady Percy's experience and reduce the power of the speech.

We can see this by exploring what her personal connection would be to some of these words:

- *God* would be experienced as a condition of faith.
- *Wars* are a familiar reality to Lady Percy: she is married to a soldier and knows the brutality of battle. In this play war is about actual bodily contact, sword on sword, not top guns in fighter planes bombing an unseen enemy. It is far more visceral than that, far more real to the senses.
- *Father* is her father-in-law – Percy's father who, terribly, has betrayed his son. And Lady Percy is living in the house of her in-laws – a difficult enough situation without the added complication of her host having been responsible for her husband's death.
- *Honours* is particularly powerful when it involves a father's duty to a son, and echoes with the betrayal of that duty. What greater obligation could have kept a father at home when he could have been defending his child?
- *All the chivalry of England*: these large words assume the specific qualities of her beloved husband as she lists those features that others copy – his bravery, his manner, his temperament and walk; even his speech. These are the intimate characteristics of her wonderful husband, whose abandonment by his father becomes even more appalling by contrast.
- *Today might I, hanging on Hotspur's neck*: the rich longing of this is tremendously moving, because it's informed by a physical memory of their intimacy which roots emotion and loss in a precise gesture of desire and affection.
- Consider too the context of the speech. From what goes before, it is clear that her father-in-law has not asked Lady Percy for her opinion. She is not expected to speak or to have anything to speak about the man's world of battles and war. But remember that in *Henry IV Part 1* she had accompanied her husband and seen him in the midst of battle, looking for his father. Perhaps she even

retrieved his body from the field, as many women did. It's a thought that would enrich the whole speech with added passion and pain. She may be out of order in her society, but she is full of courage as she witnesses the truth.

Now you have anchored yourself in the text, and placed it within the character's experience, the following exercises are designed to extend your ownership of the language in specific and focused ways.

Exercises

Peopling the Text

The aim of this exercise is to place yourself in a speech and to flesh out imaginatively the people mentioned in it.

Think and breathe a whole speech, but speak out aloud only those words that relate to people. Include personal pronouns (I, me, thou, she, my, his), proper names (like Duncan or Olivia), gods – Jupiter, Cupid – and types of person such as man, woman, fop and beggar. Ask: who are these people? Let them teem through the text, through your mouth and imagination.

- How many are there?
- What are their names?
- Who are they?
- What is their history with you?
- How well do you know them?
- Why do you speak about them?
- Do you care about them?
- Or, if no one is mentioned, is it because other people don't concern you?

Let us look at a speech from *Henry IV Part 1* by Lady Percy's husband, Hotspur. Remember that in any battle the taking of prisoners was a potentially lucrative endeavour. The higher orders were spared death in order that they could be ransomed. They were a way to make huge amounts of money. Hotspur has taken prisoners but failed to release them to the king. The king is angry: he wants the associated revenue. Here Hotspur explains why he failed to hand over the spoil.

My *liege*, I did deny *no prisoners*.
But *I* remember when the fight was done,
When *I* was dry with rage and extreme toil,
Breathless and faint, leaning upon *my* sword,
Came there a certain *lord*, neat, and trimly dress'd,
Fresh as a *bridegroom*, and *his* chin new reap'd
Show'd like a stubble-land at harvest-home,
He was perfumed like a *milliner*,
And 'twixt *his* finger and *his* thumb *he* held
A pouncet-box, which ever and anon
He gave *his* nose and took't away again;
Who therewith angry, when it next came there,
Took it in snuff – and still *he* smil'd and talk'd –
And as the *soldiers* bore dead *bodies* by,
He call'd them untaught knaves, unmannerly,
To bring a slovenly unhandsome *corse*
Betwixt the wind and *his* nobility.
With many holiday and *lady* terms
He questioned *me*: amongst the rest, demanded
My prisoners in *your Majesty's* behalf.

(I.iii)

As you people this text, you quickly realise that it is about the conflict of personalities between a very macho Hotspur and an effeminate lord sent by the king to demand the prisoners. The lord's appearance was so completely out of place on the battlefield, so incongruous and startling, that Hotspur answered the demand inappropriately. Now he expects the king – who is, after all, a soldier – to understand: 'he made me mad / To see him shine so brisk, and smell so sweet'. Many of us will have seen actors emoting through this speech without realising that it is simply about one person's gut reaction to another. One depressing aspect of war is that it is so often about personal misunderstandings and jealousies. Thousands will be slaughtered in this war because a king believes a fop instead of his greatest ally.

In *Richard III*, the deposed Queen Margaret confronts her old enemies, the Duchess of York and Queen Elizabeth. Elizabeth has just heard of the death of her two young sons and with her mother-in-law – the Duchess – is mourning her loss. Margaret enters the fray, listing all her losses. These women are united by grief and hate.

Count the number of people in each line:

Margaret: Tell o'er *your* woes again by viewing *mine*.   (2)
I had an *Edward*, till a *Richard* kill'd *him*;   *(3)*
I had a *husband*, till a *Richard* kill'd *him*:   (3)
Thou hadst an *Edward*, till a *Richard* kill'd *him*;   (3)
Thou hadst a *Richard*, till a *Richard* kill'd *him*.   (3)
Duchess: I had a *Richard* too, and *thou* didst kill *him*;   (3)
I had a *Rutland* too, *thou* holp'st to kill *him*.   (3)
Margaret: *Thou* hadst a *Clarence* too, and *Richard* kill'd *him*.   (3)
From forth the kennel of *thy* womb hath crept   (*1*)
A *hell-hound* that doth hunt *us* all to death.   (*3 or more*)
That *dog*, that had *his* teeth before *his* eyes
To worry *lambs* and lap *their* gentle blood,
[...]
Thy womb let loose to chase *us* to *our* graves.
O upright, just, and true-disposing *God*,
How do *I* thank *thee* that this carnal *cur*
Preys on the issue of his *mother's* body
And makes *her pew-fellow* with *others'* moan!

                                              (IV.iv)

To people this text accurately – and this is just a brief excerpt from the scene – all three actors need to do a course in history: the history of the characters through the three *Henry VI* plays, and the history of their relationships. Notice as you do the exercise how each of the women needs to witness the names of her dead. It seems a frightful competition for who has suffered most. Everyone who has died is named by their relationship to that person – 'husband', 'mother' – and every act of horror comes from one person: Richard III. The whole scene is peopled by the dead, and driven by the women's passionate need to witness their losses and name the perpetrator – Richard.

Notice that I have also emphasised any mention of Richard as a dog and his victims as lambs. These exercises are not to be played rigidly. You may not connect to 'dog' on the first working of the text, but you will discover the full shock value of reducing a human to a cur in due course.

The people in a speech are part of that character's world, and at times of great love or loss they can seem to take it over entirely. In *Romeo and Juliet*, Juliet is thrown into despair by the news that her beloved has killed her cousin Tybalt. Her heart and mind are filled with the people of her world suddenly at odds: those she loves are pitted against one another – so much so that first Romeo is a villain, and then Tybalt.

Juliet: Shall I speak ill of him that is my husband?
Ah, poor my lord, what tongue shall smooth thy name,
When I, thy three-hours wife, have mangled it?
But wherefore, villain, didst thou kill my cousin?
That villain cousin would have kill'd my husband.
Back, foolish tears, back to your native spring;
Your tributary drops belong to woe,
Which you, mistaking, offer up to joy.
My husband lives that Tybalt would have slain,
And Tybalt's dead that would have slain my husband.
All this is comfort; wherefore weep I then?
Some word there was, worser than Tybalt's death,
That murder'd me; I would forget it fain,
But, O, it presses to my memory
Like damned guilty deeds to sinners' minds:
'Tybalt is dead, and Romeo banished'.
That 'banished', that one word 'banished'
Hath slain ten thousand Tybalts. Tybalt's death
Was woe enough, if it had ended there;
Or if sour woe delights in fellowship
And needly will be rank'd with other griefs,
Why followed not, when she said, 'Tybalt's dead'.
Thy father or thy mother, nay, or both,
Which modern lamentation might have mov'd?
But, with a rear-ward following Tybalt's death,
'Romeo is banished' – to speak that word
Is father, mother, Tybalt, Romeo, Juliet,
All slain, all dead. 'Romeo is banished' –
There is no end, no limit, measure, bound,
In that word's death; no words can that woe sound.
Where is my father and my mother, nurse?

(III.ii)

That she calls herself 'wife' and Romeo 'husband' highlights her suffering. Just a few moments before, Juliet has been delightedly anticipating their wedding night in 'Gallop apace, you fiery-footed steeds'. But her real agony is the news that Romeo is banished, and her acknowledgement of it is made in a line that contains all the people important to her: 'Is father, mother, Tybalt, Romeo, Juliet'.

Peopling this text poignantly uncovers the scale of Juliet's world. Those close to her are her life and in a profound way her whole world has changed because all the people in it have been polluted.

Thus this exercise will help reveal a character's human pre-occupations; and it becomes clear that in speaking Shakespeare you have to talk about people or things as if you really know them, or have just met. Establishing a connection to these concrete parts of his work is easy with imagination: we all speak every day about people, places and things and, as we speak, we know them. It's what we do all the time: listen to any conversation and people will be talking about matters that are real and alive to them, not about some abstract entity.

When actors don't know the people or things they refer to, the effect is a generalised emoting. Connecting to the reality in a text both specifies and produces real rather than forced emotions. A real connection to a known human being is vivid with emotional truth rather than forced by abstract generalisation. And for all the challenges and heightened energy of Shakespeare, it's only by anchoring yourself in the text that you will understand how real is the world it creates. Once you begin to appreciate this reality, you will find there is much less in Shakespeare to be afraid of than you imagined.

Realising the Objects in the Text

Breathe and think the whole text, but this time speak aloud only the objects, places, and things, including parts of the body. The aim of this exercise is to reveal and recognise that Shakespeare's characters have a real relationship with everything they speak about. What they talk of has presence in their minds: it's not just a word or an idea.

Romeo's home is Verona. It's a real city. The lovers in the *Dream* live in and know Athens. It's not an abstract place. Lady Macbeth sees ravens every day from her castle. She has walked on the battlements. Shylock has seen and perhaps kicked the curs that sniff around the Rialto. It is his place of business.

When Macbeth says 'Is this a *dagger?*' it's not a prop to him. He would have carried one as a small boy – it is an everyday object in his life. When he tries to clutch it by its handle, he knows what it should feel like. Until the object is fully in your imagination there is no point in speaking the speech. And when it is in your imagination it is easy to speak.

Here is a speech about a dog from *Two Gentlemen of Verona*. Without the dog and the history of your relationship with it in your mind, you cannot make the speech live.

Launce: When a man's servant shall play the cur with him, look you, it goes hard – one that I brought up of a puppy; one that I sav'd from drowning, when three or four of his blind brothers and sisters went to it. I have taught him, even as one would say precisely 'Thus I would teach a dog'. [...] You shall judge. He thrusts me himself into the company of three or four gentleman-like dogs under the Duke's table; he had not been there, bless the mark, a pissing while but all the chamber smelt him. 'Out with the dog' says one; 'What cur is that?' says another; 'Whip him out' says the third; 'Hang him up' says the Duke. I, having been acquainted with the smell before, knew it was Crab, and goes me to the fellow that whips the dogs. 'Friend,' quoth I, 'you mean to whip the dog.' 'Ay, marry do I,' quoth he. 'You do him the more wrong,' quoth I, ''twas I did the thing you wot of.' He makes me no more ado, but whips me out of the chamber. How many masters would do this for his servant?

(IV.iv)

Crab the dog must be known: the speech revolves around Launce's relationship with him. Anyone who has kept a dog and loved it, particularly one that behaves badly, will be able to understand and relate to Launce at this moment of this life. But it depends entirely on the actor making the imaginative connection.

Try the exercise with this speech from *Richard II*:

King Richard: What must the King do now?
Must he submit?
The King shall do it. Must he be depos'd?
The King shall be contented. Must he lose
The name of king? A God's name, let it go.
I'll give my *jewels* for a set of *beads*,
My gorgeous *palace* for a *hermitage*,
My gay *apparel* for an almsman's *gown*,
My figur'd *goblets* for a *dish of wood*,
My *sceptre* for a *palmer's walking staff*,
My *subjects* for a pair of *carved saints*,
And my *large kingdom* for a little *grave*,
A little little *grave*, an obscure *grave* –
Or I'll be buried in the king's *high way*,
Some way of common trade, where subjects' *feet*

May hourly trample on their sovereign's *head*;
For on my *heart* they tread now whilst I live,
And buried once, why not upon my *head*?

(III.iii)

Here the isolation of the objects vividly highlights Richard's loss of material power. The grandeur of the items whittles down to a grave, 'an obscure grave'. As you connect to the objects you realise that Richard can only comprehend his fall through the exchange of rich possessions for simple ones as the station of king is replaced by the religious life, power by no power, material wealth by poverty. His relationship to the objects expresses his experience of the fall.

I knew an actor with a gambling problem who fully understood this speech. Only when the debts had grown so large that the bailiffs arrived to take his possessions did he finally have to acknowledge that he had a problem. He told me how he'd begged them to let him keep even the simplest things: a bed, a table and chair. So it is with Richard at the point of losing everything.

After adding the objects to the speech, go back and people it. You will excavate more detail and texture with each exercise.

Energising and Heightening the Text

The next exercise focuses on energising and colouring the text by concentrating on verbs, adjectives and adverbs.

Breathe and think the whole speech, but this time speak aloud only the verbs. You may find it interesting to physicalise them. You will be surprised by how many verbs there are, how active the text is. You will also move through time with the changing tenses. On your return to the whole text, the negatives will also leap out at you as the blockages to the verbs will be very apparent.

Now repeat the exercise speaking only adjectives and adverbs. This exercise usually reveals the tremendous cost to the character of their situation. It will heighten your speaking as you connect to accurate descriptions of nouns and verbs. This exercise is a great antidote to our common habit of reducing everything to 'quite good' and 'sort of nice'. It demands commitment and precision, and adds enormous colour.

In the course of these exercises, as with those involving people and objects, you may feel that you are losing the work you have done on the givens. For instance, by picking out individual words you will find yourself smashing the iambic, the line and the thought. Please don't worry. You can always go back and do the givens at any point. Indeed, you will have to – and when you do, the speeches will quickly return to their written power and rhythm, but with much more life, passion, texture and specificity.

Focus and Energy

Over the last ten years, I have been pondering ways to engage and release young actors in Shakespeare: to focus them on the text rather than deny or skid over it. One of the main problems, it seems to me, is that so many actors find it hard to go beyond the two most common kinds of energy, which I described earlier as denial and bluff. One translates broadly into devoicing and mumbling; the other into pushing and shouting. Both undermine the performance of language-based plays because they make it impossible to hear the words.

There seems to be a tightrope to be walked, a line between denial and bluff. It's a condition of real, filled energy that observes the world, gives out and takes in: a taut but released moment of connection and engagement. It's a condition that is necessary for the state of readiness, for neither denial nor bluff will serve when survival is at stake.

We've been tackling these two energies all through the book, but this last section of the imaginative work suggests another way of dealing with them. Over the years I have developed a series of exercises for voice energy focus. They revolve around what I call the three circles of concentration. Nothing in this work is rigid, but it has helped many actors practise and maintain their ability to stay ready and engaged in speaking and listening.

The *First Circle* is where you engage with yourself. Here you speak, listen and use language from and for yourself. You have no need to communicate to the world. The First Circle relates to the energy of denial. When an actor lives here, the audience can seem irrelevant. The language is secret and inactive, the voice depressed and under-energised: it's really just for you. You often speak after the impulse, so you are not on the line. Your body, breath, voice and speech collapse into yourself. There is a sinking sensation around you.

The First Circle is where many actors initially connect to the text, which is fine as long as they don't stay there! Too much work on owning the text without the givens as an ingredient will leave you in this circle. You probably don't listen to others accurately, and are slow to react to cues. You are interested above all in yourself and are withdrawn from the world. It may be that you're in The First Circle simply because of fear or shyness, but it can come across as uncaring. There's no real eye contact: often First Circle actors look glazed or shut their eyes as they speak.

The *Third Circle* is someone talking to the whole world – not to individuals, but in a general sweep to everyone. It relates to the energy of bluff. It's an attempt to connect outwardly. It can be a place of shouting, pushing, aggression, over-heartiness and general eye contact. Often the actor is ahead of the line or jumps in on other people's – forcing energy. Too much work on the givens without the imaginative owning can result in being stuck in this circle. The audience hears the text but because it's not specific or individual they don't care. Third is what most actors do if they are required to fill a space or to speak with pace before they have fully connected to the language. It's all sound and fury with no listening and no vulnerability.

The *Second Circle* is what has begun to interest me in Shakespeare. It is to do with connecting, listening and speaking to individuals. It translates into the state of readiness. It's the condition of survival: full alertness, living, breathing, listening and reacting completely in the present. It's what every martial artist describes as the only way to fight and win; or anyone engaged in sport. The Second Circle is centre, is open, is strong, is vulnerable; it is not random. In the Second Circle we speak to connect. We are prepared to listen; our voices are open and placed as we really do want them to reach someone. It is very hard not to listen to anyone connected in the Second Circle. All the finest actors I have worked with in Shakespeare are naturally in it.

Of course it's possible to shift – as we all do in life – between the circles but I believe that the constant, the place from which you should start and to which you should return, is the Second Circle. Second takes enormous concentration, emotional and intellectual, to sustain. It puts you at once on the line, reacting in the moment, accessing language quickly and vividly, seeing, hearing and speaking clearly. It is the most human energy and the most human of connections.

Indeed, I believe that all the important moments in our lives are conducted in the Second Circle; and that the great plays, because they deal with the moments that change and refocus us, are written in the same energy.

It's an energy we all of us know: any good conversation takes place in it. But it may feel outside our habits, and the following exercises are meant to help focus on it. Try them in a spirit of free and uncensored experiment.

Circle exercises

- Stand, sit or lie on the floor.
- Be aware of your breath and body.
- Be silent and still for at least two minutes.
- Place your focus on yourself.

You will feel that your body and your breath have closed around you. You are navel-gazing – and you are probably in the First Circle. If you heard a sudden noise in this state you would be jolted into Second.

Now experiment with the Third Circle.

- Still in silence, imagine your energy shifting out, pressing forward.
- Feel the shift in your body and breath as your being impinges more and more on the space around you.

You are now probably in the Third Circle. You may well have sensed yourself passing through the Second on the way from the First, and if at this point you caught sight of something in the room that interested you, you would certainly drop into it.

- Sit in front of a mirror and play with the circles – First, Third, Second.
- In the First Circle you will see yourself with a surrounding smear.
- In the Third Circle you will see a mask of yourself.
- In the Second Circle you will begin really to see yourself in the mirror, clear and *present*.

Remember that in acting it is quite possible to be in the Second Circle but assume the physical qualities of the First or Third. An animal can look relaxed while it is fully alert.

- Take a speech and speak it in the First Circle.

This will probably feel familiar: the words are trapped in your body; you are addressing yourself; and when we address ourselves we have our own language which is often not fully formed.

Eventually the decision as to what circle a character is in will rest on the language. Who is it for? Does it reach beyond you or is it just for yourself? What is it doing and who is it changing?

- Try the speech in the Third Circle.

This might feel easy, as you can pump the text out without much connection inside or specific target outside. The voice will sound bluffed. Does this generalised energy serve the specific nature of the text? Are you losing the details within the language?

- Now work in the Second Circle.

If you are on your own, imagine someone or something you are addressing. It will be immediately clear how demanding and precise this circle is. You have really to know your text in order to place it in the Second Circle. The First and Third Circles allow for a degree of randomness. The Second is precise and intense, revealing and truthful: in this circle it can be harrowing to curse and painful to love because you really mean it.

You might find yourself slipping between the three circles.

- Play with this slippage.
- Move between First, Second and Third.
- Then Third, Second and First.
- The shift of energy and focus will soon be tangible.
- Experience how each circle makes the language feel and work.
- Now experiment with each circle and some of the givens in the text.

Try the *iambic*. The First Circle will de-energise the rhythm. The Third Circle will over-stress it. The Second Circle will keep you aligned to the rhythm and meaning. Try holding a long *thought*. In First, it will probably droop and lose momentum. Third will be energised but perhaps generalised. Second will be engaged and sustained.

Now open this work out with either a partner or a group. You can replay the whole sequence of exercises with others, but let us for the moment explore another profound aspect of energy: listening.

- Make the work more complex: as your partner delivers a speech to you in First, Third and Second, change the circle you are listening in.
- Realise how annoying it is to listen attentively in Second when someone is addressing you in First or Third.
- Equally true, if you are speaking to someone in Second and they are listening in First or Third, discover how dismissive it feels. All actors know this sensation – it's infuriating to play opposite someone who is not in Second when you are.

Every great actor's aim is to engage the audience and have it listen in Second – and it's very hard for an audience to be in Second if it is being addressed in First or Third. You can lose the audience if you don't risk being in Second.

This does not mean that the actor has to be in Second with the audience the whole time – although this is what soliloquy explores – but it is always interesting to observe Second Circle communication. Look at people in any setting, and your eye will be drawn to Second Circle conversations. Even if you can't hear what is being said, the face and body in Second are compelling. Second is the engagement of the life force, and it is thrilling to feel and thrilling to observe.

For much of the work earlier in this book you will have been in Second. These circle exercises are lenses to help you in the final focusing of any heightened text.

Summary

At this stage you have investigated and exercised four main components in preparing to speak Shakespeare. The four stages are:

1. The physical preparation of your body, voice and speech muscles. This includes an awareness of being heightened, alert and curious, open and flexible. This is the starting point that will enable the text to pass through you and play you.

2. An exploration of the givens of form. This includes an understanding that form equals content. The form will help you act. It propels action and story forward, and reveals meaning.

3. Imaginative exercises to own the language and the specifics within the text. This explores the 'vertical' nature of the word and the concrete qualities of the poetry. The language is rooted in the real, not the abstract, and the emotional power of the text has been unleashed.

4. Circle exercises: know and refine the focus of your energy.

Put all these four together and you will be ready to rehearse.

Part 4 The Speeches

'Now does my project gather to a head'

(The Tempest, V.i)

The Speeches

It is now time to put our work into practice by looking in more detail at a range of Shakespearean texts, applying the principles established in the earlier parts of the book and finding what they reveal. First we will analyse eleven speeches, seven of them in verse and four in prose. Then we will explore two complete scenes; and finally we will present strategies for coping with two challenges that often pose problems for the actor: dealing with lyrically beautiful verse, and avoiding vocal pushing when under emotional stress.

Richard III Act I, Scene ii

The Context

This is the first speech of the second scene in the play. It is the first time we meet Lady Anne, the young widow of Prince Edward Lancaster, son of Henry VI and Queen Margaret. Richard, who is not yet King but still Duke of Gloucester, has confided to the audience immediately beforehand that he intends to marry 'Warwick's youngest daughter'. Although he doesn't name her directly, Anne is his victim. Warwick was a powerful man and a match with Anne would strengthen Richard's political position. He also acknowledges

> What though I kill'd her husband and her father?
> The readiest way to make the wench amends
> Is to become her husband and her father.

(I.i)

Because he has told the audience of his intentions, his wooing of Lady Anne, which immediately follows this scene, has a particularly heightened energy.

The scene takes place in a London street with attendants and guards carrying the corpse of Henry VI, and Lady Anne is the only mourner. She is, in every sense, alone in the world, her family destroyed by the York faction who are now in power. In this context the act of removing Henry's body is a courageous and political one – and yet Lady Anne is someone many character actors dismiss as insubstantial.

Such sweeping generalisations about a character are dangerous and often indicate that the actor hasn't studied the text for evidence. Removing the body of a political icon in violent and bloody times is not the act of an insignificant person. Certainly Anne has human vulnerabilities, and her loneliness and fear make her prey to Richard's flattery – but she also has gall. She has somehow mustered loyal attendants, who might have abandoned a doomed family instead of aiding her in this extremely dangerous task.

Heightened Circumstances

We all know from history how significant the bodies or graves of major political leaders can be. They have enormous importance for their followers, and can exert a power beyond death. Myths and legends can gather around them, particularly bodies that can't be found. They're potential fuel for political unrest. There is still speculation over the whereabouts of Hitler's corpse, and White Russians have only recently accepted the fate of the Tsar's family with DNA testing of their remains. In bars in the hills above Lake Como in Italy, visitors are still hushed if they mention Mussolini. Many people in that area saw what was done to his body.

Shakespeare would have known that the real Richard III's body was horribly mutilated after his defeat on Bosworth Field. Human remains are sacred to all of us. The remains of a leader have much wider implications, particularly a leader from the defeated faction and one known to be good and spiritual.

What a thrilling start to a scene. A young girl follows a body: not one safely hidden in a closed coffin but a body you can see and touch.

Lady Anne has deliberately taken a mutilated corpse from its resting place and is transporting it to where she knows the holy King would wish to rest – with the monks at Chertsey. It's no easy act, and it's fraught with risk.

In part, of course, she is merely fulfilling what she believes would be her father-in-law's final request. It is open to speculation as to whether she knows how politically inflammatory this could be. The suggestion that she does perhaps gains weight from the unusual setting – a London street. She has chosen to lament over the King's body not in a quiet country lane but in a crowded city. Is she actively bearing witness to the House of York's brutality for the benefit of London's citizenry? Remember that later in the play Richard has to win the approval of those same citizens – who are historically an anarchic group of subjects.

At the beginning of the speech she requests the men to 'set down' the body. She asks this twice. In that repetition there is a lot of potential action. The question is, why don't they obey her the first time? The acting solutions range from the mundane to the heightened. The mundane could be that the attendants carrying the coffin don't hear her the first time. The heightened could encompass rich and exciting possibilities. From the attendants' point of view, putting the body down in the street is very dangerous. It lengthens the time taken for this illegal movement of a body. Carrying it was difficult enough, but to put it down in a public highway is asking for trouble...

It you are playing Shakespeare you will always have the chance to answer textual problems with the mundane, but it is much more interesting to invest in the most heightened solutions. Do this even if you are just playing an attendant carrying the coffin, and you will have a rich history to play. You are involved in an act that could get you killed. You are either outstandingly loyal to the House of Lancaster or you are extremely unlucky, in the wrong place at the wrong time – crossing a courtyard to be stopped by Lady Anne and given this perilous task.

The Human

Every day we hear in the news or through friends of the human importance – psychological and emotional – of a body to mourning relatives. In the absence of a body to bury many people find it impossible to accept the reality of a loved one's death, or to begin to grieve, or to end. Lady Anne is fulfilling a very human need. Today, we call this complex, distressing and painful process 'closure'. She is doing what we all would do if we had the courage – placing the corpse appropriately. It is not an impossible leap of imagination for us: what Anne experiences, we all will have to go through.

In her speech she does something else so potent and human – she looks again at the body; she touches it; she talks to it. In today's more clinical world, we might not be allowed to experience death so closely but it is something we all need to do when we accept loss and grief. To say goodbye is to know that someone has gone forever. For Lady Anne this includes acknowledging that the whole House of Lancaster is also in 'ashes'. Her family has been 'cleaned out': she is able to understand this through the body of the king.

The Speech

Anne: Set down, set down your honourable load –
If honour may be shrouded in a hearse;
Whilst I awhile obsequiously lament
Th' untimely fall of virtuous Lancaster.
Poor key-cold figure of a holy king!
Pale ashes of the house of Lancaster!
Thou bloodless remnant of that royal blood!
Be it lawful that I invocate thy ghost
To hear the lamentations of poor Anne.
Wife to thy Edward, to thy slaughtered son,
Stabb'd by the self-same hand that made these wounds.
Lo, in these windows that let forth thy life
I pour the helpless balm of my poor eyes.
Curs'd be the hand that made these fatal holes!
Cursed the heart that had the heart to do it!
Cursed the blood that let this blood from hence!
More direful hap betide that hated wretch
That makes us wretched by the death of thee
Than I can wish to adders, spiders, toads,
Or any creeping venom'd thing that lives!
If ever he have child, abortive be it,
Prodigious, and untimely brought to light,
Whose ugly and unnatural aspect
May fright the hopeful mother at the view,
And that be heir to his unhappiness!
If ever he have wife, let he be made
More miserable by the death of him
Than I am made by my young lord and thee!
Come, now towards Chertsey with your holy load,
Taken from Paul's to be interred there;
And still as you are weary of this weight
Rest you, whiles I lament King Henry's corse.

The Givens

The first examination of this speech reveals it to be extremely regular. All thoughts start at the beginning of lines, and most lines are iambically regular. The flow and pulse of the text helps the flow of Anne's grief. Let it carry you on its tide and it will help in speaking – the grief washes over and through you, form releasing content. If we give vent to our feelings, they do come in waves; and once Anne sees the body her sorrow and rage are set free. The grief once released purges her. By the end of the speech she has reached a place of peace and can move on. She can continue her journey with the body.

The form is open and opening, and the actor can use the purged feeling it creates in the next stage of the scene, Anne's confrontation with Richard. She is drained of her emotion and anyone who has experienced this sensation knows that it can also give you a liberating, even foolhardy courage. A friend of mine beat off three muggers with an umbrella a week after her only son had died. She said that she had felt no fear: grief had made her fearless.

However this same openness also makes her susceptible to manipulation. Richard has quite a tussle with her, but emotionally charged people can be steered with care. The height of their emotions can be quickly swung. So the openness makes her vulnerable to him and perhaps encourages her to engage with him unwisely. Very few of us would take on the Richards of this world: if she hadn't purged herself, she might be more controlled and guarded.

One less positive consequence of the regular structure is that the actor can easily be swept along on the verse, losing textual detail and diminishing the emotional specificity of Anne's journey by generalising it. Later work on the imaginative will help prevent this, but your first aid in the givens is the structure of words.

Mouth the text, and you will notice that Shakespeare tightens articulation at the points where you might allow emotion to run away with you. The precision and repetition of the first line starts the process: 'Set down, set down your honourable load.' Five words end in consonants that hold you – *t n t n d* – and while 'your' opens out, the precision required for 'honourable' contains you again.

But look at this sequence:

> Poor key-cold figure of a holy king!
> Pale ashes of the house of Lancaster!
> Thou bloodless remnant of that holy blood!

The first section of each line moves potentially out of control, and is then reined in by the second half. Just as she catches herself emotionally tumbling, she regains balance. This effect is contained in the vowels and consonants as well as the content. In each line she moves from the personal reality of a body to the station the body held – the personal to the political. The personal is unbearable, so she moves to the impersonal to check and distance herself.

Let's examine the irregular lines. Although the first line is regular you can only make it scan by placing all the syllables on 'honourable'. It is not a particularly modern word, but its power of that word cannot but resonate if you give it the right weight in your mouth. In a play so teeming with dishonourable acts, the word has a pure poignancy when we realise that this king's honour is now merely a 'load' 'shrouded in a hearse'. It has literally been buried. Indeed, the power of 'honourable' seems to trip Anne up. 'If' starts the next line, attaching itself to honour – 'If honour may be shrouded in a hearse' – with a questioning, a lack of resolution, that seems to throw the whole concept into doubt.

'Be it lawful that I invocate thy ghost' is an eleven-syllable line, the first in the speech. The wave of the line lands on 'ghost' but is broken on 'lawful' and 'invocate'. Is she breaking a law by speaking to a ghost? She's not sure she should be calling up his spirit. The line informs her uneasiness and although the next line is regular again, the one after – 'Wife to thy Edward, to thy slaughtered son' – trips once more, but this time at the beginning with 'Wife'. Is it that she's not sure Henry's ghost will remember her? She has to place herself in the family context. Even calling across into the spirit world requires domestic clarification.

Now Anne returns to a regular flow until the heavy, stressed and repeated 'Cursed':

> Cursed the heart that had the heart to do it!
> Cursed the blood that let this blood from hence!

The first line has the powerful stress on 'Cursed' but scans quickly over 'to do it', as if astonished that the killing of a king could be so effortless and rapid. The second has only nine syllables but five of them are stressed, making the line scan but with a fearful symmetry – 'Cursed' and 'hence' are so final. And the mention of blood brilliantly sets up the later horror of the body actually bleeding in Richard's presence.

'If ever he have child, abortive be it': this eleven-syllable line stumbles messily over the word 'abortive' – as messily as an abortion – and is then made solid by 'Prodigious, and untimely brought to life / Whose ugly and unnatural aspect'. Notice how you must give full weight to 'unnatural', breaking the wave which then has to be contained by 'aspect'. The play is teeming with unnatural acts – even a hardened villain, Sir James Tyrrel, is appalled by the things he witnesses outside the laws of nature.

The only other irregular line is the eleven-syllable 'Come, now towards Chertsey with your holy lord'. This rhythm works if you match the urgency of movement from 'Come' into 'now'. Anne has finished talking to Henry; now she is addressing her attendants, and you feel her real desire to finish moving Henry's body. She is returning to the practical task in hand.

If we now count the thoughts, we will find there are fourteen – which is a lot for someone still being swept along by her feelings. Grief can be a deadening emotion that closes us down from the world so we don't have to feel any more, but the number of thoughts and the amount of detailed observation here suggest otherwise. For grief, when it thaws, can also make us more seeing and more knowing. Perhaps this is the moment Anne thaws. That's why she asks for the body to be put down in the street. Perhaps she has gone through the weeks of blood and destruction closed down, but now, in this moment, she comes alive again and in rush waves of feeling and layers of comprehension.

There is a rhythm in the thoughts that unleashes meaning. Feel this surge by intoning the text. You will sense at once the relentless quality of the thoughts – it is exhausting. By the time you arrive at 'Then I am made by my young lord and thee', you will feel spent. Your breath system will have been thoroughly worked out, just as it would be after a good cry or even a good laugh. Your voice will be stretched open by the feeling and the act of proclaiming it. Make sure that your mouth feels all the words because it is the muscles of articulation that will hold and focus Anne's passions.

By the end, Anne has finished mourning and is ready to go on to Chertsey. Little does she know that within seconds she will have to find more emotional energy to deal with Richard. Such is the power of speaking that the person she has cursed is summoned into her presence. We've seen that Shakespeare does this a lot: as a device, it's not only metaphysical but extremely theatrical.

The sequence of Anne's speech starts with one four-line thought to her attendants. She speaks a command to them and within the thought explains what she is about to do: she is about to lament. The command is unusual – hence the repetition and the explanation. The next three thoughts take in the body. There must be a reason that such a succinct writer takes three thoughts to contemplate the body. The reason is human. It's very difficult to face a body that has no life in it, a body that represents a whole dynasty and symbolises a whole family's destruction and your own.

Remember Anne's utter loneliness when she later submits to Richard. She has no one, and she needs a protector. She is not a commodity many would want and there is little she can do as a woman alone. Anyone with a spark of compassion will understand her concession: we might not approve, but in extreme circumstances we have all done things we later regret or would rather forget.

The thought sequence continues as Anne speaks to Henry's ghost. This is brought into intimate focus by the word 'thy' – 'Thy Edward', 'thy slaughtered son'. The repetition poignantly establishes her own relationship to the body by joining her to Henry through Edward – her husband, his son. Then husband and father-in-law are joined by their murderer, 'by the self-same hand that made these wounds'. This is the first mention of Richard. He is never actually named in this speech. Perhaps it's too horrible to put his name in her mouth in the presence of Henry's body. Now she describes her tears – 'the helpless balm of my poor eyes' – pouring into the body's wounds, her eyes cursed by the hand that 'made these fatal holes'.

The next four thoughts are curses that gather momentum. First she curses Richard's heart and then his blood; in this thought she is still anchored in Henry's body – 'let this blood from hence'. As the curse grows, 'more direful hap', she is still speaking to Henry – 'by the death of thee' – but the curse extends in the next thought to Richard's offspring. The final curse includes any wife of his – a terrible irony, as later in the play she will speak of the fact that she has cursed herself – and again it is focused in her attention to Henry and her thoughts of Edward.

Finally, the last thought is addressed to the attendants as she instructs them to continue their journey and promises them rest when they get to Chertsey.

Many actors are scared of this speech because they think they have to emote abstractly and in isolation. In fact, by examining the sequence of thoughts it is obvious that nearly all of the time she is talking in the Second Circle to *someone*, be it attendants or Henry's ghost. Her words are rooted in a series of actual exchanges.

Remember too that a speech is never just a speech. It is a series of steps or stages on a journey. Always take the pressure off yourself; don't think you have to do the whole speech in one emotional burst. Instead, start at 'set down' and move in concrete, particular stages until you are finished. Stay rooted in what the givens tell you. There's a stage direction, for instance, in 'Poor key-cold figure': Anne cannot say the line unless she touches the body. Equally, she must be placed over the body, close enough for tears to fall on it, for the pitiful 'I pour the helpless balm of my poor eyes' to work.

The Imaginative

Now spend time breaking all the givens! Breathe, and speak the text only when you have a particular image or sense of every word and phrase.

As with all the imaginative exercises on language your experience of the words will be unique to you. Some of the discoveries you make will be yours alone, and they will change over time.

When I did this exercise I was astonished by several words, images and connections. 'Blood' occurs three times and there is one 'bloodless'; the speech flows with blood – 'slaughtered', 'wounds', 'heart'. Then I was shocked by the word 'abortive' because I still had blood in me. I was frightened like 'the hopeful mother at the view'. 'Untimely' was another discovery: the untimely fall of Lancaster, the untimely delivery of the abortive child. So too were the two references to 'wife' – one to Anne in the past, one, unwittingly, to her in the future – and the two laments and one 'lamentations'.

Owning the Text from the Character's Point of View

The first shift you need to make might involve a full and vivid connection to 'honour' and 'honourable'. 'Lancaster' and 'holy king' refer to a man Anne knows; 'Edward' is her husband. Both men when named or referred to in the speech are real, and Anne has had a deep and intimate history with them.

Chertsey and Paul's are places: St Paul's is the church from which she has removed the corpse, but does she know Chertsey? Has she been there before? Does she know how she is going to get there or how long it will take? And remember, she is travelling on foot.

This isn't a speech where it's useful for actors to say that they don't believe in ghosts. Anne does. As she invokes Henry's, she should believe in its reality; and later in the play Richard will be visited in a nightmare by all his victims' ghosts, so the play believes in their reality too.

Peopling the Text
Within the speech there are the attendants, King Henry, Edward and Richard, Richard's child, the mother of that child, and at last Richard's wife. It must be most relevant that Richard is not named, but that Anne does name herself.

Anchoring the Text
The 'load' turns 'honour' to a weight 'shrouded in a hearse', just as King Henry and all he stood for ends up as a 'corse'. Richard's evil is manifest in the mention of his hand, twice; and 'wounds', 'windows' and 'holes' all specifically refer to the stab wounds Anne is looking at. See how emotion is translated and anchored in things in the four lines from 'I pour' to 'hence' – balm (tears), eyes, hand, holes, heart, blood – and then the same for hatred with 'adders, spiders, toads, / Or any creeping venom'd thing that lives.'

Characterisation Through Language
There are three intriguing features in the speech. On two occasions, although she is in a state of grief and despair, Anne talks to her attendants with grace. At the beginning she explains why she's asking them to deposit the corpse on a public highway, and at the end she promises them rest at their destination. Someone of her station doesn't have to explain her actions to servants.

The list of 'adders, spiders, toads' seems to spring from a youthful imagination. She starts by saying she will 'obsequiously lament', which is a formal way of describing grief, one that distances Anne from the messiness of pain. Then the touch of the body seems to send her into a visceral journey of cursing and a vivid imaginative purge. This is not an obsequious lament – it's an untempered venting that includes creeping things and an aborted child frightening its mother. It's not stately and considered language: it's fresh and raw, and has a poignant directness that highlights her youth and her pain.

Julius Caesar Act III, Scene i

The Context

At the beginning of Act III, Julius Caesar has been assassinated and we learn that although Antony was his right-hand man at the news of Casear's death he 'Fled to his house amaz'd'.

Antony's initial reaction was to run away rather than confront the murderers: a very human response but probably not one he will enjoy living with. Antony next sends a servant to negotiate with Brutus, the conspirators' leader, asking if he may safely visit them to discuss their motives. Brutus gives his word that they will not harm him although Cassius 'fears him much'. Antony arrives and it is agreed, against Cassius' advice, that he will be allowed to speak to the Roman citizens alongside Brutus, provided he does not blame the conspirators. During this scene Antony shakes their bloodied hands and Brutus then instructs him to 'Prepare the body then, and follow us'. Antony is now left alone with Caesar's body for the first time.

Heightened Circumstances

These are clear. Antony loves Caesar, a man who has been very good to him. He is frightened for his own life and in order to meet with Brutus has had to secure a safe passage. He then negotiates with Caesar's murderers and shakes their hands. Left on his own with the body, he has now to face the fact of Caesar's death, its consequences, and his own cowardice.

You are in the presence of the body of a great and famous man brutally stabbed. A messy, mutilated, freshly bleeding body – as bad as anything brought into the Emergency Department of an inner city hospital. But this body is lying in a grand, secure place, in a street outside the Roman capital.

The Human

Mark Antony has to apologise to Caesar's body for his meekness towards his butchers. He is a great soldier but he is so in fear of his life that he's prepared to debate with them and shake their hands. This isn't heroic: it's human. During the speech, Anthony has to face not only his own behaviour, but the dire consequences of the murder. He probably behaves in a way he doesn't expect. Great plays test humans. With the body he must now check, look and reflect on the consequences of his compromise.

He starts by looking at the blood-soaked earth before moving his eyes to the body and then into its wounds. This seems to me to be a very human way of taking things in. It's too demanding to look immediately at a corpse – you have move in cautiously. It's the same when people drive past a bad car crash. They take the wreckage in and then gradually the eyes approach the heart of the carnage, the broken bodies.

The other vivid image of death in the scene is of mothers cradling their dead infants. It reminds me of the harrowing television coverage of the massacres in Rwanda, where mothers nursed their babies hacked to death. Rwanda too was 'civil strife'. There were so many bodies piled up that people didn't have the energy to bury them; they just covered their faces from the stench and walked past the 'carrion men, groaning for burial'.

The Speech

> *Antony*: O, pardon me, thou bleeding piece of earth,
> That I am meek and gentle with these butchers!
> Thou art the ruins of the noblest man
> That ever lived in the tide of times.
> Woe to the hand that shed this costly blood!
> Over thy wounds now do I prophesy –
> Which like dumb mouths do ope their ruby lips
> To beg the voice and utterance of my tongue –
> A curse shall light upon the limbs of men;
> Domestic fury and fierce civil strife
> Shall cumber all the parts of Italy;
> Blood and destruction shall be so in use,
> And dreadful objects so familiar,

That mothers shall but smile when they behold
Their infants quartered with the hands of war,
All pity chok'd with custom of fell deeds;
And Caesar's spirit, ranging for revenge,
With Até by his side come hot from hell,
Shall in these confines with a monarch's voice
Cry 'Havoc!' and let slip the dogs of war,
That this foul deed shall smell above the earth
With carrion men, groaning for burial.

The Givens

The iambic pentameter is very regular except in four lines. This indicates a sure flow and ease in which Antony experiences the power and presence of the body and the visions that spring from it. The uneven lines are interesting. The second line falters and trips over 'butchers': the murderers are high-born and civilised, but this is what they have become. The one word summons up all the horror of men so accustomed to killing that they have blood under their nails and murder without heart or feeling. The clumsiness of the line ending here contrasts strongly with the next line, even and elegant in its construction and ending with 'noblest man'. The butchers versus Caesar: the former in a line with turbulent waves, the latter far steadier although there is a surge of rhythm under 'ruins'. The butchers have created the turbulence and disturbed the colour that accompanies the reign of a noble man.

The shortened line 'That ever lived in the tide of times' trips over 'lived': Caesar's life has been foreshortened. Couple this with the image of 'the tide of times', where the expansiveness of the sea and the surge of the tide can be felt beneath the second half of the line. Because you feel the rhythmical death of Caesar on 'lived', you sense that the sea has washed his life away, and this energy is emphasised as you move into the first word of the next line: 'Woe'.

The eleven-syllable 'To beg the voice and utterance of my tongue' can only scan if you skip neatly and rapidly over 'utterance'. The tongue does wag in speech: it actually must move quickly in order to say this word. The only other uneven line is the last one: 'With carrion men, groaning for burial'. Here you can feel the terrible weight of 'groaning'. A groan isn't a neat or contained sound, but disturbing and unpredictable.

The other significant rhythmic irregularity is in the three lines beginning 'Domestic', 'Blood' and 'Cry'. Breaking the thrust of the iambic so that the rhythm forces a pause at the start of the line, these three words summarise the fate of Rome as a consequence of the murder: bloody, woe-filled civil war.

Looking now at the thoughts, we find that they all start at the beginning of lines and there are only four of them. Two are of two lines, one of one line – and then the rest of the speech is one seventeen-line thought.

The first three thoughts are indications that Antony is finding his way and his rhythm. Like Lady Anne, he takes time to let his shock thaw before fully engaging his feelings. What he then sees and experiences gathers momentum with an energy that matches the image of dogs unleashed – 'let slip the dogs of war'. As dogs once off their leads will not be called back until they have run their course, so war, once started, is impossible to contain, the blood flow unquenchable until it is spent. Antony sees and knows what Caesar's death will mean, and his understanding is housed in the flow of line and thought.

Linked to this iambic and thought freedom is the openness of the vowels. If you isolate and speak them throughout the speech without consonants, you will hear groans, moans and woes sounded in most of the lines. The lament for the dead has already begun: the killing fields are inevitable because of Caesar's death.

The sequence of thoughts moves very specifically from the bloodied earth to the butchers, to the noblest man to the hand that shed the blood, to the wounds begging Antony's voice to the gathering clarity of the prophesy. 'The limbs of men'; 'civil strife'; 'Italy': these three points telescope out to encompass the whole nation. Then Antony's vision moves back into the domestic horror of war, mothers and infants; and from this appalling spectacle he sees the spirit of Caesar with Até, from hell spreading war, before the last two lines tie his whole vision together by returning to the deed and the smell it will create of unburied bodies.

The Imaginative

The language is simple and modern. The only remotely unfamiliar words are 'thou' – the familiar of 'you' – and 'Até', the daughter of Zeus (god of gods), who personifies chaos and moral blindness. The rest of the language, when you imagine and then speak it, should be conjured reasonably easily.

It's important to cement the images firmly in place, as the structure in the givens is so fast-flowing and undisturbed that there is a danger of the speech running away with you. The internal groan and motor of the text can lead actors merely to communicate an incoherent and generalised sense of woe.

As you work on the first exercise of owning the text, be very diligent about attaching yourself to the physical geography in the speech. You will realise there is an enormous journey without and within Antony's imagination. His eye and mind move like a panning camera from the earth to the body, the murderers, the wound, Italy and war, until his imagination follows the smell of the dead above the earth.

One of the reasons the givens move so quickly forward is that, left with the body of such a great and historic figure, Antony's mind races, seeing the dreadful consequences of the act. Anyone who has sat by a dead body will probably have experienced the same rush of memory and thoughts of the future. Any death fuels the mind into rapid action. Heighten the scenario from the personal to the political and you can easily imagine the dreadful implications of this murder. Caesar is not only important to Antony personally: he ruled the world, and so through the lens of his body Antony can see the destruction wrought on the world.

Try moving imaginatively between these solid, concrete images. Use them as secure stepping stones: bleeding piece of earth, butchers, ruins of the noblest man, hand, wounds, dumb mouths, ruby lips, tongue, limbs of men, civil strife, Italy, dreadful objects, mothers, infants, hands of war, foul deed, above the earth, carrion men. By plotting the speech in this way you will have peopled and achieved the text. But more importantly, when you now return to speak it with all the energy of the givens, you will discover that the power of the verse is under greater control.

Another way of harnessing the speech is to examine the different qualities of action contained in the verbs. Not only will this help differentiate the energy of the verse, but you will discover a powerful movement from the present into the past, followed by a launch into the future. The first thought is present; the second and third thoughts are past; the fourth – and longest – is all about the future.

Owning the Text from the Character's Point of View
The most fundamental shift here will probably involve connecting to

Caesar, who has been a friend, benefactor and hero to Antony.

The conspirators are also people whom Antony has known well, and there is no doubt that he respects Brutus. But now he sees this familiar and honourable man quite differently – as a 'butcher'.

Antony is a soldier, so he has seen plenty of blood, wounds and war in his time. The difference he is exploring here is that a great man has been slaughtered not on a battlefield but in a place of free debate. It's an unexpected place of death – as in *King Lear*, when Gloucester's eyes are taken out by friends in his own living room. Accordingly, the war he sees isn't fought abroad in an enemy's domain – it's at home, a domestic struggle so horrendous that any code of conduct will disappear, all pity will be choked, and Roman will slaughter Roman.

Characterisation through Language

There are two aspects of Antony's language that will help you characterise him. Remember that he fled on hearing about the murder and has negotiated with the 'butchers'. The first thing he does is to apologise to the earth – not to Caesar, but to the earth. He knows that his initial inability to confront the conspirators will scar the earth and make it bleed.

Of course the earth has Caesar's blood on it, so the reference is rooted in the concrete; but it's not actually bleeding – yet. Still, in the very idea we understand the dreadful scope of Antony's vision, for the earth is his country and it *will* bleed.

Next he admits that he has been 'meek and gentle'. Both actions in the first thought show a level of vulnerability. A lesser man might be plotting to save his own skin or to run away. Antony sees the consequences of Caesar's death beyond himself: it is bigger than his own distress. There is a generosity in his contemplation of others before his own security.

Circles

This is a soliloquy but it is rooted in the earth, the body and Caesar in the first two thoughts. The third thought is addressed to the 'hand'. In this way these thoughts are easy to focus in the Second Circle. The long last thought is perhaps more problematic. It is too easy to fall into a vague and generalised focus.

I suggest you use a Second Circle focus on the wounds to spring out into the prophecy. As long as you see all the specific detail of the curse as you speak each sight, you will be sufficiently held to move securely through the thought until you return to the wounds and body on 'this foul deed'.

Measure for Measure Act III Scene i

The Context

The play is set in Vienna and this scene takes place in a prison. Claudio is the prisoner. The plot is complex, but all Claudio knows is that the Duke of Vienna has left his dukedom and placed Angelo, a puritan – 'the precise Angelo' – in power.

One of Angelo's first actions is to reinstate an old law that condemns to death anyone who has sex outside marriage. Claudio has been arrested; his execution is scheduled for tomorrow. He has sent his sister Isabella – a novice nun – to Angelo to plead for his life.

In the course of the scene, Isabella tells her brother to prepare himself for death. She then reveals that there is a remedy for his plight – but that it is worse than the death he must undergo. Finally, she explains what the remedy is. Angelo has promised to save Claudio's life if she will have sex with him: 'yield him my virginity'. At first Claudio passionately agrees with Isabella: 'Thou shalt not do't'. He would rather die.

However, as he questions his sister about Angelo's hypocrisy and the law, Claudio begins to edge towards asking Isabella for life. He argues that Angelo – being so wise – wouldn't damn himself under his own law. Uneasily Isabella asks her brother to make himself absolutely clear: 'What says my brother?' What follows is an impassioned plea from Claudio for life, driven by his fear of death.

The physical geography of this scene is powerful, and particularly relevant to Claudio. He is in prison and contained. Isabella can easily walk away and he won't be able to follow her. Anyone who has visited a prisoner or been in prison knows the strain and tension this barrier puts on any conversation, particularly for the one behind bars. Here it works to enormous dramatic effect as a kind of emotional corset.

Shakespeare achieves a similar tension – although a happy one – through the geography of the balcony scene in *Romeo and Juliet*, where the physical separation of the lovers considerably increases the sexual power of the dialogue.

Heightened Circumstances

Both the setting and the topic are heightened. A sister bringing news to her brother that he is to die is itself extremely potent, let alone the real possibility that this is their final meeting – that they will never, in this life, meet again.

Isabella has great expectations of her brother. Earlier in the play she says:

> I'll to my brother.
> Though he has fallen by prompture of the blood,
> Yet hath he in him such a mind of honour
> That, had he twenty heads to tender down
> On twenty bloody blocks, he'd yield them up
> Before his sister should her body stoop
> To such abhorr'd pollution.
>
> (II.iv)

Not only does she intend to tell him that he is to die but, as the scene develops, she seeks his reassurance that he is willing do so for her and her virginity. She needs him to be her saviour. Their father is dead: they are alone in the world – except for each other. Most daughters expect their father's protection or, in the absence of a father, a brother's. Her mission to save Claudio has led her to be verbally ravished by the puritan Angelo. Now she expects her brother to protect her, to give her permission to save her virginity at the expense of his life.

Claudio behaves as Isabella hopes he will, as her saviour, until the moment in the scene that we are examining. Then he sees the possibility of life, and expresses his fear of death in the hope that she will let him live – which means she will have to have sex with Angelo.

All this is heightened enough, but there is one other ingredient in the mix. Isabella is about to become a nun. Her chastity is more than usually important: she is due to marry Jesus.

The Human

What could be more human than a young man pleading for life or a sister hoping her brother will protect her? Both of them have compelling and moving points of view. Both are in pain and despair and they have only each other to solve their distress.

Isabella wants comfort from her brother. She needs his strength and his sympathy after the abuse she has suffered from Angelo. Claudio tries to be brave and to face death as his sister and society expect of him; but the life force in him is too great, and so is his fear of death. He likes life, he likes his body. He is not a man who could follow his sister's route by entering a monastic order.

Never forget that Claudio is sentenced to die in a few hours. He's not on death row for years. It's now.

The Speech

Isabella: What says my brother?
Claudio: Death is a fearful thing.
Isabella: And shamed life a hateful.
Claudio: Ay, but to die, and go we know not where;
To lie in cold obstruction, and to rot;
This sensible warm motion to become
A kneaded clod; and the delighted spirit
To bathe in fiery floods or to reside
In thrilling region of thick-ribbed ice;
To be imprison'd in the viewless winds,
And blown with restless violence round about
The pendant world; or to be worse than worst
Of those that lawless and incertain thought
Imagine howling – 'tis too horrible.
The weariest and most loathed worldly life
That age, ache, penury, and imprisonment,
Can lay on nature is a paradise
To what we fear of death.
Isabella: Alas, alas!
Claudio: Sweet sister, let me live.
What sin you do to save a brother's life,

Nature dispenses with the deed so far
That it becomes a virtue.
Isabella: O you beast!

The Givens

The first physical observation about the text is that the first line is shared. Claudio picks up his sister's line and finishes it. Immediately there is a break in the next, short line, after Isabella's 'And shamed life a hateful'. There is a pause of two beats here, just before Claudio launches into an eleven-line thought. Perhaps it's there so he can gather his breath and heart to plead for life – to prepare for the fight of his life.

The other important line break is after Claudio's 'To what we fear of death'. Again there is a pause of two beats here before Isabella's 'Alas, alas!' We may imagine that his passion has knocked the usually fast-thinking Isabella off her perch.

In the other exchanges throughout the scene before this speech, all but two lines are picked up. Both siblings are articulate:

Isabella: What says my brother?
Claudio: Death is a fearful thing.

Beat this out and you will feel the full power of Claudio's pick up here, and the strong stress on 'Death'. Do the same with

Isabella: Alas, alas!
Claudio: Sweet sister, let me live.

Here you will feel Claudio's urgency in stopping his sister's lament. The heavy stress falls on 'sister', perhaps punning on their relationship and her imminent taking of holy orders. Feel too the alliteration that connects these fractured lines as the *s* draws them together in sound and breath – just as the repeated *th* in the previous exchange uncomfortably identified brother and death.

The last exchange here –

> *Claudio*: That it becomes a virtue.
> *Isabella*:   O you beast!

– puts Isabella back in control. Beat it and you will sense that she has regained the emphasis on the line. She's found her feet again, in both the rhythm and her convictions.

The scene continues with:

> *Isabella*: O faithless coward! O dishonest wretch!
> Wilt thou be made a man out of my vice?
> Is't not a kind of incest to take life
> From thine own sister's shame? What should I think?
> Heaven shield my mother play'd my father fair!
> For such a warped slip of wilderness
> Ne'er issu'd from his blood. Take my defiance;
> Die; perish. Might but my bending down
> Reprieve thee from thy fate, it should proceed.
> I'll pray a thousand prayers for thy death,
> No word to save thee.

I won't analyse this text in detail, but just note the raw, direct strength of her speech, the quick fire of thoughts and questions beneath the fragmentation of the lines. The habitually composed Isabella is speaking the unspeakable and the givens reflect the violence of what she has to say.

The disturbed lines in Claudio's speech throw certain words into startling relief. These are the words that make death concrete alongside the joy of life: 'A kneaded clod; and the delighted spirit'. Feel how the iambic wave is suppressed and dies on 'kneaded clod' before it lifts and finds lightness in 'delighted spirit'. The rhythm is clogged in the first half before it finds wings again in the second. Claudio flies on this line between death and life.

'In thrilling region of thick-ribbed ice': to make this a ten-syllable line you have to travel all the way on 'ribbed' – and giving this word full attention catches our imagination for an instant, forcing it to dwell long enough to feel Claudio's ribcage. The swing of the ribs gives us breath and life but here they are frozen and breathless. A perfectly preserved two thousand-year-old body locked in Alpine ice comes to mind – the exact fate Claudio is dreading.

The heavily broken 'Imagine howling – 'tis too horrible' sweeps us into the onomatopoeic 'howling' before we reach 'horrible', which is also linked by the *h* – a release of breath. Soon Claudio won't have any breath to release and you can feel that sense of suffocation in the *t*'s of "'tis too' as they lead into the 'horrible'.

To navigate 'The weariest and most loathed worldly life' you have to face 'loathed' – to accept that even the most loathed life is better than no life. As a word it deadens the rhythm but there is physical life and energy around it. The *w*'s of 'weariest' and 'worldly' go on in the breath and mouth, and although 'most loathed' has short vowels the long vowels in 'weariest' and 'worldly life' surround them, giving length and hope in the line.

'That age, ache, penury, and imprisonment': this eleven-syllable line moves quickly through 'age, ache, penury' but settles on 'imprisonment' – the one part of the list that Claudio knows. He hasn't yet experienced the other conditions, and maybe never will, but he is imprisoned – both in reality and in the speaking of the word.

'Can lay on nature is a paradise' is a line that scans, but feel how it tumbles towards 'paradise' and lies across it. 'Paradise' here represents life but is also connected to a place after death. Life and death meet in the one word.

So here is a list of words that peak through the rhythms in this excerpt: 'death', 'delighted', 'ribbed', 'horrible', 'loathed', 'imprisonment', 'paradise'. Feel how they create a collage of the scene and proclaim the antithesis contained in the title – the measure for measure. It's a play that examines the swings in all of us, and in society, between purity and pollution, natural and unnatural, sex and chastity, delight and disgust – heaven and hell.

In Claudio's main speech there are only two thoughts, of eleven lines followed by four lines – two huge movements of the head and heart. You feel that the first thought's length dramatically fulfils a specific purpose. Claudio keeps speaking in order to stop any intervention by Isabella. The audience already knows that she is a fearless debater. She wins almost every argument with the superbly educated Angelo. Imagine living with that: the sister who always beats her brother. Claudio knows how eloquent she is, which is why when he was first arrested he persuaded Lucio to find and send her to plead with Angelo. So in this one long thought, there is the history of a whole sister/brother relationship. Give Isabella an opening and you won't be able to finish what you need to say.

Within its energy and thrust you can feel the inevitability of death and its horror: 'Ay, but to die, and go we know not where'. Speak the vowels in this first line and feel how open they are – they need breath and they *do* send you out into the unknown. I get the feeling of a door being opened with those vowels, but one that leads only into an empty space – no room, no floor, just space, 'we know not where'.

Next Claudio contemplates a fate 'worse than worst': to be howling with the wild and lawless. This proves too terrible; his imagination has shocked him and he breaks with ''tis too horrible'. His mind, driven by imminent death, has taken him to a place of inexpressible horror. The ghost of Hamlet meets the same moment in trying to describe the torment of his afterlife torment: 'O horrible! O horrible! Most horrible.' When articulation becomes impossible, when things become indescribable and words fail us, then the real horror begins. It is a relief that his second thought pulls him back from death to life, whose worst forms will still be paradise compared to the unspeakable horror of death.

The Imaginative

Claudio is trying to communicate the unknown – the 'know not where' and 'the nowhere' – so the basic exercise of imagining the text will be difficult. Nevertheless you will get help from the simple images and their composition. In 'cold obstruction', for instance, we know what cold is and 'obstruction' does actually block the mouth in speaking. The speech moves from the familiar – 'warm motion' – and stays with the specific – 'kneaded clod'. By focusing on the everyday we are helped in venturing out to the 'know not where'.

Peopling the Text

This is an exercise that yields a number of surprises. They refer to each other with 'brother', 'sister' and 'brother's life' – but then Isabella reduces him to a 'beast'. However, in the main speech there are only two 'we's, one in the first line, one in the last. The 'we' is moving and painful because Claudio hasn't said 'I' except in the pun of 'Ay', and so he includes Isabella – and all of us – in the journey to death. How right he is: it's something we all have to face. And yet by refusing to use 'I', he is still trying to keep a distance between himself and death.

As you anchor the text, you will uncover the plethora of infinitive verbs: to die, to lie, to rot, to bathe, to reside, to be. They are part of Claudio's all-inclusive vision of death as a condition that will meet us all.

Owning the Text from the Character's Point of View

Remember first that this conversation takes place between a brother and sister. Of the issues they're discussing, the concepts of sin and virtue might need extra work to understand. Isabella is about to dedicate herself to chastity, so many contemporry Westerners will have to dig deeply into their imaginations to understand her horror of sex. As for Claudio, he might be unable to cling on to his faith – he doesn't talk about Christ or heaven – but he certainly believes that his spirit will survive.

As you read this you can be sure that somewhere on the planet a woman is facing punishment, perhaps even death, for not being chaste. In some cultures, brothers kill their sisters for this 'crime'. That may seem a strange reversal of this particular scene, but it reminds us of how profoundly significant chastity still is today for many people. It is certainly not easy for Claudio to ask his sister to sacrifice her virginity to save his life.

Characterisation through Language

In relation to the rest of the play, this is an uncharacteristic scene for both of them. They have no experience of such a situation, or of how to handle it. Claudio has never prepared himself for death before, or had to ask his sister to trade her virtue.

Claudio's language – like 'sensible warm motion' (referring to his body) and 'delighted spirit' – reveals his love of life, but it's probably the wrong choice to persuade Isabella, who is much less connected to the pleasures of her own body. As for Isabella, she isn't often lost for words as she is with 'Alas, alas!', nor does she habitually use phrases like 'you beast'. It is a strange and intensely difficult scene for both of them.

Circles

Try the excerpt completely in the Second Circle. This will be difficult but it will enable you to release its intensity and passion. However tempting it is – simply because the scene is so difficult – try to avoid slipping into First or Third.

You might discover that it is Isabella who wants to pull away from Second, disconnecting from her impassioned brother in his speech. At any rate, you can't experience this energy unless Claudio risks the Second Circle.

King Lear Act I Scene iii

The Context

This is a whole scene at the beginning of the play. It begins half-way through a conversation between Goneril and Oswald. King Lear has divided his kingdom between Goneril, his eldest daughter, and Regan, his second daughter. The division has shocked everyone: it had been the king's intention to divide his estate equally between all three of his children. His youngest and favourite daughter, Cordelia, was to get the best portion of land and Lear was to stay with her. However, Cordelia has refused to compete in terms of love with her sisters and in a rage Lear has cut her out and banished her. The King of France has, against all expectations, married her without a dowry.

After this surprising turn of events, Lear plans to stay with Goneril and Regan on a monthly rota. He is now at Goneril's house, accompanied by his hundred knights, and creating not only domestic chaos but political threat.

Heightened Circumstances

One hundred knights is a very substantial standing army. Presumably all the knights have squires, so Goneril has a house full of dangerous men. There's no telling what might happen: the guests seem out of control. They are certainly out of order.

Lear has given his daughter power, but he won't let her take it. This is bound to rankle. The first time we met Goneril, we learned how politically aware she is. 'There is further compliment of leave taking between France and him', she said to Regan, clear as to the potential danger of the new alliance between Cordelia and France. In the scene we're now looking at, it is evident that she trusts Regan only on certain matters,

'Whose mind and mine I know in that are one, / Not to be overrul'd'.

In addition to the political dimension, there is of course the personal. This scene takes place in Goneril's home. We may just about be able to bear a parent being rude to us in the parental home, but it's quite another matter when it happens in our own space. Lear's knights may be free to stomp mud over his own palace floors, but not over his daughter's. There is further heightening in the need for Goneril to face her father's ageing: he is not in control but still demands control. Remember too that he has always loved the youngest best. For a daughter to know they are not the father's favourite is a difficult under any circumstances. Here the father-daughter relationship remains unresolved – and those unresolved family ties always make our hearts beat faster.

The Human

Goneril is frequently played as a woman of sheer evil. Indeed her actions, by the end of the play, are horrendous – but what makes Shakespeare so brilliant is his understanding of cause and effect. By placing this scene near the beginning of the play, he lets us see a hurt and vulnerable woman prepare for action. Here we have a daughter, fully aware that she is not her father's favourite, dealing with his appalling behaviour in her own home. Perhaps the insult is even worse than that: we might speculate that, as eldest daughter, she should have been entitled to the whole kingdom. It seems very probable that she would have received it had she been the favourite instead of Cordelia.

It is revealing too that she discloses her frustration at Lear's behaviour to Oswald, a trusted servant, rather than to Albany, her husband. She is a woman alone, and not only emotionally. It seems that she has to control the household without any help from her husband.

Through this scene, we can enter the secret fears and heart of Goneril, and anyone who has struggled with a parent will have sympathy for her. What goes around comes around. As Edmund says at the end of the play, 'The wheel is come full circle'. Children are very likely to treat their parents in old age as they were themselves treated in childhood. Goneril has not had the best of times with her father.

The human edge of this is clear from early on. At the end of the first scene, Goneril speaks to Regan about her father. She observes that 'He always lov'd our sister most' – imagine how hurtful that knowledge must be – and 'The best and soundest of his time hath been but rash'. Both these insights must connect in Goneril in the course of this scene.

There is one other exchange, later in the play, that illuminates the complex human relationship at the heart of the scene. As Goneril enters, Lear says to her 'What makes that frontlet on? You are too much of late i' th' frown.' In front of many men, in her own house and after he has given her power, he tells her not to frown. Is it that he wants her to look pretty, approve of his behaviour, be nice? What's certain is that any daughter addressed by her father in public in such a way will feel a sharp pain and rage.

The Speech

> *Goneril*: Did my father strike my gentleman for chiding of his fool?
> *Oswald*: Ay, madam.
> *Goneril*: By day and night, he wrongs me; every hour
> He flashes into one gross crime or other
> That sets us all at odds. I'll not endure it.
> His knights grow riotous, and himself upbraids us
> On every trifle. When he returns from hunting,
> I will not speak with him; say I am sick.
> If you come slack of former services,
> You shall do well; the fault of it I'll answer.
> *Oswald*: He's coming, madam; I hear him.
> *Goneril*: Put on what weary negligence you please,
> You and your fellows; I'd have it come to question.
> If he distaste it, let him to my sister,
> Whose mind and mine, I know, in that are one,
> Not to be overrul'd. Idle old man,
> That still would manage those authorities
> That he hath given away! Now, by my life,
> Old fools are babes again, and must be us'd
> With checks as flatteries, when they are seen abus'd.
> Remember what I have said.
> *Oswald*:   Well, madam.
> *Goneril*: And let his knights have colder looks among you;
> What grows of it, no matter. Advise your fellows so.
> I would breed from hence occasions, and I shall,
> That I may speak. I'll write straight to my sister
> To hold my very course. Prepare for dinner.

The Givens

There is the potential for a riot in Goneril's palace and that possibility is clearly exhibited in the structure of this speech. There is definitely a riot in Goneril's head.

We know that she is very capable of fine, well-balanced and poetic verse. We've seen it in the first moments of the play when she answers with great skill her father's abrupt command to speak her love for him:

> *Lear*:   Goneril,
> Our eldest born, speak first.
> *Goneril*: Sir, I love you more than word can wield the matter;
> Dearer than eyesight, space and liberty;
> Beyond what can be valued, rich or rare;
> No less than life, with grace, health, beauty, honour;
> As much as child e'er lov'd, or father found;
> A love that makes breath poor and speech unable:
> Beyond all manner of so much I love you.
>
> (I.i)

Things are very different in this scene with Oswald. She starts in prose, then pulls herself into irregular verse while Oswald stays in prose. Seven out of sixteen thoughts start mid-line. Of twenty-three lines of verse, fourteen are more than ten syllables long and one is foreshortened. There are four twelve-syllable lines and one of thirteen syllables.

The kingdom has been fragmented. The family has been fragmented. The peace and order in Goneril's life have been fragmented. And her history with her father is surfacing in her house and she can't avoid it – like shrapnel worming its way out of her body.

The structure of thoughts does move towards a conclusion, but she keeps entering the debate at different points. The sequence of ideas is not straightforward, partly because Oswald keeps prodding and prompting her. With this erratic sequence of thoughts comes the possibility that she is probing deeper and deeper into the wounds she feels inflicted by her father. When the pain gets too much, she pulls out and then starts again. It's as if her fingers are exploring an open wound – a life-long father wound.

In the imaginative work you will need to embrace a great deal of history to understand this relationship, but if you try the walking exercise, turning and changing direction on each section of thought, you will immediately realise how thrown about Goneril feels. She is extremely disturbed.

Her language is mostly practical, direct and uncluttered: she is viewing the situation almost clinically. It is only by exploring the chaos in the lines and rhythms that you understand the real pain in her heart. The no-nonsense language, packed with facts, information, orders and action, acts as a lid on her trouble. If she became too poetic, she might dissolve into tears.

The opening question is in prose. Goneril has been told that her father has struck a gentleman for chiding a fool, and she wants confirmation from Oswald. The question might be an expression of amazement as a fool's role in life is to be chided – so Lear has inverted social etiquette by putting a fool above a gentleman. When Oswald confirms the fact, Goneril moves into verse to discuss the real problem with her father.

Packed into the first line is the relentlessness of his behaviour: 'day and night', 'every hour'. As you beat this line out, you will feel the swell in 'wrongs me'. That trip is the heart of the matter – a father wronging a daughter. It is an obstruction in the line, as Lear obstructs Goneril, before it continues with pace and time to 'every hour'. Content and form express the relentless aggravation of Lear and his followers.

The next four lines are uneven in syllabic weight, the first two of eleven syllables and the next of twelve. It is very unsettling. Notice how certain words surface prominently above the rhythmical chaos – 'flashes' does flash; 'gross' is joined to it by the s's. In Goneril's mouth there is a slush of distaste for her father's behaviour that continues in the next line with the rhythm and the alliteration of 'sets us', resting for a moment on 'odds' as she gathers herself to put an end to a lifetime of abuse. Feel the rhythmical certainty that combines with the strength of the t's in 'I'll not endure it'. She moves off again with energy on 'His knights grow riotous, and himself upbraids us / On every trifle', where again the s's dominate and, although there is flow in the line, waves peak on 'riotous' and 'upbraids'. This heightens her sense of danger, which is contained and brought down to small details as opposed to 'riotous' ones with 'On every trifle'.

Notice how she refers to 'my father' only once at the beginning of the scene. Thereafter she distances herself from him as he becomes 'himself', 'he', 'old man' and even by implication 'old fool'.

It's only when she decides not to speak to him on his return from hunting that she settles into a regular rhythm. For the moment, the only ease she can find is not seeing him – she isn't yet ready to tackle him. Within the regular rhythm is the relief of the idea she pursues throughout the scene, which is to get her servants to enrage him by performing slackly. This notion takes the pressure off her both rhythmically and politically. It's easy to punish someone if they behave badly. She wants to punish him, so he must be goaded into bad behaviour.

Throughout the scene, she is at her most firm and dangerous in short half-line thoughts: 'I'll not endure it'; 'Remember what I have said'; 'Advise your fellows so'; 'Prepare for dinner'. Between these strong statements and commands, she practises her feelings and ideas, using Oswald as a sounding board for her distress and pain.

The last line of the first section of verse – 'You shall do well; the fault of it I'll answer' – has eleven syllables. It's clear that she isn't finished or resolved. Oswald hears Lear coming. Her father's approach pushes her on. She instructs Oswald, and next there's a twelve-syllable line that only becomes irregular in its second half: 'I'd have it come to question'. This repeats the earlier pattern of 'the fault of it I'll answer'. Goneril trips only when she talks about herself having to deal with her father – others dealing with him can be spoken of fluently. Perhaps this is what she has always wanted to do but never achieved. It's new territory when a child takes on a parent for the first time – and very testing.

The next line is irregular on the word 'sister', perhaps a reflection of Goneril's deep distrust of Regan. Then, in the next five lines the main rhythmical trips occur on 'Not to be overrul'd' and 'Now, by my life'. Both show her beginning to harden – a determination in the first, and a firmness in the second that echoes the imminence of her action to stop her father.

The next twelve-syllable line – 'with checks as flatteries, when they are seen abus'd' – moves rapidly forward. It is the first time that Goneril actually speaks about checking Lear. The ease in this line seems to settle her. She knows what to do to constrict him, and is somehow convincing herself that her approaching cruelty is a form of kindness. A baby has to be scolded for its own good. 'Checks' and 'flatteries' rise out of the line; 'checks' is a gentle admonishment, not on the level of the 'riotous' 'upbraids', 'gross crime' or 'wrongs' she has suffered. Her ease is further strengthened by the rhyming couplet: 'us'd' and 'abus'd' are connected. This couplet seems to end her discussion with Oswald, but she wants confirmation after it – 'Remember what I have said'. After his assuring

'Well, madam', she is off again, reiterating her plot and then introducing her sister and the need to prepare dinner.

All the final five lines are irregular. Goneril's mind is swinging on to all the issues and people discussed in the scene. In this way it is a resolve, but a messy one. The next twenty-four hours or so are not going to be easy or pleasant.

When you people the text, you will realise that in her first two speeches she includes her father, herself, his knights, her servants and her sister. In the last section Lear is absent. She has somehow dealt with him. He no longer figures.

The Imaginative

The imagery in this scene is sparse, which might give you the impression that it lacks meat. In many speeches it's the imagery that guides you to the imaginative heart of a character. Here it's different.

The real intensity of the scene is found in three givens. First, look at the evidence of the text. Here is a daughter talking about her father, a constant figure in her life. The evidence is that he is a man who loves Cordelia, but wrongs Goneril and constantly criticises her. I remember working on this with an actress who, suddenly connecting to the domestic tragedy of an unloved child, announced, 'It's not about hating Lear, it's all about loving him.' This came to her because she realised that 'father' is only used at the beginning: she felt that it was too painful for Goneril to call him that again.

Second, the fragmented nature of the verse implies that Goneril hasn't been able to speak about these things before. It is a new experience openly to criticise her father, and it is safe to reason that she can only do so once he has given her power. Now that she has it, she can imagine speaking out against him. Hitherto she hasn't even dared to think of challenging him, the all-powerful father.

Third, there has to be some real connection between Oswald and Goneril. She feels safe enough with him to reveal her vulnerability – she trusts him. Whatever the relationship, it is intriguing to find that such a powerful woman is so comfortable with a servant.

As you come imaginatively to own this speech you will probably discover that through all its structural chaos Goneril remains very clear-headed. She has the kind of brain that makes a good organiser and politician. She understands how dangerous the situation is – setting the whole court at odds. She knows that the best way to tackle Lear is to encourage his bad behaviour so that she can be seen to act in the best interests of the kingdom. She knows she has to strike with her sister, and within the scene plans the crucial letter to Regan. Only then is she able to get on with the domestic running of the court – 'Prepare for dinner'. She is a very competent woman. She would probably make a very efficient queen.

Owning the Text from the Character's Point of View

The father-daughter relationship is of course central here, but if you walk the speech you will come across certain ideas and words that might need extra imaginative care. Goneril's relationship with her sister is crucial; so too is that with her 'people'.

Her father has struck a gentleman – not a lowly servant – and gentlemen can carry arms. The knights too are armed, and riotous; later she clearly implies they are also drunk. If Goneril's men start to react against Lear's, there will be bloodshed. By instructing Oswald to allow her men to show insolence, she is not only challenging her father but appeasing her followers.

Peopling the Text

This exercise will reveal all Goneril's preoccupations. Her mind is bursting with people: her father, his knights, herself, her men, Regan, Oswald, and, at the beginning, the Fool. She doesn't name any of them and she uses the royal 'us' twice. She's practising her royalty. Oswald repeatedly calls her 'madam'. The only line in the whole scene that doesn't refer to a particular person is 'That still would manage those authorities'. Every other line contains specific references to people: he, I, us, you, fellow, knights and so on. It is all the more striking that Albany, her husband, is not present in any of her thinking. There is no help for her from that quarter.

The people anchor the text and the movement of thought is strikingly clear in the reduction of Lear from 'father' to fool and even babe. The process is mirrored by the things in the speech which, though less dominant are powerful when they appear: day, night, hour, crime, trifle, services, fault, negligence, authorities, life, matter, occasions, dinner.

Characterisation through Language

Goneril's use of language reflects her political skill and ability, but she never allows herself to speak rich, poetic verse. Might this open her heart too much? Throughout the play we sense that her language has been emotionally stunted – she speaks efficiently, not emotionally.

Circles

On first examination, Goneril in this scene could be completely in the Second Circle. However, there might be a swing between First and Second. If she trusts Oswald completely, it's possible that she might feel able to spend some time in First as he listens attentively.

King Lear Act II Scene iii

The Context

Edgar is the Duke of Gloucester's legitimate son – which makes him the most powerful young man in the kingdom. Up to this moment we have only met him in two short scenes with his illegitimate brother Edmund. Edmund is plotting against Edgar's life: he wants his land and inheritance. In those two scenes Edgar appears to be something of a pushover, easily manipulated by his brother's lies.

In their first (prose) scene together, Edgar speaks only ten short thoughts as Edmund manages to persuade him that Gloucester, their father, is angry with him and that he should go into hiding in Edmund's lodging. As Edmund says, in verse, after Edgar's exit, 'My practices ride easy'. At this moment Edgar appears almost spineless, unable to react with any sense of survival. Why doesn't he just go and confront his father? That, of course, is a clear indication of his dysfunctional relationship with Gloucester. There are two dysfunctional and highly powerful families in this play.

In their second scene Edgar has only one prose thought, and Edmund deals with him so efficiently that he gets Edgar to run from the Court – making him a fugitive. Later in the scene there is a price placed on his head for his capture, dead or alive. Within this scene it would be perfectly feasible for Edmund to kill his brother and be done with it. Letting him live and run off to the heath is an indication of how weak a threat Edgar is to Edmund. He's not even worth killing. Edmund has called him a fop in his first speech, and obviously doesn't think he can survive the elements – he'll probably be dead in a few days. This will be Edmund's greatest misjudgement in his plot for power.

As we have seen, if the two brothers were to fight at the beginning of the play, Edgar wouldn't stand a chance. By this scene, however, Edgar is on the run and during the speech he decides to survive.

Heightened Circumstances

This speech is about survival. A once affluent and extremely powerful young man is facing the fact that he has been proclaimed an outlaw and is being hunted down to his death. Remember that he is not someone who has ever expected to be in this position, given the privileges of his class.

In the course of this scene Edgar realises that the best disguise is to transform himself into a mad beggar. It's a brilliant disguise because most of us never closely look at a beggar, particularly one who is disturbed. We're either embarrassed by their distress or frightened of their potential power. Once we accept this fact, the 'fop' Edgar immediately becomes a more interesting young man. He has noticed in tremendous detail the suffering of those on the lowest rung of society.

Once when I was teaching in southern India, some of the actors were discussing their favourite characters in Shakespeare. To my surprise many of them named Edgar. When I asked why, they said that his journey was the journey of Buddha. He gains enlightenment and strength through suffering. From this perspective, this is a pivotal scene: Edgar decides here to survive through suffering. And perhaps the end of the play is, in this light, hopeful: the kingdom is to be ruled by a wise man who, through suffering, has found truth and enlightenment.

Edgar's quest for survival takes place in rapid time. Sometimes life-changing decisions are made in split seconds, including the decision to live and escape rather than lie down and die. There are people who do metaphorically stand up again when they've been knocked down. Any animal being hunted or attacked has to keep standing, has to keep getting up. Edmund believes Edgar isn't capable of it. In this scene, we discover that he's wrong.

The Human

Survival is a universal theme. Plays revolve around it and regularly our newspapers offer further remarkable stories of those who make it against the odds. They're heroes. Edgar knows the odds: he lists the forces against him before making his decision:

> No port is free; no place
> That guard and most unusual vigilance
> Does not attend my taking. Whiles I may scape
> I will preserve myself;

We have all fought for our own survival in various ways. They may involve leaving a painfully claustrophobic relationship or quitting a suffocating job rather than something as dramatic as a literal escape from death – but in essence they are about the common human experience of wanting to live.

We also all understand that we might have to sacrifice everything – have nothing, be nothing – in order to achieve something. That nothing can give us all is part of Edgar's universal appeal. And finally, as we've already seen, it's very human to avoid looking at – or even seeing – those who have less than us. They are part of what we fear, together with the notion that we could be one of them at any time.

The Speech

> *Edgar*:   I heard myself proclaim'd,
> And by the happy hollow of a tree
> Escap'd the hunt. No port is free; no place
> That guard and most unusual vigilance
> Does not attend my taking. Whiles I may scape
> I will preserve myself; and am bethought
> To take the basest and most poorest shape
> That ever penury in contempt of man
> Brought near to beast. My face I'll grime with filth,
> Blanket my loins, elf all my hairs in knots,
> And with presented nakedness outface
> The winds and persecutions of the sky.
> The country gives me proof and precedent
> Of bedlam beggars, who, with roaring voices,
> Strike in their numb'd and mortified bare arms
> Pins, wooden pricks, nails, sprigs of rosemary;
> And with this horrible object, from low farms,
> Poor pelting villages, sheep-cotes, and mills,
> Sometimes with lunatic bans, sometimes with prayers,
> Enforce their charity. Poor Turlygod! Poor Tom!
> That's something yet. Edgar I nothing am.

The Givens

The first line has six syllables and three iambics: 'I heard myself proclaim'd'. Its curtailment surely reflects the enormity of Edgar's realisation as his proclamation begins to settle in his mind. This privileged young man has to take beats of time fully to comprehend that he is now an outlaw – literally outside the law. The first thought continues from this line with its built-in pause to the happy (meaning 'lucky') hollow of a tree in which he has escaped the hunt. The word 'hunt' conjures dogs baying, men with weapons: but nature has sheltered him. The heath is on his side.

Notice the *h*'s: the alliteration in 'heard', 'happy', 'hollow', 'hunt'. It gives the sensation of breath; perhaps Edgar is out of breath, trying to catch it in this small window of respite from the chase.

Of nine thoughts in the speech, only one starts at the beginning of a line and there are four in the last two lines. These four thoughts have no flow but state almost savagely his reduced circumstances. Only short sharp thoughts can clearly anchor him in the reality of his life. 'Poor Turlygod' – 'poor' might open him with its long vowel – is closed down by the *t* and *g* and the short vowels in 'Turlygod'. The same pattern occurs in 'Poor Tom'. Any self-pity is being curtailed: he won't survive if he feels sorry for himself. The last line seems to start with hope, in sense and in rhythm – 'That's something yet' – but is checked again by the brutal realisation, 'Edgar I nothing am'.

The syllabic weight of the lines falls mostly into an even ten syllables apart from the first line and 'Does not attend my taking. Whiles I may scape'. This eleven-syllable line is Edgar's turning-point – the moment he decides to preserve himself. The next eleven-syllable line is 'That ever penury in contempt of man'. Beating this out, you will feel the power beneath 'penury' and 'contempt'. Here is a rich man realising the full horror of poverty. The trips on the words highlight a theme explored throughout the play: that poverty reduces humanity, that it is a crime against the dignity of the race. The degradation is experience physically in the consonants here – the *k* and *t*, and the *b*'s and *t*'s of 'Brought' and 'beast' as the thought finishes on the next half-line.

The next eleven-syllable line, 'Of bedlam beggars, who, with roaring voices', gives a swell when beaten out to 'who' that continues with 'roaring voices'. The vowels and buoyant rhythm beneath these words will take you, as you breathe and speak the line, nearly to a scream of despair. Leading on, you will be struck by the violence of 'strike', a violence you can sense in your mouth and in the rhythm of the line as it continues with 'numb'd' and 'mortified'. You can almost feel objects piercing into flesh; and although the next line is ten syllables, the pace within the iambic of 'Pins, wooden pricks, nails, sprigs of rosemary' gives a real, concrete horror to the items pushed into the beggars' arms. Each object begins with a consonant that you have to thrust through to complete the word, just as a pin must be pushed through skin before it slides into the body. Pins, pricks, nails, sprigs: all have that energy and pattern. There is some relief as you land on 'rosemary'; it's a much more gentle word to make and imagine. The next extended line, however – 'And with this horrible object from low farms' – gives full weight to the grotesque horror, settling in the mouth as you attach yourself to and feel the weight of 'horrible'.

The last eleven-syllable line, 'Sometimes with lunatic bans, sometimes with prayers', moves through 'lunatic' to land on 'prayers' which in turn propels you forward to 'Enforce their charity. Poor Turlygod! Poor Tom'. It is the most chaotic line in the speech. With twelve syllables and three thoughts, it is the moment when Edgar loses himself and becomes 'Poor Tom'.

Try beating the whole speech and you will begin to release the pace and urgency of Edgar's decision. His heart and mind are racing. The transitions of thought and feeling happen very rapidly. Accordingly, the sequence of thoughts is clear and uncluttered. There is no time for indulgence or self-pity; only in the penultimate line, with the words 'charity' and 'poor', do you sense that Edgar is dwelling for a moment in sadness. 'Poor' in particular, in its repetition and echo of the earlier 'poor pelting villages', is pregnant with meaning, from impoverished to unwell to pitiable, and in its very sound reinforces the sense of sorrow.

The journey Edgar takes in this speech is very direct, which harnesses and focuses the speed of the iambic. It goes in the following sequence: he realises he is proclaimed and that by luck he has escaped; the pursuers are vigilant and want his capture; he decides to survive by disguising himself as a bedlam beggar; he describes his disguise; he notes and remembers the beggars he has seen and describes their behaviour, moving from himself to others; he continues this movement and becomes Poor Tom; finally he discards himself.

Of course, each of these stages contains more detail and movement, but what is clear is that the scene is about transformation, not emoting, about action to survive, not unfocused panic or self-pity. Understand this – trust the givens – and you will be safe in playing it.

The Imaginative

As soon as you breathe and imagine this speech you realise how many places and objects it involves. The people in it are Edgar and the beggars – and then Edgar becomes a beggar. He doesn't mention his father or brother – he hasn't time to reflect.

Here is a summary of the people, places and objects in the speech: I, hollow of a tree, hunt, port, place, I, I, basest, shape, man, beast, face, I, loins, hairs, winds, sky, country, beggars, voices, arms (punning with 'alms'), pins, pricks, nails, sprigs of rosemary, object, farms, villages, sheep-cotes, mills, Turlygod, Tom, Edgar, I. Connect imaginatively to each of these and the main body of the speech will be in place. In Edgar's heightened state, he sees and remembers everything clearly.

Isolating the verbs is most revealing. What's immediately startling is the clear movement of tenses from the past via the future to finish in the present. The past is held in 'heard', 'proclaimed', 'escaped'; the future in 'I will preserve' and 'I'll grime'; and the present is 'Edgar I nothing am'.

Owning the Text from the Character's Point of View

To connect to this speech from Edgar's point of view requires an imaginative journey into a wasteland. I suppose most city dwellers have seen the degradation of the homeless, but the horror Edgar has observed is in a rural setting and the wretches he refers to as 'bedlam beggars'. They are from the asylum. They are not on tranquilisers, they're not settled in mind. They have inserted fearful objects into their arms; they are roaring and almost naked.

The other important thing to understand is that Edgar has never expected to be chased by authority – indeed, he represents it. Whole sections of society are familiar with the threat of being stopped on suspicion by the police. Edgar isn't: he assumes that his innocence will protect him. Before the play starts, he has never imagined being on the wrong side of the law. In fact, his family makes the laws! There is nothing streetwise about him – if there was, Edmund wouldn't have been able to dupe him so effortlessly, and Edgar would have been alert enough to dispatch him.

To understand Edgar, you have to start with his status and his innocence.

Characterisation through Language

Given Edgar's status, it is extraordinary that he has noticed beggars at all. He has observed them closely and with sympathy. It is an insight into this young man's being.

Take note as well of the fifth line of the speech; here he discovers that he wants to live and preserve himself. We might say that he discovers his manhood at this moment. Given what we've seen of him previously, it is a huge shift in character – a rite of passage. No longer a victim of events, he has decided to mould them to his own ends – to take control of his destiny.

Circles

This is a perfect example of a soliloquy in which the character speaks to the audience as his only friend. Many actors elect to do this in the First Circle. This can work, but try it in Second or Third and you will realise that Edgar's need is to find something outside himself in order to survive – and particularly after he reaches out to the beggars of the world to help him.

Try starting in First, moving through Second into Third and then back to First on the final line. It's not the only way to do the speech, but as an exercise it will help you connect Edgar's inner turmoil to the outer one.

As You Like It Act III Scene v

The Context

Before the start of the play, Rosalind's father, the Duke, has been usurped by his brother Frederick. The Duke now lives in exile in the Forest of Arden. Rosalind has remained at court at the request of Frederick's daughter, Celia – Rosalind's cousin and best friend.

Also in the equation is Orlando, who is being appallingly treated by his elder brother Oliver and risks his life in battle with the court wrestler in front of Frederick. Orlando wins both the wrestling match and Rosalind's heart, but in so doing angers Frederick who banishes his niece. Celia defends her friend but to no avail. The girls plot to run away to Arden, Rosalind in disguise as a boy – Ganymede, a shepherd – and Celia as a shepherdess.

In Arden they settle into pastoral life and discover that Orlando has littered the forest with love poems to Rosalind. She meets him disguised as Ganymede and challenges his love for Rosalind. Orlando agrees that Ganymede should try to cure him of loving her.

Meanwhile the real rural inhabitants, Phoebe and Silvius, are having a lovers' tiff. Phoebe has been cruel about Silvius' protestations of love for her. Rosalind – still in disguise as Ganymede – intervenes and chides both Phoebe for her unkindness to Silvius and Silvius for his infatuation with Phoebe.

Heightened Circumstances

It's always dangerous for an outsider to interfere in a lovers' quarrel. Silvius has met Ganymede before, but Phoebe hasn't. Rosalind, newly in love, is appalled that Phoebe should misuse Silvius. She's not, in Rosalind's opinion, beautiful enough or of high enough status to behave so badly towards her lover, dismissing him in such a high-handed way. Her speech, accordingly, is brutally clear as she tells Phoebe exactly what she thinks of her.

Rosalind is in disguise, which heightens her intervention on several levels. It liberates and gives her courage: most of us would be more honest and straightforward if we were in disguise and didn't have to answer for our remarks as ourselves. There is in addition the thrill of being a woman playing a man in a man's world – freeing her body, her self-esteem and her aggression.

As far as Phoebe is concerned, here is a young man possessed of a woman's insights into her relationship and her self. The chances are that if a woman were to say these things, Phoebe would attack back – but it's very different coming from a man. Ganymede's words have truth in them – which is why the audience finds them funny – and that truth is somehow a relief to Phoebe's ears. That is why, in the course of this speech, she starts to fall in love with the beautiful 'young man'.

Another aspect of the heightened circumstance is that female words are coming from a male body. In many of his plays, Shakespeare toys with this sexual ambiguity. It is always intriguing and often strangely attractive to meet a cross-dresser or transsexual: the relationship between outside appearance and inside knowledge carries a particular frisson of energy and engagement.

The Human

Rosalind is in love, and it's all she wants to talk about. It's new to her and – like so many of us on our first acquaintance with it – she thinks she is an expert. Combined with this, there is an arrogance of youth in Rosalind that both makes her cruel and also to some degree excuses her behaviour in this speech. In an older person, it would be less forgivable. Much of what she says is elitist and harsh, but at a human level her dislike for the Phoebes of the world is at least understandable.

Rosalind sees Phoebe's manipulations of Silvius as only another woman can; and Phoebe falls in love with the person who tells her the truth. Rosalind is shielded in her speech by her disguise, her class and her fine education, but she will be punished for her boldness. By the end of the scene she thinks the matter is over, that she has dealt with Phoebe and Silvius. She hasn't considered that Phoebe will plot to complicate her life. You can't interfere in this grand way without repercussions!

It's a speech that contains six questions and a lot of stop-starts in the verse structure. This seems to indicate that Rosalind expects a reply, a sort of verbal joust with Phoebe and then Silvius. She is used to high-powered exchanges with Celia and probably doesn't expect such passive listeners. However, the more she gets away with it, the meaner and wittier she becomes. It's a very human temptation, and very enjoyable – for Rosalind at least.

The Speech

Rosalind: And why, I pray you?
Who might be your mother,
That you insult, exult, and all at once,
Over the wretched? What though you have no beauty –
As, by my faith, I see no more in you
Than without candle may go dark to bed –
Must you be therefore proud and pitiless?
Why, what means this? Why do you look on me?
I see no more in you than in the ordinary
Of nature's sale-work. 'Od's my little life,
I think she means to tangle my eyes too!
No, faith, proud mistress, hope not after it;
'Tis not your inky brows, your black silk hair,
Your bugle eyeballs, not your cheek of cream,
That can entame my spirits to your worship.
You foolish shepherd, wherefore do you follow her,
Like foggy south, puffing with wind and rain?
You are a thousand times a properer man
Than she a woman. 'Tis such fools as you
That makes the world full of ill-favour'd children.
'Tis not her glass, but you, that flatters her;
And out of you she sees herself more proper
Than any of her lineaments can show her.
But, mistress, know yourself. Down on your knees,
And thank heaven, fasting, for a good man's love;
For I must tell you friendly in your ear:
Sell when you can; you are not for all markets.
Cry the man mercy, love him, take his offer;
Foul is most foul, being foul to be a scoffer.
So take her to thee, shepherd. Fare you well.

The Givens

Before examining the structure here, just take in what Rosalind is saying: it's quite unpleasant. It's so easy to think of this as a witty, clever speech without absorbing what she actually says to Phoebe and Silvius. The real – and shocking – meaning is a given.

Who are you? What is your parentage? You have no beauty, you will have to go to bed in the dark. You are ordinary. Silvius is foolish. People like you have ugly children. It's a horrible attack, yet I've worked with numerous actors who had no concept of how vile Rosalind is being – she's not politically correct! This lack of understanding comes about partly because it's easy to be caught by the wit in this play, and not dig deeper to see how cruel it is. Many witty people manage to say unpleasant things without being appropriately challenged. Often, as in this case, they are not attacking an equal, which makes it an unfair exchange. The fact is that, however enjoyably, Rosalind is abusing her power, her disguise and her wit. She's not being a good Shakespearean heroine – but she is being very human.

Play what's in the text and the person will be revealed. Avoid playing your romantic notion of these characters. It is human to have such delight in demolishing those we perceive as cruel. The humour is in this liberated meanness. The more you enjoy the shock factor in the text, the funnier the speech becomes.

The speech has sixteen thoughts, six of which are questions and six of which start mid-line. Try tracing the sequence of these questions and comments – bridge each thought to plot Rosalind's journey.

The first thoughts are questions. They might be rhetorical but I think they're more human and active than that. I think Rosalind expects a reply from Phoebe, and when she doesn't get one she has to go on – and as she goes on she gets worse, prodding harder and harder. She has come in on an intimate lovers' quarrel, and no one will respond or help her out. If she doesn't continue speaking, she will begin to look foolish. The lack of response – other than Phoebe's looking at her – is itself amusing. Rosalind just isn't getting the interaction, the debate she thrives on.

It's a sequence of frustration that drives her to address both lovers. After 'Why do you look at me?' yields no reply, she goes back to Phoebe and describes her ordinariness – still no response. With ''Od's my little life, / I think she means to tangle my eyes too!' Rosalind is talking either to Celia or the audience before she returns to Phoebe with a six-line question – the longest thought in the speech. The first part lists Phoebe's imperfections; the second asks Silvius why he follows her.

The next three thoughts are addressed to Silvius; and then back to Phoebe for a further three. The last of these is a rhyming couplet, which would normally signal the end of a speech:

> Cry the man mercy, love him, take his offer;
> Foul is most foul, being foul to be a scoffer.

But this turns out to be a false ending. She has to return to Silvius – or perhaps she imagines that the couplet concludes her business with Phoebe (little does she know what she's set in motion!) and frees her again to address Silvius – 'So take her to thee, shepherd. Fare you well.' Those last words could be to Silvius alone or to both him and Phoebe.

By this simple tracing of the speech, you can immediately unlock the circles. There are only two thoughts that are ambiguous- the last one and "Od's my little life, / I think she means to tangle my eyes too!' The rest are clearly addressed to either Phoebe or Silvius, and in this way the speech is very directly focused.

The rhythmic structure is also revealing. Twelve lines out of twenty-nine have eleven, twelve or thirteen syllables. These lines heighten Rosalind's unease at not being answered and are placed when she changes tack, while the regular lines flow when she feels confident and reveal how easy it is for her to be mean. There is no hesitation when she speaks cruelly to Phoebe. The difficulties lie in the lines when she isn't being answered.

Even more is revealed as you beat out the iambic and observe where the rhythmical trips and swells are. Feel the scornful texture of these moments: 'your mother' (the end of an eleven-syllable line); 'wretched? What though you have no beauty –' (twelve syllables); 'ordinary' (this word creates thirteen syllables); 'worship' (at the end of eleven syllables); and 'wherefore do you follow her'. These last seven syllables at the end of a twelve-syllable line crackle with Rosalind's disbelief at Silvius' devotion to one who so easily manipulates him.

The next eleven-syllable line continues this theme, with the iambic highlighting the last two words: 'You are a thousand times a properer man'. There are another eleven syllables in 'That makes the world full of ill-favour'd children', where the iambic hovers over 'full' – a startling vision of the world teeming with these unfortunate progeny.

'And out of you she sees herself more proper' is the same length, and the iambic unease here falls on 'more proper'. Rosalind feels uncomfortable with the consequences of Silvius' flattery, which in turn contributes to his own pain. The unevenness continues in 'Than any of her lineaments can show her', where 'lineaments' – Phoebe's physical attributes – surface sharply in the line with the full belittling force of Rosalind's emphasis.

Rosalind tries to finish off and extricate herself from the scene with three uneven lines –

> Sell when you can; you are not for all markets.
> Cry the man mercy, love him, take his offer;
> Foul is most foul, being foul to be a scoffer.

– in which the weight falls on 'you are not for all markets', 'love him, take his offer' and 'Foul, foul, foul'. These lines are the only ones in the speech that start with substantial words that do not immediately spring the lines forward. They make an interesting collage: sell, cry and foul.

The Imaginative

Rosalind's language is direct, and perhaps deceptive in its directness. Work to experience each of the images she tosses at Phoebe and Silvius; feel the power of each insult; and feel at the same time how simply Rosalind expresses the insult and has solutions for this couple. From her point of view, their options are easy. They are not banished, in love with a man who is also an outcast and who has been deceived by his lover's gender disguise.

'Take her', 'Cry the man mercy' and 'marry him': this simplicity about such a complex issue as love and marriage is one of the main features when you consider characterisation through language and ideas. That, and Rosalind's naïve belief that you can interfere with other people's hearts without fermenting trouble for yourself – a sign of her innocence and youth.

Peopling the Text

There are three main people in the scene – Rosalind, Phoebe and Silvius – but the interesting detail lies in the starkness of address Rosalind uses. Phoebe is successively 'you, you, you, you, you, you, she, mistress, mistress, you, you, you'; and Silvius 'you foolish shepherd, you, you, you, you, you, thee, shepherd' ('thee' being more familiar). Even when Phoebe isn't being spoken to directly, she's frequently just a dismissive 'she' – even though it's in her presence.

Littered among these are equally stark references to others – mother, man, woman, children, man, fools, scoffer – and to objects: candle, bed, nature's sale work, life. Then we move into bits of the body: eyes, brows, hair, eyeballs, cheek (Phoebe will make a list of these insults later in the scene, so she has taken them all in!) and thence to south, wind, rain, glass, lineaments, knees, love, ear, markets. We travel from domestic objects to Phoebe's face to the weather and then back to a glass, other bodily parts and end on 'market', a place for buying and selling. It's insistently unadorned and wonderfully reductive, simple, funny, and almost naïvely cruel. It's rather like when a child tells you the truth: the potency is in the directness, and the charm is in the lack of apology.

Much Ado About Nothing Act II Scene iii

The Context

The first setting of the play is Leonato's house. Hero is his daughter, and Beatrice his niece. A messenger announces the imminent return from war of a victorious Don Pedro with his attending soldiers. These include Claudio, Benedick and Don Pedro's wayward brother Don John.

There is history between the men and women. Claudio is obviously attracted to Hero – she comes with wealth – and Benedick has a sharp sparring relationship with Beatrice. They are constantly engaged in edgy exchanges.

The soldiers are home from war. They are relaxed and love is in the air. Entertainments are sought – parties and dancing. But Benedick can't believe how quickly Claudio's thoughts are turning from life as a professional soldier to women and affairs of the heart. His own experience with women – Beatrice – is not going well. She gets the better of him in every meeting.

Heightened Circumstances

Most of the first half of the play is in prose. Perhaps everyone is too relaxed, too off their guard, to notice that the villainous Don John is busy plotting. If they were still battle-ready they might be alert enough to see through him – to question him further when he slanders Hero later in the play, claiming that she was unfaithful on the night before her wedding. Equally, Benedick is talking about love and Beatrice too casually. His guard is down and he too is vulnerable to being duped.

The subject matter is heightened: Benedick is mourning the loss of a friend to a woman, of a soldier to a lover. He debates in prose his own ability to fall in love and marry. He's not taking the possibility seriously enough. Cupid likes to be taken seriously, as Berowne discovers in *Love's Labour Lost*. If you don't treat Cupid with respect he will take his revenge:

> Go to; it is a plague
> That Cupid will impose for my neglect
> Of his almighty dreadful little might.

(III.i)

Heightened passions require heightened speech forms. Benedick hasn't learnt this yet.

The Human

It is human to lament the loss of a friend to a member of the opposite sex. Instead of spending time with us as they used to, they'd rather be with their new partner. We've been replaced as the preferred company. I remember how difficult it was when two of my students 'got together'. The group dynamic was fractured, their friends were unsettled, and one boy was visibly distressed at losing his best mate. 'He doesn't even want to come to the football with me,' he lamented. Just so is Benedick bemoaning the loss of Claudio.

It's also an ordinary human matter to ponder marriage and settling down. Do I want to do it? If so, who with? What will it mean? Do I have to grow up? Certainly Benedick is maturing through these explorations. He is growing up. He and Beatrice may be late starters in the subject of sex, and indeed their age is something that Shakespeare explores with great wit, but Benedick is starting to catch up.

Benedick has long talks to the audience, probably in the Second Circle. He has got no one else to confide in. He has lost Claudio. He's alone with only the audience interested in him, and his use of prose rather than verse adds to the intimate, conversational quality of his contact with us.

The Speech

> *Benedick*: I do much wonder that one man, seeing how much
> another man is a fool when he dedicates his behaviours to love, will,
> after he hath laugh'd at such shallow follies in other, become the

argument of his own scorn by falling in love; and such a man is Claudio. I have known when there was no music with him but the drum and fife, and now had he rather hear the tabor and the pipe; I have known when he would have walk'd ten mile afoot to see a good armour, and now will he lie ten nights awake carving the fashion of a new doublet. He was wont to speak plain and to the purpose, like an honest man and a soldier, and now is he turn'd orthography; his words are a very fantastical banquet, just so many strange dishes. May I be so converted, and see with these eyes? I cannot tell; I think not. I will not be sworn but love may transform me to an oyster; but I'll take my oath on it, till he have made an oyster of me he shall never make me such a fool. One woman is fair, yet I am well; another is wise, yet I am well; another virtuous, yet I am well; but till all graces be in one woman, one woman, shall not come in my grace. Rich she shall be, that's certain; wise, or I'll none; virtuous, or I'll never cheapen her; fair, or I'll never look on her; mild, or come not near me; noble, or not I for an angel; of good discourse, an excellent musician, and her hair shall be of what colour it please God. Ha! The Prince and Monsieur Love! I will hide me in the arbour.

The Givens

The givens to follow here are the thoughts, the sequence of thoughts, the use of opposites to illuminate meaning, and the humour of a list.

Benedick's attempt to analyse and control what most of us know to be beyond reason – falling in love – gives the speech its humour. But it's unconscious: he is not trying to be funny. Rather, as with all soliloquies, he is trying to solve a problem – to understand why and how Claudio has changed, and whether or not he himself will ever be similarly transformed.

There are ten thoughts in the speech, and their arrangement and sequence are interesting. Three long thoughts concerning Claudio are followed by a question that places the emphasis on Benedick – can it happen to me? – and then three long thoughts about himself and his relationship with women. The speech concludes with three short thoughts as he is interrupted by Claudio and Don Pedro, from whom he hides.

As you trace the journey of each thought, it is important to acknowledge how logical and precise it is and how it moves towards the centre of the problem. This is the same thought structure that we find in verse and it must be given the same focus and drive. It might be harder to locate in prose, but it is essential to attend to it.

The first thought opens by referring to men in general – men who laugh at fools who fall in love, and then fall in love themselves – before turning specifically to Claudio. On the principle that we are what we speak, however, Benedick is on the very road he so despises. In mocking Claudio he is, by an unconscious irony, preparing himself to be mocked and ridiculed. By devoting time to the issue of love, he has declared himself interested in it.

The second thought charts Claudio's changed behaviour as Benedick swings from the past 'I have known' to the present 'and now'. This opposition highlights Benedick's unease and is used too in the third thought to describe the altered Claudio as an instance of the enormous changes love imposes on a man. It's changed Claudio's taste in music, his taste in clothes and even the way he speaks.

It's obvious that Benedick prefers the old Claudio and finds his new behaviour distasteful. Then comes the question: 'May I be so converted and see with these eyes?' Perhaps the implications of this question shock Benedick: 'converted' has religious connotations, possibly even of a change made under duress or torture. And to 'see' differently 'with these eyes' is a startling notion – that the same eyes in the same head might see in a different way.

The next three thoughts try to respond to the horror of this possibility. Benedick doesn't think he can be converted. He takes an oath – 'but love may' is an area of doubt. Only when he is transformed into an oyster will he be made into a fool. It's an interesting choice of image. This curious life form is easily swallowed, but also makes pearls. Hidden in Benedick's dismissiveness is the potential for great beauty and value – love – though he doesn't realise it yet.

The next thought homes in on women. He lists their qualities with the repetition after each of 'yet I am well'. He is not going to 'catch' love from fairness, wisdom or virtue – the conventional, courtly requirements for women and love. Indeed, by implication, and unconsciously again, Benedick is establishing his readiness to fall for the unconventional charms of Beatrice. The movement continues as he plays with the idea of grace – in women and himself – and then goes further towards a deeper contemplation of marriage. The fact is that in doing so he isn't excluding love, but exploring it more deeply.

The list continues, alternating her possible attractions with his immunity, until what appears to be the final off-handedness of 'good discourse, an excellent musician and her hair shall be of what colour it pleases God' – at which point he is interrupted by 'Monsieur Love'. Benedick seems to be abandoning the picture, but perhaps he's really entered it. He's removed himself from the equation, and left it all up to God. There's a sense of completion here – matters are out of his hands – which is deliciously complemented by his farcical and slightly childlike rush to conceal himself in the trees.

The Imaginative

To appreciate how much Benedick thinks Claudio has changed, you might have to research certain words and phrases. There's a difference in music between 'the drum and the fife' and 'the tabor and the pipe', as there is between a straight-talking soldier and the 'orthography'.

Most of the language, however, is familiar and immediate, and as you own the text you will feel the conversational rhythm and style. Without the strictures of iambic pentameter, you will feel an accommodating rhythmic ease which runs as a counterpoint antithetical swing of Benedick's thoughts and debate. Walk the speech, imagining the positives in his argument lined up on one side of the room and the negatives on the other. Try to find the right pace as you speak the speech. Once you've found and felt it, this pacing will inform even the most relaxed delivery.

Peopling the Text
I, man, fool, Claudio, woman, prince, Monsieur Love: the most startling observation is that there is no mention of Beatrice – she is not directly in Benedick's thoughts. His world is peopled by himself and Claudio, by man as a fool in love and then by woman in the abstract.

The objects in the speech for the most part highlight the clash of two worlds: the world of war – a man's domain – and the world of the court, where women intrude.

This exercise thus emphasises Benedick's preoccupation: the loss of his friend, not merely to a woman but from the world of men.

Characterisation through Language
The act of listing a woman's qualities as though you can go to a shop and buy one is a clear indication that Benedick doesn't really know

women. They are a kind of abstraction – or rather, summarised by their conventional virtues, they are abstractions, not real people. Furthermore, while a woman who satisfies convention might be enough for Claudio, it's clearly not enough for Benedick. That is, as we find, appropriate because Beatrice – like Benedick – is anything but conventional. He and she are oddities in their worlds. They don't fit the stereotypical mould of a 'man and a woman': they don't conform. So to this extent, Benedick is pondering the fashions or conventions of his world.

Perhaps, in fact, he's already in love with Beatrice. She gets to him, annoys him – and her absence from the speech might signify that she isn't part of the courtly love world he is describing – a world, as he sees it, full not of real people but of fools who change overnight to accommodate new scenarios. Beatrice is bigger than that, and more troublesome. Benedick might be immature in his view of the world, of love and men – but equally he might be extremely mature, unwilling to conform with neat little social categories. His list of womanly virtues makes mockery of a society which categorises people in terms of their 'assets'. When Claudio's love is tested in the play, it fails because it is conditional on all these things. Benedick's doesn't – it is unconditional, defying convention and power.

The language demonstrates that Benedick is his own man, and the moments later on when he lets go of himself create a great deal of human humour. At this point in the play he has a beard. When he hears about Beatrice's love for him, he shaves it off. We have all known men who only start to wash when they're hot in pursuit of a lover!

The Merchant of Venice Act III Scene i

The Context

In order to secure the loan of a huge amount of money for Bassanio, Antonio has made a bond with his enemy Shylock to forfeit a pound of his flesh if he can't meet the payment date. However, Antonio's ships have failed to return in time and the payment is now due. Venice, the financial centre of the world, is outraged that Shylock, whose daughter Jessica has run away with a Christian and taken much of his fortune, is sticking to the bond and demanding his payment in flesh.

Just before this speech, Salanio and Salerio, two of Antonio's friends, have been goading Shylock about his daughter's flight. Then Salanio brings up Antonio:

> *Salanio*: But tell us, do you hear whether Antonio have had any loss at sea or no?
> *Shylock*: There I have another bad match: a bankrupt, a prodigal, who dare scarce show his head on the Rialto; a beggar, that used to come so smug upon the mart. Let him look to his bond. He was wont to lend money for a Christian courtesy; let him look to his bond.

Shylock's answer is one thought, fluent, passionate and structured with a natural rhetoric, the simple repetition of 'Let him look to his bond' a powerful counterpoint to and reminder of Antonio's past behaviour.

It is Shylock who brings up the word 'Christian', and in his next speech he will compare Jew to Christian. He needs to talk about his faith because he is an outsider. Salerio and Salanio are Christians: they live in a Christian state with all the rights and privileges that gives them. Shylock takes time to educate them about his state – where he lives with regard to the law. They have no idea what it's like to be without power and redress, a second-class citizen. So when Salanio goes on to ask 'Why I am sure, if he forfeit then wilt not take his flesh; what's that good for?' Shylock will tell them.

Heightened Circumstances

There are many factors at stake here, not just revenge for the loss of an only daughter to a Christian or for a lifetime of being despised and baited.

Antonio has mocked Shylock in his place of work, threatening his very livelihood on a daily basis. The only living Shylock can hope to forge is through money-lending; Antonio has not only attacked him for it, but lent money gratis – free of interest.

He's caught Shylock in a pincer movement. Only Jews can lend money with interest – it's a sin for Christians. The state of Venice needs the service for its economy, but the Jews are hated by the likes of Antonio. And yet, when Antonio needs to borrow money, he comes to Shylock. His actions have been imposed on him by the Christians, and now the Christians are shocked at the consequences.

Shylock's speech is so heightened that you can physically feel its thrust. The flow of ideas is palpable. It's clear that he doesn't usually address Christians like this. He's been pushed up against a wall, not only by the goading of these two friends of Antonio, but by Christians all his life – and now he can give vent to his feelings.

The Human

Anyone who has been wronged merely because they belong to a group labelled as inferior will understand this speech. Shakespeare manages to inhabit the skin of every oppressed human being, and the relevance of Shylock's words sings as clearly now as ever.

It is even more remarkable, given the extent of anti-Semitic prejudice in Shakespeare's London, that he has managed to enter the sensibility of an outcast with the to express empathy and compassion for him. Even better, he has that outcast explain humanity to the Christians in the play – and presumably to anyone in the audience prepared to listen beyond their prejudices.

I don't know whether you can get a better plea for humanity than this – or a clearer statement of the appalling reality that abuse breeds abuse. Revenge is taught. If you push someone too hard for too long, they will eventually push you back.

The Speech

Shylock: To bait fish withal. If it will feed nothing else, it will feed my revenge. He hath disgrac'd me and hind'red me half a million; laugh'd at my losses, mock'd at my gains, scorned my nation, thwarted my bargains, cooled my friends, heated mine enemies. And what's his reason? I am a Jew. Hath not a Jew eyes? Hath not a Jew hands, organs, dimensions, senses, affections, passions, fed with the same food, hurt with the same weapons, subject to the same diseases, healed by the same means, warmed and cooled by the same winter and summer, as a Christian is? If you prick us, do we not bleed? If you tickle us, do we not laugh? If you poison us, do we not die? And if you wrong us, shall we not revenge? If we are like you in the rest, we will resemble you in that. If a Jew wrong a Christian, what is his humility? Revenge. If a Christian wrong a Jew, what should his sufferance be by Christian example? Why, revenge. The villainy you teach me I will execute; and it shall go hard but I will better the instruction.

The Givens

There is a huge amount of energy in this speech: you can feel the thoughts tumbling out of Shylock. One of the fundamental decisions the actor has to make here is whether this is the first time he has ever given vent to these thoughts. It's probably the first time he's expressed them to Christians – but they come out under such pressure it seems likely that they've built up over years of resentment.

Such is their vitality that the old acting note of speaking prose quickly works well here. Notice, even on a first reading, the abundance of rhetorical devices Shylock uses. In prose he is a very fine speaker. He has all the devices of good storytelling. He has to be good to keep the attention of these Christians. They don't want to hear what he has to say. Give them any opportunity and they might switch off.

The idea in the first thought that Antonio's flesh could be used for fish bait is shocking, and heightened by the repetition of the 'feed'. Repetition is used to great effect in the speech: 'If it will feed nothing else, it will feed my revenge'. Bait, fish, feed – the cycle of revenge.

The next thought is a long question that lists Antonio's offences against Shylock's life in Venice – 'laugh'd at my losses, mock'd at my gains, scorned my nation, thwarted my bargains, cooled my friends, heated mine enemies' – leading adroitly up to 'And what's his reason?' Within this thought notice the abundance of antitheses – losses/gains, cooled/heated, friends/enemies. Then note the catalogue of verbs that chart Antonio's behaviour. It is a fearsome list – laughed, mocked, scorned, thwarted, cooled, heated – but it is also in the past tense. Since Antonio's imprisonment Shylock has not been abused by him in these ways and he intends never to be again.

Whether he expects an answer to his question is up to the actors and director in rehearsal to decide. There's an issue about whether Antonio's friends have ever heard Shylock's side of the story before, known about Antonio's behaviour to him. Whatever decision is made, Shylock answers himself: 'I am a Jew'. Then follow more questions, about being a Jew and the similarities between people – eyes, hands, organs, dimensions, senses, affections, passions – and their common needs and vulnerabilities: food, 'hurt with the same weapons,' healed similarly, affected by the weather, hot or cold. The focus narrows to precise and involuntary physical reactions in a crescendo of questions: 'If you prick us, do we not bleed? If you tickle us, do we not laugh? If you poison us, do we not die?'

And then suddenly Shylock, having produced indisputable physical evidence, turns as if by necessary consequence to the moral issue – 'And if you wrong us, shall we not revenge?' It's a breathtaking conclusion. The next thought is not a question, but a statement: 'If we are like you in the rest, we will resemble you in that.' Coming after all those questions, the words are solid and intractable.

Next come two questions and two answers – and the thought in each short answer is 'revenge' – before Shylock concludes on 'The villainy you teach me I will execute' (and the thought moves further forward with) 'and it shall go hard but I will better the instruction'.

Shylock takes us through a clear and structured journey, a finely ordered argument. The flesh feeds my revenge. He has wronged me. Why? I am a Jew. But aren't Jews the same as Christians? If a Jew wrongs a Christian, the Christian seeks revenge. If a Christian wrongs a

Jew, why shouldn't the Jew seek revenge? You taught me this and I'll perform the instruction better.

Click, click, click, it goes, with impeccable power and logic. It's completely apt that the Christians have no time to debate this with Shylock as a servant enters to bid them go to Antonio's. Or is it that they are too shocked to speak – and then the servant enters?

The Imaginative

The power of Shylock's argument is easily accessed by anyone who has been wronged. The only major shift needed to own it from the character's point of view is the attachment to Jew or Christian if you are not of the appropriate faith – and particularly to the history of anti-Jewish prejudice.

Peopling the Text

The surprising revelation as you people the text is that Shylock never mentions Antonio by name. He avoids it in the scene as a whole, perhaps as an act of distancing. It's harder to kill someone who has a name.

Furthermore, Antonio is only mentioned directly in the second thought – 'He hath disgrac'd me and hind'red me half a million'. This is a further distancing. From then on the people fall into categories of Jew and Christian. Shylock appears three times as 'I', but mostly the Jews are 'we' and 'us'. It's not only Shylock who's wronged, it's a whole people. The Christians are 'you' – both a singular accusation and a general plural. 'The villainy you teach me' is to one of the Christians, and to all – and then there is 'me', Shylock alone as a Jew facing one who has instructed him in revenge.

Turning to the objects in the speech, the first jolt is the word 'fish' and that Antonio's flesh is merely 'it'. The fish is an early Christian symbol. Jesus is a fisher of men. Shylock has taken over Christian imagery. He knows his enemies better than they know him, as the oppressed must know their oppressors to find their weaknesses.

The objects also reveal Shylock's broad concerns, his world of finance and people – losses, gains, nation, bargains – and as you do the exercise, you will see how tangible Shylock's hurt is and in what concrete terms he sees the world. His life concerns are all our concerns: our bodies, food, weather.

We've seen the verbs and how they list Antonio's unpleasant behaviour; the other verbs extend to common sensations, reactions and needs. It's a surprise to find, in this catalogue, tickling and laughing. At first they seem out of place: we never really imagine our enemies in such innocent pleasure. That Shylock talks of such things is unexpected – but it dramatically humanises the image he is creating in his speech.

Characterisation through Language

Shylock is passionate and his passion is held within strong rhetorical devices and sequential thought; but he speaks in prose. He is formal in the informal structure of prose. Why? Is it that he feels more at home in prose or is it that he doesn't respect the mocking Christians enough to address them in verse? And yet later in the scene he stays in prose to talk to a fellow Jew, Tubal, when he hears news of his daughter spending his hard-earned money.

The first time in the play that we meet Shylock, the scene begins in prose as he discusses the loan with Bassanio. When Antonio enters, the scene shifts into verse and it is Shylock who makes the change, turning formal in an aside to the audience about his hatred for Antonio. Although the verse scans well, Shylock expresses himself less fluently in it, and more carefully. It is as though the form masks his true feelings rather than releasing them. Later this will put him at a distinct disadvantage in the courtroom scene which, being a formal setting, is conducted in verse. Speakers unused to formality in speech are more trapped in any heightened setting – we can see the evidence of this in any courtroom today. It's not that Shylock can't speak verse, but his use of it is less spontaneous. The rhythms don't sit easily with him. Within his house, interestingly, he addresses his daughter in verse – but this is perhaps a reflection of their troubled relationship.

An actor I worked with recently made the observation that verse was Shylock's business code. All you can do is note that Shakespeare has made a deliberate choice of form – and that his writing decisions are acting decisions.

Circles

At first this seems straightforward: Salerio and Salanio, having pestered Shylock, are receiving an answer delivered in the Second Circle. However, if you assume that Shylock is surrounded by Christians – including the audience – then your options are open to move into Third. You can then take us all in.

Othello Act II Scene i

The Context

This soliloquy is the third contact Iago has with the audience. On the basis that those characters who have no one else to speak to use the audience to ponder their problems, we have become absorbed in and involved with Iago. We have witnessed the development of his plot to destroy Othello; we know that he is not honest, although everyone in the play thinks he is; and our involvement makes us to some degree complicit in his actions.

Iago has been overlooked for promotion: Michael Cassio, a young and inexperienced officer, has been appointed Othello's lieutenant over him. As a result, Iago hates Othello, but appears to serve him well and loyally. Othello, unaware of the true situation, believes him to be a good and true companion.

Just before this speech, Iago is conversing with Roderigo, a foolish young gentleman in love with Othello's wife Desdemona. Roderigo has wealth that Iago uses as he steers this boy at will like a decoy to catch his prey.

Heightened Circumstances

In his own way, Iago believes he is fighting to survive. By destroying Othello and Cassio, he believes he will ease the pain of his hatred. He is not in any immediate physical jeopardy, but he does feel attacked and under threat. Unfortunately for all concerned, he is incapable of acting openly and confronting the failures in his life face on. The insults he cannot deal with openly are what fuel his heightened need to survive.

The Human

Iago has been passed over for promotion, in spite of his long and well-noted service, in favour of the totally inexperienced Cassio. The pain he reveals to Roderigo about this in the opening moments of the play is palpable, and many of us will at some time have experienced it. But there's more. Iago also believes that Othello and Cassio have slept with his wife. His hatred of Othello is not just career disappointment, but emotionally heightened. Add to it the fact that the black Othello has married the most beautiful white girl in Venice, and Iago's rage begins to boil with the combined human heat of racial prejudice, sexual jealousy and professional humiliation.

Cassio by contrast, in Iago's view, wins women and promotions easily. Roderigo – the 'trash of Venice' – has money. Sex, power and money are all whirling around this play and around Iago – and he isn't getting any of them. He feels impotent, poor and excluded – and he wants revenge on the people on the inside track.

Look in any tabloid paper any day, and you'll find evidence of an Iago or the results of his actions.

The Speech

> *Iago*: That Cassio loves her, I do well believe it;
> That she loves him, 'tis apt and of great credit.
> The Moor, howbeit that I endure him not,
> Is of a constant, loving, noble nature;
> And I dare think he'll prove to Desdemona
> A most dear husband. Now do I love her too;
> Not out of absolute lust, though peradventure
> I stand accountant for as great a sin,
> But partly led to diet my revenge,
> For that I do suspect the lustful Moor
> Hath leap'd into my seat; the thought whereof
> Doth like a poisonous mineral gnaw my inwards;
> And nothing can nor shall content my soul
> Till I am even'd with him, wife for wife;
> Or failing so, yet that I put the Moor
> At least into a jealousy so strong
> That judgement cannot cure. Which thing to do,

If this poor trash of Venice, whom I trash
For his quick hunting, stand the putting on,
I'll have our Michael Cassio on the hip,
Abuse him to the Moor in the rank garb –
For I fear Cassio with my night-cap too;
Make the Moor thank me, love me, and reward me,
For making him egregiously an ass,
And practising upon his peace and quiet
Even to madness. 'Tis here, but yet confus'd:
Knavery's plain face is never seen till us'd.

The Givens

Every thought starts mid-line. A general scan of Iago's speeches throughout the play will reveal that most of his thoughts similarly begin mid-line, fracturing the harmony of the verse. Thirteen of the twenty-seven lines are between eleven and thirteen syllables. This high percentage of extended lines is another characteristic feature of his speech. There is no physical harmony in his speaking – a direct reflection of the disorder in his soul.

Notice after you mouth the text how violent his words are in feeling. The first four lines are stretched between the violent *t*'s at the ends of words – 'That', 'it', 'apt', 'credit', 'howbeit', 'not', 'constant'. This underpinning is relieved only in the fifth line, 'And I dare think he'll prove to Desdemona / A most dear husband', where it gives way to an unnerving kind of sneer in 'dear'. But of the twenty-seven lines only five are without the *t* propelling and dominating the energy. Iago is spitting his words out in lines that feel aggressive and dirty. The *t*'s are an aid in his attempt to control the world around him, and his internal rage.

A look at those lines not held by t's reveals the parts of the world Iago cannot control, yet wants to. In 'And I dare think he'll prove to Desdemona', there is a hint of control around 'to Desdemona', but 'Doth like a poisonous mineral gnaw my inwards' is a flowing, unstoppable description of the pain he cannot contain, the length of the line depending on how strongly you dwell on 'poisonous'.

The other three lines – 'I'll have our Michael Cassio on the hip' and 'Make the Moor thank me, love me, and reward me, / For making him egregiously an ass' – refer to the future and are yet to be worked out. For the rest, *t*'s nail words and events with terrifying efficiency.

Turn now to beating out the iambic rhythm of the speech and something intriguing is revealed. We already know that there is distress and disorder in the verse but on first beating the lines there seems to be an overriding flow to them. Iago has a rhythm that covers the real roughness of the structure of his verse. He deludes us with a seeming scansion and, although on closer inspection the rhythm reveals his true intent, he is good enough with the iambic to hide the sludge under the surface, to mask his true self. It's like a thin layer of plaster that decorates a rough-hewn wall.

Beat out the speech again to examine closely the less obvious discord in the verse. The swell in each line reveals Iago's hatred of all that is good in the world. Notice how the rhythm falls off certain words and phrases: 'loves her', 'apt', 'great credit', 'howbeit', 'constant, loving, noble nature', 'dear husband', 'absolute lust', 'even'd', 'cure', 'rank garb', 'night-cap', 'thank me, love me and reward me', 'practising', 'Even to madness', 'knavery's'.

Of course there are other words that spring through the rhythm but it is as though anything virtuous unsettles Iago; although he tries to keep his rhythm on an even keel, he wobbles on goodness.

You will feel as well that the rhythm is swift. Iago thinks very quickly – he is bright. People who wish us no good are much more dangerous when they are as intelligent as Iago. This swiftness is married to the fact that he is rarely extravagant with vowels. His are short and containing – remember that longer vowels open the heart more readily. Equally revealing is the fact that he starts only two lines with substantial words – 'Abuse' and 'Knavery'. They're both unnerving words, even more startling because they are embedded at the beginning of a line while the rest of the lines start with regular words that kick them easily forward.

Equally disturbing is the rhyming couplet at the end of the speech, with 'confus'd' and 'us'd'. The first line is broken, and the second line struggles to start with 'Knavery', but within this difficulty the couplet provides an easy energy. It makes the destruction of Othello seem casual. The form tells us that the plotting is difficult but the active evil, once embarked on, will be easy – that confusion is only banished when knavery is used. This is the upside-down moral world of Iago. Peace in his soul comes with the destruction of others.

There are five thoughts, three long ones sandwiched between two short. The length of those three central thoughts confirms not only the speed of Iago's brain but the emotional rush he experiences in thinking out his tactics. There is a momentous focusing and gathering of energy as he propels himself through the speech. He is turned on by the darkness he plots. It excites him.

However, perhaps the most chilling aspect of Iago is manifested in the sequence of thoughts. He is like a chess master who pushes human pieces around his board. The first thought starts with Cassio and Desdemona. The second starts with Othello and Desdemona. The third starts with Desdemona and himself. Othello may be the target of Iago's hatred but his mind plays with everyone – all to get to Othello. They're all pawns to be sacrificed to feed his revenge. And so he dehumanises them. Othello becomes 'the Moor'; divorced from his name, his human individuality. Roderigo is merely 'trash'; Iago's own wife Emilia isn't named. To destroy them, Iago cuts them off from their identity.

The Imaginative

The first revelation as you work this speech is how little imagery Iago uses. The language is workmanlike, simple, direct and practical. It's full of himself and those he sees as competitors. He is known as an honest, direct man. But if his language is direct it is also devoid of poetry – a sign perhaps of the malaise in his heart.

Peopling the Text

In the first two thoughts, Iago's focus on people – the chess pieces – moves like this: Cassio, her (Desdemona), I, she (Desdemona), the Moor, I, I, he (Othello), Desdemona, husband (Othello). He anchors on the three people he is obsessed with, and in the centre of this threesome his 'I' is a potent reminder of Iago's ego.

The third thought moves from Desdemona on to Iago's own wife and then back to Othello: I, her (Desdemona), I, I, Moor (Othello), I, wife for wife (Desdemona, Emilia), I, Moor (Othello). Along the way 'my' is used four times.

The fourth thought travels: trash (Roderigo), I, I, Michael Cassio, him (Cassio), I, Cassio, Moor. There is one 'my', and 'me' is used three times. Desdemona has moved out of his mind.

The final thought has no one personal except the frightening presence of 'Knavery' with a 'plain face'.

This exercise yields some revelations. The first is that each of the long thoughts constantly returns to Othello. Iago's obsession with this man burns in him. He can't be distracted for long with anyone else – his mind keeps returning to him.

Secondly, there is a strange crossover from people to objects. Emilia becomes 'my seat' – he suspects Othello of leaping on to or into her. By the end of the fourth thought, Othello has become an ass. Roderigo is trash and Cassio's possible sexual encounter with Emilia is viewed through a 'night-cap'. It's a reduction that dehumanises Emilia – though the detail of Cassio wearing his night-cap in his bed with his wife is so personal that it's also powerfully human.

Finally, every person that Iago's mind settles on is viewed negatively and lined up for destruction. The workings of his mind are so thorough and cold that to be caught in his line of vision would send a shudder through the soul.

Characterisation through Language

Our initial impression that Iago's language is not poetically rich offers a direct insight into his character. His words distance him from people, and this unemotional connection is what enables him to destroy them. It's all the more noticeable by contrast when the language does become vivid. 'Doth like a poisonous mineral' bursts through the calculating and practical voice, and for once and exceptionally in this play we hear an uncensored description of Iago's pain and hell. The thought of Othello in bed with his wife churns his stomach. In that image lies the emotional fuel that drives Iago.

The problem many actors have in playing Iago is that they depict him as evil and judge his actions. Both are lazy and inappropriate choices. He is dangerous precisely because he doesn't appear evil, and doesn't judge his own actions. Use your imagination to connect to the language from Iago's point of view and you will quickly uncover his uncluttered, yet topsy-turvy view of all the qualities most of us value. The goodness in people is to be polluted, and Iago's distress visited on us all. Love, constancy, nobility must be consumed by Iago – 'diet my revenge' – so that his soul can be contented. Judgement must be made powerless against the strength of jealousy, peace and quiet driven into madness.

He is prepared to sacrifice the world in order to gain his revenge on Othello. Individual victims on the way are trivial against the great plan – the revenge he plans on Cassio is reduced to a wrestling term, 'on the hip' – flip him over, but get Roderigo to do the work for him.

Desdemona is to be had sexually – or at least made to suffer the consequences of Othello's jealousy. Iago's view of his own wife appears to be so inconsequential that she is not even worth the dedication of revenge.

All this clear, direct and unemotional contemplation of how to wreak havoc on living beings is delivered in an almost conversational tone. Iago isn't struggling with himself or the problems of his conscience: the main energy in the speech is how to do it – 'which thing to do'; 'Tis here, but yet confus'd'.

Read any reports on the trials of cold, calculating murderers and you will find Iago. Neighbours call them honest and useful, wives seem not to know, friends defend them. Police are shocked at how unremorseful they appear, how they discuss their deeds rationally and practically. Their victims are commodities to serve their lust, their hatred of the world.

Circle
The thought of Iago addressing me personally in the Second Circle is terrifying. It will be too intense, but try the speech to an individual or group, always fixing on them in Second, and see what happens.

Henry V Act II Scene iii

The Context

This speech describes the death of Falstaff. It comes in the second of only two scenes in which the Hostess appears in *Henry V*.

The Hostess appears throughout *Henry IV Parts I* and *II* as Mistress Quickly. She is now married to Pistol. *In Henry IV Part II*, she says she has known Falstaff for twenty-nine years; their relationship has been a long and turbulent one. From the Henry IV plays, we have a great deal of evidence about the reality of their lives together. The Hostess runs the Boar's Head Tavern. Through Falstaff she knows the Prince – now King Henry V – and through Falstaff she has a glimpse of glamour in her hard life. Bankruptcy and arrest for running a brothel and serving meat through Lent are the daily threats this woman faces. Falstaff eats, drinks and whores under her supervision. He borrows money from her, which he rarely repays. She pawns valuables to supply his needs, gives him clothes, dresses his wounds. He, at appropriate moments, promises to marry her – to make her a lady. On occasions, she defends him from the law and on occasions calls the law to arrest him, so she can recover money, goods and her dignity. Through all the ups and downs of their relationship, there is constant affection on her part.

At the end of *Henry IV Part I*, Falstaff is rejected by the new King, his old friend Prince Hal. In her first appearance in *Henry V*, a boy arrives with news that Falstaff is ailing:

> *Boy*: Mine host Pistol, you must come to my master; and your hostess – he is very sick and would to bed...
> *Hostess*: The King has kill'd his heart. Good husband, come home presently.
>
> (II.i)

She goes at once to Falstaff but returns shortly, telling everyone to come in urgently to Sir John. This evidence suggests that Falstaff has come to the Boar's Head to die. Earlier in the scene, Pistol has scorned the idea of taking in lodgers. If Falstaff is not lodging with them, his decision to be near the Hostess is even more poignant.

Two scenes later Falstaff is dead and the Hostess is bidding farewell to her husband, who is off to war. Pistol's attitude to Falstaff's death is practical – 'For Falstaff he is dead, / And we must earn therefore' – while Bardolph wants to be with him 'either in heaven or in hell.' It is at this point that the Hostess describes the manner of her old friend's death.

Heightened Circumstances

Within the context of the scene, the Hostess could easily side with her husband's view of Falstaff, or consign the man who owes her so much to hell. Bardolph and Pistol are leaving on men's business – war – and it must take energy and passion to focus on the details of Falstaff's death at such a time. That her own husband is also off to his possible death – though on a battlefield, not a bed – contributes to the heightened quality of the description.

The Human

The scene takes place in a street, and the public–private contrast adds a dimension to her very precise, intimate account; but the greatest human need you feel in this speech is to record the fact that she was there. Legends are growing around his death and what he called for, but she was with him to witness it, and every detail is clear, observed and ordered. We tend to remember our last leave-takings with great clarity: they can be etched in the mind for ever. Her compassion overrides all the troubles of their past and she finds poetic language to heighten Falstaff's last moments on earth. But she doesn't sentimentalise. Throughout their relationship in the *Henry* plays she and Falstaff have laughed together. In spite of all their quarrels, they have had warm fun and it remains with her in the bawdy evidence of his death, found as her hand moved up his cold body.

The surprise of the speech is that we haven't heard the Hostess speak poetry before – her language reveals something we haven't seen in her until now. She has flirted and laughed, been angry and awed – but here we see her compassion. She doesn't speak of her own feelings or loss, but of Falstaff. The others speak indirectly of themselves. Bardolph misses him; the boy, later in the scene, misses his jokes; Pistol mourns the losses he endured with him. The Hostess stays directly on Falstaff and the manner of death.

We all know that eventually we will face what Falstaff faces, and we all hope that someone who loves and knows us will be there to help us on our way. That is perhaps the most human aspect of the speech.

The Speech

> *Hostess*: Nay, sure, he's not in hell; he's in Arthur's bosom, if ever man went to Arthur's bosom. 'A made a finer end, and went away an it had been any christom child; 'a parted ev'n just between twelve and one, ev'n at the turning o' th' tide; for after I saw him fumble with the sheets, and play with flowers, and smile upon his fingers' end, I knew there was but one way; for his nose was as sharp as a pen, and 'a babbled of green fields. 'How now, Sir John!' quoth I. 'What, man, be o' good cheer.' So 'a cried out 'God, God, God!' three or four times. Now I, to comfort him, bid him 'a should not think of God; I hop'd there was no need to trouble himself with any such thoughts yet. So 'a bade me lay more clothes on his feet; I put my hand into the bed and felt them, and they were as cold as any stone; then I felt to his knees, and so upward and upward, and all was as cold as any stone.
> *Nym*: They say he cried out of sack.
> *Hostess*: Ay, that 'a did.
> *Bardolph*: And of women.
> *Hostess*: Nay, that 'a did not.

The Givens

This is a prose speech. The Hostess never once speaks verse in any of the three plays. If she could, this would be the moment for it. Pistol has previously been in verse in the scene but no one else can or wishes to attempt the formal code.

However, her prose is precisely structured. From an immediate assertion that Falstaff is in heaven, she takes us sequentially and in detail, without diversions, through the exact record of his last moments.

There are six thoughts in the speech. The main body of the story is held in three long thoughts. A short thought answers Bardolph and then the two short thoughts in the middle coincide with and reflect Falstaff's distress as he calls to God, shattering the peace of his drifting away.

The Hostess will have heard good storytelling in her tavern every night. She knows that the keys to a good tale are sequence and repetition, particularly when the story is so personal and emotional. Sequence and repetition sustain us and help keep the tears at bay.

She opens the account with the general statement that ''A made a finer end, and went away an it had been any christom child.' Next she moves into specific detail: the hour – between twelve and one – and then the moment the tide turned. She lists the order of his last actions – fumbling with the sheets, playing with flowers and smiling as he observes his fingers' ends. It's hard not to be touched by these images.

Observing these things, she knows there is only one way for her old friend, a knowledge confirmed by noticing how sharp his nose looks – the flesh is shrinking on his face – and his babbling of green fields. At this point she intervenes and talks to him, trying to cheer him up. He calls to God and she tries to tell him that it's not necessary, yet. Then he asks her to put more clothes on his feet – and as she feels how cold they are, she runs her hand up his body and the coldness tells her that he is dead.

It's a precise sequence, within which repetition effects a series of refrains – 'Arthur's bosom', 'ev'n', 'God', 'as cold as any stone', 'upward'. The last are in her two closing replies to Nym and Bardolph. She admits he called for sack, but denies he called for women. Is she choosing to censor the facts, making herself the only woman he needed; or did she just not think the sack important?

The rhythm of the speech flows with an iambic pulse. Not only does this regular beat reflect the inevitability of death – like the tide, the waves shifting at its turn – but it is comforting. It holds until it is shattered by 'God, God, God' – which probably also shattered the Hostess as she heard it. Quickly she comforts him, and steers her words back into the supportive rhythm of the iambic tide that is soon to stop.

It's deliberate – a given – that she says 'Arthur's bosom'. The Hostess often uses malapropisms by accident. She means 'Abraham's bosom', just as later in the scene she will mistake 'incarnate' for 'carnation'. We can laugh at her for this but she is trying to heighten the story with biblical references. Her intentions are good, and she moves on to describe his end like 'any christom child'.

The Imaginative

When you own this speech from your point of view you realise how simple and direct it is. It is not difficult at all. The details are mostly accessible and relevant to us all. The real imaginative leap comes with owning it from the Hostess's point of view. At that moment, the details become very vivid. She's sitting up with him into the early hours: "a parted ev'n just between twelve and one, ev'n at the turning o' th' tide'. Remember the tavern is in the City of London beside the River Thames, and that the Thames is tidal. The turning of the tide was something she could hear, smell and know, a real detail that corresponds with the metaphorical turning of the tide in Falstaff's life. She saw him 'play with flowers' – someone had placed flowers near him, probably the Hostess. He babbled of 'green fields': it is enormously poignant to hear a man who lived for the delights of the city remembering at such a moment an innocent, rural past.

The greatest revelation, however, is how intimately the Hostess has known Falstaff in their twenty-nine years. It's clear that she knows well his feet, knees and 'upward and upward'. He was a life force: finding him now as 'cold as any stone' must be full of the warm history of their relationship.

Characterisation

In many ways the Hostess's character is revealed in the context of the speech: her need to witness with dignity the fineness of his passing, the omission of details like the crying for sack that might have been expected. She stayed up with him, brought him flowers, comforted him; she doesn't filter the story through her own feelings, but places him centre stage. The detail tells us she watched him attentively and tended him compassionately. She isn't making herself important through the telling. Like many of Shakespeare's 'low life' characters, she shows herself to have more humanity than some of the better educated ones. The Hostess has had a tough life. She's worked hard and always lived close to ruin, but here we hear her shining grace and honesty.

The Winter's Tale Act IV Scene iv

The Context

Autolycus first appears in Act IV of this play, in Bohemia. He is a thief, a con artist, a scoundrel. From the evidence of the text, he has been at the Bohemian court but has disgraced himself there and has had to leave. Now he lives day to day, not worrying about the future, just getting by. He is down on his luck and will steal anything to survive – but is too scared of being hanged or severely punished to risk major thieving as a highwayman. Instead he chooses to rob the poor.

We first meet him singing: he sings a lot. Part of what makes people vulnerable to his thieving is the fact that he is so amusing and entertaining. But when he's not singing, and although he has been at court, he speaks only in prose. Interestingly, he is very reliant on the audience. He has six soliloquies and seven asides to us. We are privy to this rogue's plotting and morality.

In our first encounter with Autolycus we see him duping the Clown, who his on the way to a sheep-shearing festival. Autolycus pretends to have been mugged – by a villain called Autolycus! The Clown assists the traveller, gives him money and offers to help him on his way. As he does so, Autolycus steals his purse. After the Clown leaves him to go shopping – with money he doesn't now have – Autolycus plots, with the audience, to go to the festival to steal from everybody.

When he gets there, he's disguised as a peddler with a pack full of ballads – the latest songs – and trinkets. We watch him operate. He's a good con merchant. He gathers the workers around him with songs and banter and then draws them away. In this speech, he comes forward to boast of his achievements and to lament the fact that he would have managed to steal from them all if the Old Shepherd hadn't interfered with the 'whoobub'.

Heightened Circumstances

Both the heightened circumstances and the human considerations require a topsy-turvy approach to morality. Autolycus is a thief. Not only does he steal but he steals from those who have little. He operates in a pastoral setting, among people who have to work very hard for a living, for while Autolycus has to survive he is frightened of stealing from those who could really punish him.

In the speech, he is energised because it has been so easy, so simple to beguile the fools who are honest and trusting. The only disappointment is that he has been disturbed. Autolycus gets a thrill from stealing and deceiving.

For the audience, the heightened quality is more troubling and complex. He addresses us, trusts us, reveals to us his fears and pre-occupations – and yet as we get to know this singing, entertaining man, we are in no doubt that he is undermining two of the qualities that keep society connected and safe: honesty and trust. In his own way, Autolycus is preaching anarchy.

We can all imagine the feeling of outrage that comes with being pickpocketed. It's heightened even further when we're the victims of a conman whom we helped or invited into our home. And yet here we are, listening with interest to Autolycus. Of course, it's interesting to enter the mind of such a person, but he is laughing at and mocking us all.

The Human

Part of the human quality Shakespeare captures in Autolycus derives from the conversational style of his speech. It is not formal verse: he is talking normally about manipulation and thieving.

Autolycus manages to challenge the fabric of our morality as though it's nothing. He sees nothing wrong in it – only being caught is troublesome – and can therefore chat away to us without any difficulty or awkward judgement.

Most of us have had the experience at some time in our lives of talking informally to someone, and only realising seconds later that they have said something fundamentally immoral. The shock and power of such a moment is exactly what Autolycus achieves with us. He has no problem with his views, and he takes us along with him – his immorality sounds so reasonable.

You can go into almost any bar and hear Autolycus discussing cons, bargains and deals over a casual pint of beer. A colleague of mine used often to buy stolen goods from a few lads in her local pub. She thought nothing about it until she went on holiday and came back to a ransacked apartment. Yes, she had told them she was going away, and no, she had no proof it was them – but suddenly the reality of what they were about came home to her. They were thieves, and they steal from us all.

The Speech

Autolycus: Ha, Ha! what a fool Honesty is! and Trust, his sworn brother, a very simple gentleman! I have sold all my trumpery; not a counterfeit stone, not a ribbon, glass, pomander, brooch, table-hook, ballad, knife, tape, glove, shoe-tie, bracelet, horn-ring, to keep my pack from fasting. They throng who should buy first, as if my trinkets had been hallowed and brought a benediction to the buyer; by which means I saw whose purse was best in picture; and what I saw, to my good use I rememb'red. My clown, who wants but something to be a reasonable man, grew so in love with the wenches' song that he would not stir his pettitoes till he had both tune and words, which so drew the rest of the herd to me that all their other senses stuck in ears. You might have pinch'd a placket, it was senseless; 'twas nothing to geld a codpiece of a purse; I would have fil'd keys off that hung in chains. No hearing, no feeling, but my sir's song, and admiring the nothing of it. So that in this time of lethargy I pick'd and cut most of their festival purses; and had not the old man come in with a whoobub against his daughter and the King's son and scar'd my choughs from the chaff, I had not left a purse alive in the whole army.

The Givens

This is a very straightforward speech – that's its power. There's no chaos or doubt in the structure, as there is no doubt in Autolycus. Don't be worried about 'Ha, Ha': it's simple, happy. He is coming forward laughing. He's just made a killing. Honesty is a fool; bonded with trust, it's a simpleton.

From 'I have sold all my trumpery' onwards, notice how the rhythm flows, how easy the text is to speak. There is an excited pace and fluidity to it – like a knife through butter. Autolycus is on a high. It's perhaps the most successful venture he has been on in years. Everything goes to plan until the old man's grief intervenes.

The structure of the thoughts highlights Autolycus' pride in his skills: he is boasting. He starts by telling us he's sold all his trumpery – they've bought rubbish, counterfeit stones and everything else in the list. His use of 'fasting' in relation to his pack alerts us to the fact that he is aware of the suffering he will cause his victims. Stealing their money will impose a fast on many families.

The next thought emphasises his skill – and his scorn for the dupes. They throng as if to buy religious relics – one of the oldest cons in the world. But the great benefit to Autolycus is that he can see who has money and where they keep their purses. It's a technique still used wherever there are cash dispensers.

Then he moves on to the next stage of his operation. The Clown is perfect to con – he's lacking in reason. Autolycus picks out carefully those who are most susceptible, be they old or distressed or disabled in some way. The Clown is bent on learning a song, and as he does so the rest are drawn to Autolycus, and their awareness dulled while they are absorbed in the music.

Indeed, as we learn in the next thought, they were so senseless that he could have stolen purses from the most intimate parts of their bodies. 'Placket' can mean a woman's private parts or the opening in the apron that covers them; and Autolycus certainly cuts ('gelds') a purse from a codpiece. He reckons he could have filed keys off their chains, so taken is everyone by the Clown and his song – which, in Autolycus' opinion, is a load of rubbish.

The last thought is the realisation that he could have had all of their purses. They were carrying more money for the festival, money most of them had earned shearing sheep. Notice how he distinguishes between picking and cutting the purses. To pick a pocket is more difficult than to cut a purse with a knife. It was considered, among thieves, a higher level of stealing. Autolycus does both happily, and would have taken the lot if he hadn't been disturbed.

The Imaginative

The first discovery as you explore this speech from your own point of view is the way the language reduces the victims of Autolycus' robbery to animals and birds. Not only does he dehumanise them, he makes them particularly stupid, dirty and ugly. 'They throng' is the first example of faceless people crowded like animals; the Clown's feet become 'pettitoes' – trotters; and from pigs we move to cows as the throng becomes a herd. 'Geld' is the word for castrating a horse or bull, and 'scar'd my choughs from the chaff' evokes scavenging birds at a pile of empty husks. Birds pecking at rubbish: that's how stupid Autolycus thinks his victims are.

Peopling the Text

Just as his victims become animals, so honesty and trust become foolish, simple brothers. No one is given the dignity of a name. The Clown becomes 'my clown', a fool to be abused because he lacks the reason of a 'man'. Two girls become 'wenches', and then the Clown ironically 'my sir' – Autolycus controls the host of the feast. Hierarchy in Autolycus' world is turned upside down. The 'old man', 'his daughter', 'the King's son' aren't named – they are merely a threesome that has stopped his crime.

Suddenly the 'choughs' become a 'whole army'. Autolycus's contempt for order in society makes him believe he could have robbed an entire army. This disdain in all his references begins to characterise him through language. He and whoever he's telling – the audience – are on the outside of society, looking in at it, mocking it, and taking it for everything it can offer. That's the world of Autolycus – we are all ripe for picking. That's why there are 'I's and one 'you' in the speech. It all revolves around him, and the 'you' could be directed at the audience, inducting us into the brotherhood of thieves.

Now explore the objects in the speech. Investigate each one. The goods listed for sale are still the types of thing we buy at markets – not necessary but useful, and for the shepherds in the play, small treats and luxuries: 'counterfeit stone', 'ribbon', 'glass', 'pomander', 'brooch', 'table hook', 'ballad', 'knife', 'tape', 'glove', 'shoe-tie', 'bracelet', 'horn-ring'. They are all objects that give some pleasure or joy – pretty things that enhance life. The most common objects, though, are purses. Purses are mentioned four times. Autolycus's obsession is with getting them and the money they contain.

Already you have entered, through the people and objects, Autolycus' world. He is not a complex man: he just wants money without working for it and without putting himself at too much risk.

Accordingly he has to steal from those he thinks are simpler and less worldly than him. Later in this scene he encounters Camillo and Florizel. They frighten him because they are his perceived betters – intelligent and knowing. He enjoys himself and is at the height of his skills when he dupes the lower orders of society. Maybe that is why we can laugh at him. He is a rascal but he doesn't ultimately threaten the world order.

Try to own the speech from Autolycus's point of view. Probably the key moment, and the hardest, is the opening 'Ha, Ha! What a fool Honesty is!' If you can connect to this idea, the rest of the speech will move forward with the desired thrill and energy. It's a statement of the dangerous and amoral philosophy by which Autolycus lives. He is a bully in the sense that he relies on people's honesty and goodness to survive. We might not conduct our own lives in this light, but most of us have probably at one time enjoyed deceiving someone to our advantage – even if it was just a colleague who took the call when we rang in 'sick', and offered us sympathy. There's a small, self-satisfied thrill as we put the phone down and take a day off. We all know that if someone more worldy or cynical had answered the phone, we might not have been able to deceive them so easily.

In this way Autolycus is right. We have to know our own dishonesty to catch it in others. His duping only works on the really honest people. He won't take on equals.

Circles
I don't think there is any power in this speech unless it is addressed to the audience. Not only does it make us complicit in Autolycus' thieving, but it gives him the opportunity to brag to us. Second or Third Circle works – First doesn't.

Macbeth Act II Scene ii

The Context

The play opens with three witches intent on meeting Macbeth. Then we hear from a messenger reporting to King Duncan that Macbeth has bravely beaten the rebellious army of Macdonwald.

> *Messenger*: For brave Macbeth – well he deserves that name –
> Disdaining Fortune, with his brandish'd steel
> Which smok'd with bloody execution,
> Like valour's mission, carv'd out his passage
> Till he fac'd the slave;
> Which ne'er shook hands, nor bade farewell to him,
> Till he unseam'd him from the nave to th' chaps,
> And fix'd his head upon our battlements.
>
> (I.i)

It is a clear picture of Macbeth the soldier – the killing machine. Macbeth is used to killing.

We meet the witches again before we set eyes on Macbeth. They predict on meeting him not only his promotion and new title – the Thane of Cawdor – but that he will be king. The witches call themselves 'weird', in its old sense of fateful. Fate moves, and as the witches vanish a messenger enters and proclaims Macbeth 'Thane of Cawdor'.

We first meet Lady Macbeth as she reads a letter from Macbeth describing his meeting with the 'weird sisters', his promotion and his potential greatness. The letter, at first, frustrates Lady Macbeth:

> Glamis thou art and Cawdor; and shalt be
> What thou art promis'd. Yet do I fear thy nature;
> It is too full o' th' milk of human kindness
> To catch the nearest way.
>
> (I.v)

She wants to be queen and yet she has lived with Macbeth long enough to know that he promises things he cannot deliver. But the frustration turns to ecstasy as a messenger enters with the news that 'The King comes here tonight.' In her delight, she asks for supernatural aid to block any compassion that might impede her ability to murder.

With Macbeth's arrival begins the plot to murder Duncan. Macbeth tries to resist, but his will is overwhelmed by that of his wife. He knows it is wrong to murder – and yet he will do it. This knowledge is one of the keys to the play's tragedy.

Act II scene ii begins with Lady Macbeth awaiting the return of Macbeth after 'the deed'. It is important that their meeting takes place in a public part of the castle. They could be discovered at any time with blood on their hands. From the text we also gather that she is downstairs: he descends to her. It is also important to understand the actual geography of the murder – the details of the physical journey Macbeth has made to achieve it. The Macbeths live in a castle: cold, draughty buildings at the best of times, military fortifications designed to protect those inside from harm. King Duncan sleeps in an inner room. There is an outer room with two people, including Donalbain, lodged together. Guarding these two rooms are two grooms.

Lady Macbeth has drugged the grooms' 'possets' (a hot, milky drink). From the details of her first speech, we learn that she's been in Duncan's room and seen him asleep, but been unable to kill him because he looked like her father. Macbeth has to get to Duncan, kill him, creep out past the two lodged together, cover the grooms with blood and leave the daggers beside them so it appears that they committed the murder. The scene takes place in the silence of night – except this night is not so silent. Owls shriek, doors are pounded on and Macbeth hears voices.

Heightened Circumstances

All murder is heightened but that of a good man by his trusted host has an extra edge. The fact that he is asleep makes it worse.

There's a lot of pressure. Two people are involved in this bloody plot. The one should commit the unthinkable is bad enough but two is far worse, their collusion in an evil act greater insult to the powers of reason and goodness. More dreadful still, one of these conspirators is a woman – the gentler, more compassionate sex. That she is married to the other goes deeply into our sense of the unnatural, the taboo.

This harrowing scene is also about the breakdown of the marriage. Lady Macbeth, although active in the plotting of the murder, has not been present at its performance. Macbeth is thus more heightened in mind and language than she is, and reaches out to her on a different level. His cries for help are answered only by her pragmatism, her urgent need to leave the scene of the crime. They miss each other and fail to fulfil each other's heightened needs; and yet they are bedfellows forever in this crime. They are trapped together in a marriage of knowledge and guilt but their marriage of love is shattered throughout the scene. At this crucial moment in their relationship, they are incapable of answering each other's deepest needs – and in letting each other down, they signal the end of their union.

Macbeth's horrific realisation, minutes after the murder, that it was wrong and he will never sleep again is matched by her reason – what is done cannot be undone. He is covered in blood and she discovers that he has forgotten to leave the daggers with the grooms – the vital evidence to incriminate them. It speaks volumes for his condition – like a getaway driver forgetting the car in his panic, the mugger leaving his passport with his victim. She has to return the daggers and squeeze more blood from Duncan to smear on them: a woman in absolute, cold control. Nonetheless, she is exposed, in her soliloquy, as being startled. She is not without fear, but she cannot show it to her husband.

The Human

This scene is messy and bloody. That is part of its brilliance. I have worked with murderers in prison, and their response to the scene is how true it is – the mess and chaos, the panic, pace and seeming incoherence. Murder is rarely clean and contained; it is muddled and its immediate aftermath horrendously inefficient. The murderer panics, the conspirator tries to order events and destroy clues that might convict him. In fact, this concern is so great that Lady Macbeth doesn't see that her husband is carrying the weapons until way into the scene. This often confuses actors and only becomes explicable when you rehearse with daggers and achieve the scene's intensity. His behaviour seems so unusual to her, her need to get him away is so great and the castle so dark, that she only notices them when she looks at his bloody hands. We know he's not afraid of blood on the battlefield – but he can't cope with it at home. It's up to her to handle it on the domestic front. They both feel let down by the other in this scene: she by his failures, he by her pragmatism.

The Scene

Lady Macbeth: That which hath made them drunk hath made me
                                                            bold;
What hath quench'd them hath given me fire.
Hark! Peace!
It was the owl that shriek'd, the fatal bellman,
Which gives the stern'st good-night. He is about it.
The doors are open; and the surfeited grooms
Do mock their charge with snores. I have drugg'd their possets,
That death and nature do contend about them,
Whether they live or die.
Macbeth [*Within*]:   Who's there! What, ho!
Lady Macbeth: Alack! I am afraid they have awak'd,
And 'tis not done. Th' attempt, and not the deed,
Confounds us. Hark! I laid their daggers ready;
He could not miss 'em. Had he not resembled
My father as he slept, I had done 't.
Enter Macbeth.

                                        My husband!
Macbeth: I have done the deed. Didst thou not hear a noise?
Lady Macbeth: I heard the owl scream and the crickets cry.
Did you not speak?
Macbeth: When?
Lady Macbeth: Now.
Macbeth: As I descended?
Lady Macbeth: Ay.
Macbeth: Hark!
Who lies i' th' second chamber?
Lady Macbeth: Donalbain.
Macbeth: This is a sorry sight.
[*Looking on his hands.*]
Lady Macbeth: A foolish thought to say a sorry sight.
Macbeth: There's one did laugh in's sleep, And one cried, 'Murder!'
That they did wake each other. I stood and heard them;
But they did say their prayers, and address'd them;
Again to sleep.

Lady Macbeth: There are two lodg'd together.

Macbeth: One cried 'God bless us', and 'Amen' the other,
As they had seen me with these hangman's hands.
List'ning their fear, I could not say 'Amen'
When they did say 'God bless us!

Lady Macbeth: Consider it not so deeply.

Macbeth: But wherefore could not I pronounce 'Amen'?
I had most need of blessing, and 'Amen'
Stuck in my throat.

Lady Macbeth: These deeds must not be thought
After these ways: so, it will make us mad.

Macbeth: Methought I heard a voice cry 'Sleep no more'
Macbeth does murder sleep' – the innocent sleep,
Sleep that knits up the ravell'd sleave of care,
The death of each day's life, sore labour's bath,
Balm of hurt minds, great nature's second course,
Chief nourisher in life's feast.

Lady Macbeth: What do you mean?

Macbeth: Still it cried 'Sleep no more' to all the house;
'Glamis hath murder'd sleep; and therefore Cawdor
Shall sleep no more – Macbeth shall sleep no more'.

Lady Macbeth: Who was it that thus cried? Why, worthy Thane,
You do unbend your noble strength to think
So brainsickly of things. Go get some water
And wash this filthy witness from your hand.
Why did you bring these daggers from the place?
They must lie there. Go carry them, and smear
The sleepy grooms with blood.

Macbeth: I'll go no more:
I am afraid to think what I have done;
Look on't again I dare not.

Lady Macbeth: Infirm of purpose!
Give me the daggers. The sleeping and the dead
Are but as pictures; 'tis the eye of childhood
That fears a painted devil. If he do bleed,
I'll gild the faces of the grooms withal,
For it must seem their guilt.

[*Exit. Knocking within.*]

Macbeth: Whence is that knocking?
How is't with me, when every noise appals me?
What hands are here? Ha! they pluck out mine eyes.
Will all great Neptune's ocean wash this blood
Clean from my hand? No; this my hand will rather

The multitudinous seas incarnadine,
Making the green one red.
Re-enter Lady Macbeth
Lady Macbeth: My hands are of your colour; but I shame
To wear a heart so white. [*Knock*] I hear a knocking
At the south entry; retire we to our chamber.
A little water clears us of this deed.
How easy it is then! Your constancy
Hath left you unattended. [*Knock*] Hark! more knocking.
Get on your nightgown, lest occasion call us
And show us to be watchers. Be not lost
So poorly in your thoughts.
Macbeth: To know my deed, 'twere best not know myself. [*Knock.*]
Wake Duncan with thy knocking! I would thou couldst! [*Exeunt.*]

The Givens

Even a mere glance at the text reveals its rough texture. They are stumbling over rocky ground in the dark, and yet they are travelling quickly. They are playing fast and discordant music.

The scene is in verse. There are seventy-four lines, of which only thirty-four have ten syllables and thirty-nine are broken or unfinished. They share nine lines each picking up the energy of the verse. Six lines create pauses, holes in the vigour of the scene. In these seventy-four lines there are seventy thoughts – up to four thoughts in one line. Thirty-seven thoughts start mid-line. All this adds to the sense that they are trapped in a maze.

Lady Macbeth starts the scene with a ten-syllable line – monosyllabic words – in a heightened attempt to contain the uncontainable: 'That which hath made them drunk hath made me bold'. The suggestion is of intoxification and the tight hold is typical of someone, even slightly drunk, over-focusing to stay in control.

We seem to have arrived half way through her waiting for Macbeth. The second line is broken and as you beat it you will feel the emphasis of 'quench'd' and 'fire', in a mood which is then interrupted by 'Hark! Peace!' Her heart is jumping but she tries to calm herself in the third line although the extra syllable in 'bellman' thrusts you forward into the 'stern'st good-night' of death, and the irregular 'He is about it' reins her in over the word 'about'. Line eight is finished starkly by an off-stage

Macbeth – 'Who's there! What ho!' Lady Macbeth holds herself with 'Alack! I am afraid they have awak'd': after resting on 'Alack', she restores herself with a ten-syllable line.

She is trying to calm herself but in the next three lines, her heart's pounding is revealed not only in the rhythm but in words like "tis', 'Th' attempt', 'miss 'em' and 'done 't'. Halfway through the thirteenth line Macbeth enters, and she finishes with 'My husband!'. It is a twelve-syllable line and the fact that she manages to hold onto the end is perhaps a signal of her iron determination.

Line sixteen is extraordinary, with four thoughts in a frantic exchange:

> *Lady Macbeth*: Did you not speak?
> *Macbeth*:   When?
> *Lady Macbeth*:   Now.
> *Macbeth*:   As I descended?

Three of these thoughts are questions, and since entrance, three of Macbeth's thoughts have been questions. All is unease, uncertainty, doubt. Then follows a remarkable exchange: Lady Macbeth's 'Ay' – four beat pause – and Macbeth's 'Hark' – four beat pause. Shakespeare is doing in verse and silence what Hitchcock did with music and camera angles: creating enormous suspense and tension.

After this pause Macbeth asks the first question relating directly to his experience in the room where the murder took place. There is a short cut in the words – a desperation: 'Who lies i' th' second chamber?' The line is finished by Lady Macbeth with 'Donalbain', but she doesn't complete his next unfinished line, 'This is a sorry sight.'

This is the first direct reference in the scene to Macbeth's despair at the deed. After the pause Lady Macbeth speaks a rare – for this scene – regular line that attempts to regain calm and stability: 'A foolish thought to say a sorry sight'. But the echo of his 'sorry sight', creates an uneasy tone in this striving for calm.

In Macbeth's next speech, although the verse and thought structures are fractured, he is trying to be coherent to his wife about the horror he has experienced, about how close he was to being caught in the act. He finishes with a foreshortened line which she doesn't complete. After a short pause, she responds instead in practical terms to his terrible experience: 'There are two lodg'd together'. This starts a pattern of factual replies to her husband's emotional distress. Undeterred, he continues the description of standing, covered in blood, in the room of the 'two lodg'd together'. This time she doesn't pause, although she creates a long and clumsy line – 'Consider it not so deeply.' It is as though she will not tolerate any indulgent pause. It is time to press on. They are, after all, in a public place and could be discovered at any time. From her point of view a metaphysical discussion about Macbeth's inability to say 'Amen' is both impractical and dangerous.

Macbeth seems unaware of her unwillingness to respond and carries on in the same vein. She too continues her pattern of reply, finishing his line 'Stuck in my throat' with 'These deeds must not be thought after these ways: so, it will make us mad.' It is as if she has a balancing act to perform. She wants to silence him but knows that too harsh an answer might push him over the edge completely.

Undaunted or unaware, Macbeth pays no heed and pursues his description of how he heard voices. He is warming to his topic. This is his longest speech to date in the scene, and his longest thought. There is a real momentum not only in the thought but in the rhythm. He is trying to give vent to all his fears and feelings.

Five and a half lines into his speech she seems to intervene with a direct question: 'What do you mean?' Even this doesn't stop Macbeth and he continues for the next three lines before she has to take charge, asking 'Who was it that thus cried?' Simple and straightforward, this question feels like an attempt to shake Macbeth back into his senses.

Now she addresses him as 'worthy Thane', echoing the titles he has heard cried – Glamis and Cawdor – and then delivers her opinion of his experience: 'brainsickly'. Notice how the multi-syllabic weight of that word gives texture to the line, which is the only one of eleven syllables in this speech. The rest are ten – an unusual concentration in this scene. She uses them to deliver instructions – the practical consideration of washing hands. Only now does she discover that he has brought the daggers with him. As soon as she tells him to go back, he finishes her line with a strong rhythm and a direct refusal.

Beat out this speech and feel the power of his resistance in the weight of 'think', 'done', 'on't', 'not'. Feel the acceleration through the word 'Look'. Macbeth's resistance seems to throw her off course because although she finishes his line with 'Infirm of purpose!' it is a wobbling twelve syllables. But she recovers herself with steely firmness – taking the daggers and leaving to return them.

Now comes the given of the knocking – the outside world intruding. Still he manages to finish her line – its last word 'guilt' – with 'Whence is that knocking?' In the next seven lines, Macbeth has six thoughts, four of them questions. He has nine questions in all in this scene and only one of them is answered – 'Who lies i' th' second chamber?' The rest are unanswerable, because he has done the unthinkable.

When Lady Macbeth returns, she is moved into fast action by the insistence of the knocking, giving orders even under the impending danger of discovery. There are three rebukes to shame her husband: she starts with one and ends with one and there is one located at the centre of the speech. Macbeth doesn't finish her last line. The rhythm of his first line tempts us to anticipate that a rhyming couplet will end the scene but instead we get an eleven-syllable, broken line, which is both unsatisfying and unresolved. The ramifications of murder have yet to be worked out.

The verse, as we have seen, is distressed and diseased throughout and needs very precise handling if you are not to rush and stumble incoherently. Do play the scene with all the pauses Shakespeare orchestrates, and work carefully at the concrete details of the language.

On one level, the scene is about listening, night and silence. 'Hark' occurs three times, and 'listening' and 'peace' once, 'heard' twice and then there is 'every noise appals me'. This attention to sound has its counterpart in silence, which is constantly being ruptured. There is the repeated knocking and the questions it raises; the shrieking of the owl, the snores of the grooms, 'the crickets cry'; 'one did laugh in's sleep', 'one cried Murder', 'they did say their prayers'; and the unworldly voice that Macbeth hears – 'Methought I heard a voice cry', 'still it cried', 'Who was it that thus cried?' By all of these the silence of night and sleep is pierced.

The longing for peace comes through in repetitions. Macbeth uses 'Amen' four times, as if closing a prayer, and 'sleep' ten, while Lady Macbeth talks of Duncan resembling her father 'as he slept', the 'sleepy grooms', and finally the ultimate silence with 'the sleeping and the dead'. She also uses 'snores' and 'night gown' but all this imagery of sleep explodes as Macbeth speaks his last line in the scene – 'Wake Duncan with thy knocking! I would thou couldst!' These opposing aspects – sleep as both peace and death – are to some degree reflected in the image of water, which for Macbeth is unstoppable – 'the water of the seas', 'great Neptune's Ocean'. Sleep itself becomes a form of water, 'sore labour's bath'. By contrast, Lady Macbeth's references to water are more prosaic: it is for washing blood off hands.

> Go get some water
> And wash this filthy witness from your hand [...]
> A little water clears us of this deed.

Only, later, as she sleepwalks, does she realise that her hands can never be clean.

'Deed' is used four times – twice by both – and 'deeds' once by Lady Macbeth. This 'deed' is the murder of Duncan but 'murder' is only used when Macbeth relates what was cried in the chamber by someone else. It is as if 'murder' is unutterable so 'deed' replaces it.

By looking at the given of repetition in the scene, we have started to unlock the imaginative language.

The Imaginative

Take time, and speak the whole scene only when you have fully experienced the detail of every image. By doing this, you will gain a physical insight into their different use of language. They are linked by certain words and phrases, but the overall effect is of two people who are intimately connected, yet speaking to each other from different sources of language. If Romeo and Juliet are effectively married by the speaking of a sonnet on their first meeting, this married couple is breaking apart.

Lady Macbeth's language is mostly about action and practicalities – she does not use it to connect to feeling. Macbeth wants to explore his feelings – his language verges on the epic. He may be distraught, even unhinged, but he gets no sympathy from her, only hard practicalities. Though he has been through a transformingly horrific experience, she refuses to understand – and in any case this is not the time or place to discuss it. It's a painful misunderstanding for both of them, and reveals through their language not just the state of their relationship, but their characters.

Peopling the Text

Surprisingly, perhaps, Duncan – the victim – is only mentioned by name in the last line of the scene, in Macbeth's only reference to him.

Elsewhere he is merely 'he' for Lady Macbeth, with 'Had he not resembled my father as he slept' and 'If he do bleed'. Macbeth himself is present to Lady Macbeth in various forms – referred to as 'He', then addressed as 'My husband', 'you', 'us', 'you', 'Worthy Thane', 'you', 'we', 'us', 'you', 'us' and 'us'. She is determined to keep his attention.

By contrast, Macbeth only refers directly to Lady Macbeth three times. He is lost in contemplation of himself, with 'thou' and 'thy'. He has eleven I's compared to her seven; twice he names himself 'Macbeth' and twice by his titles. He is also preoccupied with parts of his body, 'hangman's hands', 'throat', 'eyes', 'hands', 'hand' and 'hand' – all constant reminders of his crime.

Lady Macbeth is more connected to people around her who are involved in the plot – which is why the mention of her father is so shocking. The grooms are referred to as 'grooms' three times and eight times as 'them', 'their' and 'they'. She mentions 'Donalbain' and again in 'the two lodg'd together'. Macbeth is concerned by the 'two' in the context that they will call on God.

The objects in the scene are equally revealing. Lady Macbeth's thoughts are full of them. She mentions daggers three times – Macbeth never refers to them. Her concern is with real things: 'possets', 'owls', 'crickets', 'water', 'the faces' of the 'grooms', 'the south entry', 'our chamber', 'water', 'nightgown'. Macbeth's reality is very different. The voices he hears are what's real to him. His anchoring is in prayers, God, sleep, death, life, minds, nature, oceans. It is further evidence that they are alone in different worlds with their own horror and pain, and yet bound together forever through their shared knowledge of the deed of murder.

Circles

The obvious focus for this scene is to play it all in the Second Circle, and you should certainly try this. But you will also reap rewards if you try other options. Experiment with Lady Macbeth staying in Second on Macbeth, but with Macbeth connected somewhere else in First, Second or Third. This will heighten her need to deal with him, and vividly reveal his transformation – for her it will have the strange effect of dealing with someone you think you know but suddenly don't. Then reverse the focus and have him fixed on her with Lady Macbeth's attention elsewhere, and you will reveal his pain and need.

Like all the work on the Circles, the aim is eventually to enhance the specific thoughts and needs in each line, but experimenting will enhance your energy choices from moment to moment.

Twelfth Night Act I Scene v

The Context

Viola and Olivia have both recently lost a brother, and before that a father. Olivia, now a wealthy lady, is in mourning and has shut herself away from the the world. Viola, who has been shipwrecked on the shores of Illyria, has had to survive by going into disguise as a young boy and is now serving Orsino, the Duke of Illyria. She has fallen in love with her patron but he is in love with Olivia. Orsino sends Viola, in her disguise as Cesario, to woo Olivia in his name.

The scene takes place in Olivia's house. She has no desire to hear from Orsino and it has been difficult for Viola even to gain an audience with her. Olivia is attended by a bevy of waiting ladies and just before Viola's entrance they all veil themselves so that Olivia is unrecognisable as the lady of the house.

Also in the scene is Maria, a waiting woman to Olivia.

Heightened Circumstances

We know that Viola has fallen in love with Orsino after agreeing to woo for him:

> *Viola*: I'll do my best
> To woo your lady [*Aside*] yet a barful strife!
> Whoe'er I woo, myself would be his wife.
>
> (I.iv)

While she might find it interesting to inspect her rival from the safety of a disguise, it cannot be comfortable. Still, a disguise itself is a heightening device as it liberates the wearer. As a boy, Viola can be more outspoken and difficult than a girl could be. Nonetheless, her survival is dependent on Orsino so she must perform her wooing well. Nothing is easy. It has been a struggle to get to Olivia, it is a struggle to get her to reveal her face, and then it's a struggle to be left alone with her.

Olivia herself has had a troubled day, disturbed by her fool Feste, and her uncle, Sir Toby Belch. Feste has challenged her need to mourn her brother and shut herself away and her uncle is a tiresome drunk, constantly breaking her peace. Malvolio, her steward, seems unable to keep order in her household – he's the one Viola argues with to gain entrance. The men around her are useless and she is bothered by the entreaties of Orsino. There is no peace for her.

Thus the scene starts from a heightened situation of turmoil and frustration in both these women, each struggling with grief and loneliness.

As it progresses, Viola has to hear Olivia mock not only love, but the man she is in love with. This triggers a passion in her that so affects Olivia that it moves her to love.

Olivia for her part meets a beautiful young man who speaks frankly to her, but with intimacy and an understanding of female energy, refusing to play the usual games of love. Viola, behind the safety of her disguise, can speak the truth to Olivia – and Olivia, unprepared for such insight from a man, hears and responds from her heart.

The Human

Viola has the human desire to see and challenge her rival, even questioning her beauty and calling her proud. Olivia hears the truth about herself expressed with passion and falls in love as a result. She is used to being wooed in fine but insubstantial words; like all of us, she is susceptible to those who show real feeling and attention. Both women's hearts are pounding: Viola's with indignation that Olivia is so contemptuous of being loved and Olivia's with the passionate oxygen that Viola brings into her cloistered house. Although they both start the scene in some way veiled, both by the end are exposed.

The Scene

> *Viola:* The honourable lady of the house, which is she?
> *Olivia:* Speak to me; I shall answer for her. Your will?

Viola: Most radiant, exquisite, and unmatchable beauty – I pray you tell me if this be the lady of the house, for I never saw her. I would be loath to cast away my speech; for, besides that it is excellently well penn'd, I have taken great pains to con it. Good beauties, let me sustain no scorn; I am very comptible, even to the least sinister usage.

Olivia: Whence came you, sir?

Viola: I can say little more than I have studied, and that question's out of my part. Good gentle one, give me modest assurance if you be the lady of the house, that I may proceed in my speech.

Olivia: Are you a comedian?

Viola: No, my profound heart; and yet, by the very fangs of malice I swear, I am not that I play. Are you the lady of the house?

Olivia: If I do not usurp myself, I am.

Viola: Most certain, if you are she, you do usurp yourself; for what is yours to bestow is not yours to reserve. But this is from my commission. I will on with my speech in your praise, and then show you the heart of my message.

Olivia: Come to what is important in't. I forgive you the praise.

Viola: Alas, I took great pains to study it, and 'tis poetical.

Olivia: It is the more like to be feigned; I pray you keep it in. I heard you were saucy at my gates, and allow'd your approach rather to wonder at you than to hear you. If you be not mad, be gone; if you have reason, be brief; 'tis not that time of moon with me to make one in so skipping a dialogue.

Maria: Will you hoist sail, sir? Here lies your way.

Viola: No, good swabber, I am to hull here a little longer. Some mollification for your giant, sweet lady.

Olivia: Tell me your mind.

Viola: I am a messenger.

Olivia: Sure, you have some hideous matter to deliver, when the courtesy of it is so fearful. Speak your office.

Viola: It alone concerns your ear. I bring no overture of war, no taxation of homage: I hold the olive in my hand; my words are as full of peace as matter.

Olivia: Yet you began rudely. What are you? What would you?

Viola: The rudeness that hath appear'd in me have I learn'd from my entertainment. What I am and what I would are as secret as maidenhead – to your ears, divinity; to any other's, profanation.

Olivia: Give us the place alone; we will hear this divinity. [*Exeunt Maria and Attendants*] Now, sir, what is your text?

Viola: Most sweet lady –

Olivia: A comfortable doctrine, and much may be said of it. Where lies your text?

Viola: In Orsino's bosom.

Olivia: In his bosom! In what chapter of his bosom?

Viola: To answer by the method: in the first of his heart.

Olivia: O, I have read it; it is heresy. Have you no more to say?

Viola: Good madam, let me see your face.

Olivia: Have you any commission from your lord to negotiate with my face? You are now out of your text; but we will draw the curtain and show you the picture. [*Unveiling*] Look you, sir, such a one I was this present. Is't not well done?

Viola: Excellently done, if God did all.

Olivia: 'Tis in grain, sir; 'twill endure wind and weather.

Viola: 'Tis beauty truly blent, whose red and white
Nature's own sweet and cunning hand laid on.
Lady, you are the cruellest she alive,
If you will lead these graces to the grave,
And leave the world no copy.

Olivia: O, sir, I will not be so hard-hearted; I will give out divers schedules of my beauty. It shall be inventoried, and every particle and utensil labell'd to my will: as – item, two lips indifferent red; item, two grey eyes with lids to them; item, one neck, one chin, and so forth. Were you sent hither to praise me?

Viola: I see you what you are: you are too proud;
But, if you were the devil, you are fair.
My lord and master loves you – O, such love
Could be but recompens'd though you were crown'd
The nonpareil of beauty!

Olivia: How does he love me?

Viola: With adorations, fertile tears,
With groans that thunder love, with sighs of fire.

Olivia: Your lord does know my mind; I cannot love him.
Yet I suppose him virtuous, know him noble,
Of great estate, of fresh and stainless youth;
In voices well divulg'd, free, learn'd, and valiant,
And in dimension and the shape of nature
A gracious person; but yet I cannot love him.
He might have took his answer long ago.

Viola: If I did love you in my master's flame,
With such a suff'ring, such a deadly life,
In your denial I would find no sense;
I would not understand it.

Olivia: Why, what would you?

Viola: Make me a willow cabin at your gate,
And call upon my soul within the house;

Write loyal cantons of contemned love
And sing them loud even in the dead of night;
Halloo your name to the reverberate hills,
And make the babbling gossip of the air
Cry out 'Olivia!' O, you should not rest
Between the elements of air and earth
But you should pity me!
Olivia: You might do much.
What is your parentage?
Viola: Above my fortunes, yet my state is well;
I am a gentleman.
Olivia: Get you to your lord.
I cannot love him; let him send no more –
Unless perchance you come to me again
To tell me how he takes it. Fare you well.
I thank you for your pains; spend this for me.
Viola: I am no fee'd post, lady; keep your purse;
My master, not myself, lacks recompense.
Love make his heart of flint that you shall love;
And let your fervour, like my master's, be
Plac'd in contempt! Farewell, fair cruelty.
[*Exit.*]
Olivia: 'What is your parentage?'
'Above my fortunes, yet my state is well:
I am a gentleman.' I'll be sworn thou art;
Thy tongue, thy face, thy limbs, actions, and spirit,
Do give thee five-fold blazon. Not too fast! Soft, soft!
Unless the master were the man. How now!
Even so quickly may one catch the plague?
Methinks I feel this youth's perfections
With an invisible and subtle stealth
To creep in at mine eyes. Well, let it be.
What ho, Malvolio!

The Givens

The dialogue starts in prose and then Viola shifts it into verse. This shift parallels the emotional development of the scene, and is the first sign of rejuvenation in the play. The bantering flavour of the prose is something we have earlier grown accustomed to in Illyria. It's a country full of fools, hints of plague and madmen, and the tone of its language is world-weary. Orsino speaks in ornate poetry, Sir Toby and Feste overwork their wit, and Olivia is cloistered away from the world in the prime of her youth. Viola, an outsider in this society, brings a freshness to the language that challenges its codes and disarms all who meet her. She has just out-manoeuvred Malvolio to gain access to Olivia and in an earlier scene we learn that in only three days she has deeply affected Orsino. As he says, 'I have unclasp'd to thee the book even of my secret soul.' Entering a world that is linguistically artificial and cruel, breaks its conventions and thereby wins hearts.

With this in mind, let's look at the prose section here. Olivia and the ladies of the house, all veiled, greet this young man. The power of all that female energy would unnerve most youths but the first break in form is that the disguised Viola seems to have no problem with it and asks a direct question: 'The honourable lady of the house, which is she?' Olivia responds in her first engagement with the youth. Immediately before Viola's entrance she has said, 'We'll once more hear Orsino's embassy', so it seems likely that she anticipates another poetic protestation of the Duke's love. It's an expectation that's quickly challenged, for while Viola starts with her prepared speech – 'Most radiant, exquisite and unmatchable beauty' – she swiftly breaks off, gently mocking the conventions of wooing. Viola wants to know who Olivia is and where she is: 'I would be loath to cast away my speech; for besides that it is excellently well penn'd, I have taken great pains to con it.' With that swipe, she clears away all the tired artifice that Olivia expects from Orsino, and at the same time she disarms any potential for being mocked: 'Let me sustain no scorn'. Perhaps only a woman could understand how effective a weapon that 'sinister usage' can be in the hands of other women.

This unpredictable start leads Olivia to show her first real interest in Viola – for if Viola is out of her part so is Olivia when she asks, 'Whence came you, Sir?' It's not just that she's interested in someone else; there is a practical consideration. This youth is different. Is he foreign and unable to understand the conventions of Illyria? Viola blocks this question brilliantly: it's not part of her script. Then she pursues for the third time her quest to discover who is the real Olivia.

Olivia responds with another question about Viola's identity – both have joined a game of 'who are you?' Olivia is sufficiently composed to wonder whether the youth is a comedian, someone who makes light of events or is possibly even mad. Viola immediately establishes her 'profound heart' – her seriousness – but then confounds even more by saying she is not what she plays. Literally, of course, she's not a man, but the meaning is obscure for Olivia, though the conundrum is given metaphorical bite 'by the very fangs of malice', a warning image that shows Olivia she has teeth, and sharp ones.

For the fourth time Viola asks 'Are you the lady of the house?' Olivia cannot answer directly but uses another violent image in conceding: 'If I do not usurp myself, I am.' Viola picks up on the phrase and for the first time in the scene talks to Olivia knowingly about the way she perceives her in the world. To usurp is to take another's place by force. Viola has taken a risk with this paradoxical observation, and pulls back – 'But this is from my commission. I will on with my speech in your praise, and then show you the heart of my message.' However, Olivia doesn't want praise, she wants what is important. Viola insists: she's learnt the speech and ''tis poetical'.

Olivia is now fully engaged. She is growing impatient and perhaps even annoyed. Viola is beginning to get to her – which is sometimes an overture to love. She reprimands him for his sauciness and rudeness at her gate. If he's not mad, he's out of order. Olivia is in no mood for 'so skipping a dialogue'.

Here Maria steps in to get rid of Viola. We have already seen earlier in the play how efficiently witty Maria can be, but Viola trumps her when she asks 'Will you hoist sail, Sir? Here lies your way', calling her a 'swabber' – a sailor who cleans up – and using 'hull' for 'to stay'. She is playing close to the bone, but remember that Viola has recently been shipwrecked at sea. Olivia intervenes and utters her most direct request: 'Tell me your mind'. Viola's resistance has made her stop playing games, and she is answered equally directly with a no-nonsense 'I am a messenger'.

Now Olivia's language changes tone: 'hideous matter' and 'fearful' show her deeper, darker self is engaged. 'Speak your office' is her first clear acceptance that she will have to hear the whole of Orsino's wooing. Viola must sense that a battle has been won, as she asks to be left alone with Olivia and then reassures her that there is nothing alarming in her words.

Olivia begins to spar. This youth has been rude but she is interested enough to ask two questions of him. Viola doesn't answer but justifies her rudeness by the way she has been treated at the household. She asks again to be left alone with Olivia. Daringly, she uses the word 'maidenhead' and then lifts the discourse into the realm of 'divinity'. Surprisingly, Olivia agrees to entertain 'divinity': she is already linked to Viola.

Alone with Olivia, Viola starts her speech and is rapidly interrupted. Olivia isn't as interested in the words as in the heart of the text. Viola brings Orsino's heart into the play and again they spar with Viola picking up the 'method' Olivia uses. Olivia uses the word 'heresy' to debase Orsino's love, but she is still matching the language of divinity. Perhaps she already wants to hear from the youth's heart, not his master's. She demands, 'Have you no more to say?'

At this Viola asks her to remove her veil. As a woman, she must be longing to see her rival's face. Olivia gives in, with a mild irony: 'Is't not well done?' The outrageous wit of Viola's response must be unexpected – 'Excellently done, if God did all.'

Very few men would ask a beautiful woman if she has made herself up. Olivia comes back – she is now engaging, almost flirting, enjoying herself. It's probably the most fun she's had since the death of her brother: ''Tis in grain, sir; 'twill endure wind and weather.' It is at this moment that Viola moves into verse and speaks so directly. Her next four lines flow regularly and with great ease and freedom. Yet within this ease, she opens up two complex ideas. The first that beauty is cunning, and the second is of Olivia's cruelty if she doesn't procreate – she will die and take her beauty to the grave. Remember that the grave is an immediate image for them both.

Viola leaves space for Olivia to finish her verse line – 'And leave the world no copy' – but Olivia is not yet ready to take herself seriously. She stays in prose and continues a game. She will make a highly ironic catalogue of her charms. Only after starting this belittling list does she ask 'Were you sent hither to praise me?' Perhaps she is waiting for praise from Viola. She doesn't get it.

Instead, Viola stays in verse and calls her proud. Again, the ease of the rhythm hides this tough observation. However, the verse trips and breaks in the third line, 'My Lord and master loves you – O such love'. This irregularity falls after 'loves you' – she stumbles as the words compress the pain of her own love for Orsino with his for Olivia. She has to recover herself in the next line: great love should be recompensed even if its object is the most unparalleled beauty in the world.

Viola is still stinging Olivia; it is not enough merely to be beautiful. Again she leaves a line that could be picked up by Olivia – it is as though she is asking her to heighten her responses to Orsino, to raise herself. Olivia resists and asks, still in prose, 'How does he love me?' Viola then, aptly, produces an incomplete line of eight syllables, for she is again facing Orsino's passion for Olivia. She recovers a regular form in the next line – recovering her composure.

Suddenly Olivia moves into verse. Although her thoughts all start at the beginnings of lines, only two are regular – she is struggling to find form. Maybe she hasn't felt the need to speak verse for some time. Nonetheless, her thoughts are well argued. She cannot love him, although she can list his virtues without the irony with which she listed her beauty earlier. Still, she repeats, 'I cannot love him', and concludes, weary of his pressure, 'He might have took his answer long ago.'

Viola – who knows the power of love – cannot be stilled by such a denial. Her next speech moves swiftly on with only a stumble on 'suff'ring', again a reminder of her own. This surge of energy compels Olivia for the first time to finish Viola's half-line, with 'Why, what would you?' Notice how these four words struggle to contain the line. With the three *w*'s and the open vowels in 'why' and 'you' you begin to sense the opening of Olivia's heart. The *t* on 'what' and *d* on 'would' are needed to hold it in. Viola responds with a rush of energy: a free, flowing eight-and-a-half line thought, full of open, long, yearning vowels.

Just try speaking the vowels in this speech and your heart will ache. Remember, Viola has had no one to talk to about love. It's an appalling deprivation when you are in love, but now she can vent all her passion and it is this strength of feeling that excites Olivia. Her immediate response – 'You might do much' – not only finishes the line but admits how effective Viola's words have been, how touching her emotions.

Then, as if from nowhere, a practical question: 'What is your parentage?' Olivia seems already to be vetting Viola's class and status – the first stage of marital preparation. Viola responds with a three-stage answer, a puzzle that enhances her mystery. Olivia again jumps in to finish her line, but this time with a very final dismissal for Orsino: 'Get you to your Lord. / I cannot love him; let him send no more.' But immediately she has to engineer an opportunity to see Viola again: 'Unless perchance you come to me again / To tell me how he takes it. Fare you well.' The abrupt goodbye is the first mid-line break Olivia has had so far in the play, and a sign of her difficulty now.

Although she has bid Viola farewell in words, she cannot leave it there and offers her money. Viola's response is immediate with a strong, even and relentless rhythm. Rejecting the money, she asks love to infect Olivia so that she may know the pain of it unrequited, and departs on the bravura of a rhyming couplet.

As so often in Shakespeare, what is spoken comes to pass – Olivia is falling in love but it is with a woman and doomed to be unrequited. In her soliloquy, she opens by reviewing her all-important question to Viola and the answer she received. The rest of the speech is rhythmically irregular except for the last two-and-a-half lines. All her original thoughts start mid-line. She uses the familiar 'thou' instead of the more formal 'you', and then lists his physical graces. The order is interesting: tongue, words, face, limbs, actions and spirits. They imply a 'blazon' – a gentleman's coat of arms. He seems a multiple of virtue. At this point, she brakes herself with 'Not too fast! Soft, soft!' but the attempt to contain her passion escapes through a twelve-syllable line, the energy of which throws her into the next line: 'Unless the master were the man'. Here is the first admission that she might marry him. Immediately, and within the same line, she has to acknowledge what she has felt – 'How now!' and then raise the question, 'Even so quickly may one catch the plague?'

The next two and a half lines describe how Viola's perfections have seized her: 'invisible', 'stealth' and 'creep' mark an insidious, unstoppable invasion, like a disease. The direct and practical conclusion – 'Well, let it be' – signals her acceptance, and at once she begins to plot by calling her steward: 'What ho, Malvolio!' There is something light hearted and yet determined in the internal rhyme 'ho' and 'Malvolio'.This is a woman on a mission and the open vowels carry her happily forward.

The Imaginative

Begin by owning every image and you will quickly discover a striking quality in the language. This is a love scene and yet it is filled with images of death, cruelty and disease. It is about different levels of passion, of seeing and not seeing, of veils and disguises. Both girls have recently been acquainted with death and it is partly Viola's understanding of that darkness that Olivia loves. Examine the text for the opposites of light and dark, and speak only those words that refer to them. As with all these exercises, you will reveal more texture each time you do it and sometimes the words will encompass both sides. Here are some of the swings of each character experiences.

Viola: Honourable, radiant, exquisite, beauty, pray, loath, excellently, pains, beauties, scorn, sinister, good, gentle, modest assurance, heart, fangs of malice, usurp, praise, heart, pains, poetical, mollification, war, taxation, homage, peace, rudeness, divinity, profanation, sweet, heart, good, excellently, beauty, sweet, cursing, cruellest, graces, grave, proud, devil, fair, loves, love, crown'd, beauty, adorations, tears, groans, thunder, love, fire, love, suff'ring, deadly life, denial, no sense, soul, loyal, love, dead, pity, fortunes, state is well, love, heart of flint, love, fervour, cruelty.

Olivia: comedian, usurp, forgive, praise, feigned, saucy, mad, reason, hideous, courtesy, fearful, rudely, divinity, heresy, commission, negotiate, endure, hard-hearted, beauty, praise, love, cannot love, virtuous, noble, great estate, fresh, stainless, free, learn'd, valiant, gracious, cannot love, cannot love, pains, give, plague, perfections, subtle stealth.

You will find more, but what these reveal is Viola's energy and freshness in language – she is alive. Olivia's speech is more controlled, until the flame of love starts to burn and sear off the reasonable words. Notice too that the images Viola introduces later in the scene – flames, air, earth, tears and babbling – suggest nature, creation and expansiveness. Nature moves through Viola, while Olivia's life and language deny it. She prefers lists which can control and order feelings. Her extraordinary image for falling in love is of catching the plague. The two women experience the world very differently, and Shakespeare characterises them precisely through their language.

Circles

I would try an intense Second Circle run of the scene. This should reveal the places where one of them is less focused in Second than the other. Viola probably starts in a strong Second but moves away later. Olivia is likely to be the reverse – less involved at the beginning of the scene, but becoming intensely focused by the end.

❀

Shakespeare is full of beautiful poetry but that can create its own problems. Sometimes we hear the lyricism rather than what it serves – the language hides what is going on rather than reveals it. We will look next at two speeches that can easily create the 'beauty trap'! You should do all the exercises on each text, but the focus here will be on work that helps roots poetry in action. This is not to deny the beauty but to make it real and active, and to discover why it's there.

A Midsummer Night's Dream
Act II Scene i

The Context

Two supremely powerful supernatural beings – Oberon and Titania, king and queen of the fairies – are arguing. Their quarrel is creating climatic changes on the planet, flooding and shifting seasons. The argument centres on a little boy Titania is rearing for her much-loved but now deceased mortal servant. Oberon wants the boy. He is jealous. Titania won't part with him and Oberon cannot get his way.

We have just witnessed the passion of their row in a scene at night in the woods outside Athens where Titania offers three times to make peace – but not to hand over the boy. She leaves, and Oberon is left alone with Puck.

It is important to note that while Puck is a follower of Oberon, he's not always reliable – he gets waylaid. Puck is never fully in anyone's control and he gets things wrong.

Heightened Circumstances

A being of supremely powerful force cannot get his way: that is the heightened circumstance. Part of the frustration is that Oberon has locked horns with his equally powerful wife. We will see that he can only triumph by devious means, not by straightforward confrontation. Oberon also has a pressing need of Puck. He needs him to bring the exact herb – the main body of the speech is a very precise description of it and where it is so that Puck can get it right.

The Human

Oberon is not human. Being the supernatural power that he is, he can see mermaids, Cupid and leviathans (sea monsters) but he does have human emotions that we all understand. He feels injured and seeks revenge.

The Speech

> *Oberon*: Well, go thy way; thou shalt not from this grove
> Till I torment thee for this injury.
> My gentle Puck, come hither. Thou rememb'rest
> Since once I sat upon a promontory,
> And heard a mermaid on a dolphin's back
> Uttering such dulcet and harmonious breath
> That the rude sea grew civil at her song,
> And certain stars shot madly from their spheres
> To hear the sea-maid's music.
> *Puck*:   I remember.
> *Oberon*: That very time I saw, but thou couldst not,
> Flying between the cold moon and the earth
> Cupid, all arm'd; a certain aim he took
> At a fair vestal, throned by the west,
> And loos'd his love-shaft smartly from his bow,
> As it should pierce a hundred thousand hearts;
> But I might see young Cupid's fiery shaft
> Quench'd in the chaste beams of the wat'ry moon;
> And the imperial votaress passed on,
> In maiden meditation, fancy-free.
> Yet mark'd I where the bolt of Cupid fell.
> It fell upon a little western flower,
> Before milk-white, now purple with love's wound,
> And maidens call it Love-in-idleness.
> Fetch me that flow'r, the herb I showed thee once.
> The juice of it on sleeping eyelids laid
> Will make or man or woman madly dote
> Upon the next live creature that it sees.
> Fetch me this herb, and be thou here again
> Ere the leviathan can swim a league.
> *Puck*: I'll put a girdle round about the earth
> In forty minutes. [*Exit Puck.*]

The Givens

I suggest you examine the givens in this speech only after you have anchored its magic in reality and geography – in the reality of Oberon's world.

Take your time: dwell on every concrete reference you can find and believe everything. In beautiful speeches and speaking the audience may be enchanted but they must also believe – because you believe. With 'thy way', for instance – 'thy' is Titania and 'way' is an actual woodland path as well as her will; equally 'this grove' is a specific cluster of trees. You have to imagine the reality of each detail.

Oberon's desire to torment Titania is real, as is his injury. He did once sit on a promontory or peninsula. A mermaid rode on a dolphin's back, singing so beautifully that the rough sea was tamed and stars shot from their positions in the sky to hear her music. These things happened – they're not just poetic words – and Oberon was with Puck at the time and is determined by the exact nature of his description to jolt Puck's memory. Puck does remember, so Oberon can continue.

Oberon saw, though Puck couldn't at that time, Cupid, heavily armed, flying between the moon and the earth. Cupid took a specific aim and shot his arrow with tremendous force – a force that would enter a hundred thousand hearts. Oberon saw the fire in the arrow's shaft quenched by the moon's beams, and its target – a virgin votaress – passing on, unaware and unwounded. He saw where this arrow landed on a little white flower, which turned purple from the wound and is now called 'Love-in-idleness'. That's the flower Oberon wants and he has shown it to Puck before. Its juice laid on a sleeper's eyelids will make the sleeper fall in love with the next creature he or she sees on waking.

To paraphrase the speech like this of course makes it seem mundane, and loses the richness of the verse and its poetry. However, what becomes clear is how practical and specific it is. Oberon wants the herb so desperately to revenge his injury that he gives Puck clear instructions on how to find it and tells him what it can do.

Go back and speak the speech with all those details and realities embedded in your imagination. On the first reading, it is possible that the verse will feel shattered and the thoughts disconnected from one another. Now beat the lines out: feel the iambic, but don't lose the geography of the text or Oberon's need for revenge and the flower. What should be apparent is the gorgeous melody of the verse matching, initially, the 'harmonious breath' of the mermaid. It's a melody continues broken only by 'Cupid, all arm'd', 'Yet mark'd I', 'Fetch me that flow'r', and 'Fetch me this herb'.

Oberon is very seductive with the iambic. He can lull us with rhythm but now underneath the surface the beauty of his speech, you should be anchored in the underbelly of his desires. He is an attractive, but dangerous man. To understand the danger, the cosmetic charm of his verse must marry with the specificity of his world.

The same charming deceit is contained within the structure of his thoughts. He leads us down a beautiful winding pathway whose gentle turns conceal his darker intent. Consider the next section of the scene, after Puck has gone:

> *Oberon:*   Having once this juice,
> I'll watch Titania when she is asleep,
> And drop the liquor of it in her eyes;
> The next thing then she waking looks upon,
> Be it on lion, bear, or wolf, or bull,
> On meddling monkey, or on busy ape,
> She shall pursue it with the soul of love.
> And ere I take this charm from off her sight,
> As I can take it with another herb,
> I'll make her render up her page to me.

There are two thoughts here. Beat the lines and allow yourself to be wooed by the flow and charm of the rhythm. Take each of the thoughts and sustain the energy through them but observe how, within the physical harmony of each, the sense wends itself around the horror of his plot. It slips like honey out of his mouth and it's only when you analyse the givens and anchor in the realities of the text that you realise, with the appropriate shock, how vile his plan really is. He is scheming for his wife to fall in love with a lion, wolf, bull, monkey or ape, and to keep her in this state until he gets his way and has possession of the boy. Shakespeare knows what he is doing – beautiful speakers can be dangerous. Their words and rhythms can beguile us and hide their true intentions.

To serve this text you must be prepared to sound beautiful and at the same time stay specific. Through basic work on the givens and the imaginative, you will discover not only how to do this but why the character needs to access beautiful language – there is always a dramatic purpose involved.

Antony and Cleopatra Act II Scene ii

The Context

The mighty Roman Antony has been seduced by Cleopatra and, to the fury of Caesar, been kept by her in Egypt, away from his duties – Rome, power and politics.

> *Caesar:*   he fishes, drinks and wastes
> The lamps of night in revel.
>
>   (I.iv)

Sex, idleness and langour has occupied Antony and kept him from Rome and duties. He is only roused to leave her by news of the death of his wife Fulvia and of impending civil war at home. Enobarbus, Antony's loyal follower, returns to Rome with him and witnesses his first scene with Caesar. In this Caesar tackles Antony for his absence and for failing in his oath to bear arms for Caesar. The altercation is solved when Antony agrees to marry Caesar's sister, Octavia. These negotiations are conducted in terse and rugged verse.

At the end, Antony, Caesar and his followers depart, leaving Enobarbus with two of Caesar's followers, Agrippa and Maecenas. The scene relaxes into prose as the men question Enobarbus about his time in Egypt. They talk at first of drink and food, and then of women and at last of the woman who has so engaged the great Antony. Both men have heard reports of Cleopatra – she was probably the most discussed woman in Rome – including stories about how she won Antony.

It is at this point that Enobarbus puts them straight. In doing so, he moves into the most poetic verse.

Heightened Circumstances

All three men have just witnessed a politically dangerous confrontation between two of the most powerful men on earth – a bad outcome would affect them all. The argument has been resolved by the agreement that Antony will marry. All present know of his passionate attachment to Cleopatra, so the relief of the resolution is reflected in the prose and the content of the discussion – wine, food and women.

It is Enobarbus who heightens the scene by going into verse. Notice how the line 'I will tell you' breaks, creating a pause to get their full attention before he embarks on the true version of events. In moving to a heightened form, he also heightens Cleopatra – she is not a woman to be discussed in prose. This could be a way of defending Antony, for the verse clearly signals that he was not kept from Rome and political obligations by any ordinary woman. Bear in mind that Antony has just agreed to marry Octavia, described just previously as one

> whose beauty claims
> No worse a husband than the best of men;
> Whose virtue and whose general graces speak
> That which none else can utter.

(II.ii)

Enobarbus has heard that description and by comparison his account of Cleopatra renders Octavia a dry morsel for Antony. Perhaps he is simply motivated by his loyalty and liking for Cleopatra. After all, he knows her well.

The Human

Egypt was an exotic and erotic place for the Romans and Cleopatra was its jewel. It is absolutely human for Agrippa and Maecenas to want to hear what it is like from someone who has been there. It is equally natural for Enobarbus to deliver with relish his first-hand experience of a rare vision. People often describe encounters with celebrities in a similar manner. They may not do it in verse, but they access heightened language to serve the occasion.

The Speech

Enobarbus: I will tell you.
The barge she sat in, like a burnish'd throne,
Burn'd on the water. The poop was beaten gold;
Purple the sails, and so perfumed that
The winds were love-sick with them; the oars were silver,
Which to the tune of flutes kept stroke, and made
The water which they beat to follow faster,
As amorous of their strokes. For her own person,
It beggar'd all description. She did lie
In her pavilion, cloth-of-gold, of tissue,
O'erpicturing that Venus where we see
The fancy out-work nature. On each side of her
Stood pretty dimpled boys, like smiling Cupids,
With divers-colour'd fans, whose wind did seem
To glow the delicate cheeks which they did cool,
And what they undid did.
Agrippa: O, rare for Antony!
Enobarbus: Her gentlewomen, like the Nereides,
So many mermaids, tended her i' the eyes,
And made their bends adornings. At the helm
A seeming mermaid steers. The silken tackle
Swell with the touches of those flower-soft hands
That yarely frame the office. From the barge
A strange invisible perfume hits the sense
Of the adjacent wharfs. The city cast
Her people out upon her; and Antony,
Enthroned i' the market-place, did sit alone,
Whistling to th' air; which, but for vacancy,
Had gone to gaze on Cleopatra too,
And made a gap in nature.

The Givens

It is appropriate that this speech should sound beautiful but it must also be real and specific. There might be an element in Enobarbus which wants to tease or provoke his fellow Romans – he's seen something they couldn't begin to approach – but let's begin by serving the text clearly, believing what he says and seeing it as you speak it.

The first difference between this and Oberon's speech is that the vast majority of thoughts here start mid-line. Use this hesitancy to give texture to its fluent beauty by picking up the energy of each mid-line with vigour. The structure also suggests that this is not a well-practised piece of poetry, but sincere, in the moment – a genuine attempt to witness the wonder of Cleopatra and of Antony's beguilement.

Notice how luxurious and languishing the rhythm feels – this iambic is almost hypnotic in the same way that Cleopatra drove sense out of men. The effect is partly achieved by long and open vowel sounds. Take time just to speak the vowels and feel how they create a sound pattern of open gasps and exclamations.

The soldier Enobarbus was entranced and wants to do full justice to the beauty and extravagance of Cleopatra in his language and delivery. Equally important, however, are the tangible and concrete details of his description. To anchor yourself in these, trace and trust the sequence of the speech. The order will harness your journey and help you look where he looks.

He starts with her entrance and his first view of her on her barge, which has turned into her throne. The full wonder is first conveyed by the perception that it burns on water. The next thought returns to solid realities although they are more exotic – a golden poop and perfumed purple sails. At this point, however, Enobarbus shifts from real things to the fancy of the wind being lovesick with the sails. Indeed, throughout the speech, he avails himself of precise descriptions only to be blown, within a thought, into the realms of the extraordinary. This displacement is the constant effect Cleopatra has on everyone who encounters her. It is the same in the next thought, which moves from the silver oars, keeping stroke to flutes and beating the water to follow faster, to the water becoming people who follow the stroking oars in love.

Next Enobarbus' eye moves onto Cleopatra – but she cannot be described. What an effective stroke this is: that a man with such poetic language at his disposal is unable to give us the specific details of her face and body. This is more exciting than frustrating – she is indescribably beautiful, and her quality can only be represented through her impact on her surroundings.

Accordingly, the eye now goes around her, to where she lies in her pavilion made of a gold-threaded fabric. To entice and tease us more, we are told she surpasses the paintings of Venus – and we know those paintings lie because they are works of the imagination grappling to record a mythical reality. Again, he has moved into realms outside everyday experience.

Back he comes – the pretty dimpled boys standing on each side of her. They are like smiling cupids with their multi-coloured fans fanning Cleopatra but in a paradox worthy of this extraordinary woman, the cooling fans made her cheeks glow – in other words, made heat, undoing what they did.

At this point, Agrippa interrupts, finishing Enobarbus' line in what may be a sign of spontaneous excitement: 'O, rare for Antony'. Enobarbus is not waylaid. He picks up the descriptions where his eye and memory had left it, returning to the gentlewomen around Cleopatra, who themselves seem transformed into sea-nymphs and mermaids. Next he looks at the helm, here steered by 'a seeming mermaid'. The lines between reality and perception are growing very blurred. The tackle is silken and even the helmsman's hands are flower-soft.

Now he moves away from the barge to the air around it, which is invisibly perfumed – but of course all perfume is invisible. We realise that it must have been so tangibly present that Enobarbus can't believe he didn't see it as it hit the wharfs. The lens of Enobarbus' eyes widens to take in the city and its people, which are cast as though in a net around her. All are drawn, almost without choice, to her as to a magnet. Antony, however – Enobarbus' first mention of him – is enthroned alone in the market place. Her throne is a burning barge, his a market place. Here Antony whistles to the air, and if nature didn't abhor a vacuum that air itself would have gone to gaze on Cleopatra too.

Use the progression of thoughts to lead you through the richness of this text. Root yourself in details before you let the shifts into other realms take you to the extremes of description. Anchor in the thoughts while allowing the rhythm to sustain the hypnotic wonder of Cleopatra's entrance, and the sheer lyrical beauty of the text will not run away with you.

Coriolanus Act I Scene iv

The Context

Caius Martius (later Coriolanus) is a proud, strong man, disdainful of weaker beings. At the beginning of the play, some of the citizens of Rome are plotting to get rid of him as they fear him being elected tribune. They know he disapproves of their demands for corn and their reluctance to do military service. The fact that Rome needs his power and bravery is illustrated by the news that the Volscians have raised an army. Caius Martius is the only soldier who can possibly take on this enemy: the Romans' constant dilemma is that they need his military skill but dread his domestic policies and presence. He leads an army to the city of Corioli, and this speech takes place after the first attack on the Volscians when the Roman soldiers have run back to their trenches.

Heightened Circumstances

Any reaction is bound to be heightened in the midst of a battle. The stage instruction here is often for Caius Martius to enter cursing. This fearless soldier has just watched his army flee and is full of contempt for them. He has no liking or respect for these men, unlike the morale-boosting of Henry V's: 'Once more unto the breach, dear friends'. There are no dear friends here, just cowards and deserters to be cursed and threatened.

The Human

Anyone willing to stand their ground or fight for anything is likely to be disgusted by those who run away. Deep down most of us would love to behave like Caius Martius and let rip, but are hindered by a feeling of our own powerlessness. Arrogance and disdain for others are curiously liberating. If you don't care what people think of you, you can do and say what ever comes into your head.

Barely in Control: The Pushing Trap

There are some speeches that push you right to the edge of delivery. They are always highly charged and deal with the venting of extreme passions – rage, loss and grief. Such speeches are dangerous for actors because, without the right focus and control, they can end up shouting or pushing incoherently, straining and at worse damaging their voices and certainly alienating the audience. Shouting may be a valid acting choice, but please make sure it is just that and not a one-way street with no opportunity for a U-turn.

All highly charged moments have a highly charged energy structure that can create – if the actor isn't vocally free enough, or sufficiently connected to the language – a 'pushing trap'. We will look at three speeches that fall into this category, and see how to use the physical givens in the text to hold you in these desperate moments and stay passionate but clear and free.

The first point to make is that in very heightened moments, you don't have to work on your emotions but you have to survive. The characters aren't trying to feel – in fact they are feeling so much that they are trying to focus emotion into words in order to channel the feeling and move through it. So whatever you do, don't pump yourself into a frenzy of trying to feel: you could do yourself – and others – damage. In Shakespeare, the words reveal the exact quality of an emotion. Trust that as you start to work.

As always in your work, but especially in this situation, you must stay free in your body and voice and have a strong and consistent sense of support.

The Speech

> *Caius Martius*: All the contagion of the south light on you,
> You shames of Rome! You herd of – Boils and plagues
> Plaster you o'er, that you may be abhorr'd
> Farther than seen, and one infect another
> Against the wind a mile! You souls of geese

That bear the shapes of men, how have you run
From slaves that apes would beat! Pluto and hell!
All hurt behind! Backs red, and faces pale
With flight and agued fear! Mend and charge home,
Or, by the fires of heaven, I'll leave the foe
And make my wars on you. Look to't. Come on;
If you'll stand fast we'll beat them to their wives,
As they us to our trenches. Follow me.

The Givens

One of the symptoms of high temper is that you change direction very quickly and don't censor your feelings or words. There is also a perverse pleasure in venting anger and spleen.

Speak the speech with a fully supported voice. You will feel the adrenalin of battle surge through you and the text. That surge must be there but it may well have led you to a near shout, flattening out the specifics and the journey of the speech. The task in hand is to keep the surge in your support, but to focus on the text so it lands specifically on our ears.

Although you should use all the exercises to release any speech, three in particular will help focus this one. Shakespeare has written a broken and very physically fractured text to help you keep control and avoid shouting through it.

Mouth the text with support but no voice. You will find that there is a host of strong consonants holding you in check – *t*'s, *d*'s, *p*'s, *b*'s: he is spitting. Even better, you will feel the relish in the words. He's having fun in his mouth, which is a reflection of the pleasure you get telling someone exactly what you feel.

The mouthing also reveals the rhythmic pattern. Eight out of thirteen lines are severely shattered. This internal physical struggle will give you strong anchors to rein in the adrenaline surge.

'Crunchy' moments are followed by a sweep of rhythm. It's as though he struggles to find words, and through the struggle grows fluent and lucid. This is not simply one very long shout:

                    You herd of – Boils and plagues
Plaster you o'er, that you may be abhorr'd
Farther than seen, and one infect another
Against the wind a mile!

Walk the journey of the speech, aiming to find as many changes of direction as you can. By the end, you should feel thrown about and physically disordered. It's this disorder, embedded in the text, that you must obey. At some points he is lost for words and curses – 'Pluto and hell!' – but the main reason for the chaos in the structure is his struggle to express his horror at his fellow Romans' cowardice. It is not a free-fall outpouring.

Lastly, look at the sequence of thoughts. Some of them are very complex and express vivid ideas, rather than mindless rage. He starts by asking that 'All the contagions of the south light on you, / You shames of Rome!' conjuring disease from the unwholesome warm, southern mists that bring plague. He continues with a splutter 'You herd of –' but then gets into his stride with the elaborate and even gleeful wish that boils and plagues should so plaster the men that they will be abhorred even before they are seen – presumably because of the stench of their disease (Caius Martius has a pre-occupation with the smell of the lower orders, a wonderful character note) – and infect others from a distance.

While there is a clumsiness in the structure of this thought, it only underlines the extent of his struggle to be coherent in his state of passion. Then the argument develops: they have the souls of geese although they look like men, and they run away from slaves – the Volsces – that even apes could have beaten. This contemptuous reduction of the men to animals – herd, geese, apes – is characteristic of Caius Martius throughout the play, but after the curse 'Pluto and hell', there is a change of temperature in his thoughts and language. 'All hurt behind' is mocking but with a pinch of humour: if you are running away, your back is vulnerable, and there is also something ridiculous about having a red back and a shivering (agued) white face. Then for the first time in the speech he actually says what he wants them to do: 'Mend and charge home'. He wants them to make up for their retreat by charging back at the enemy. Only now does he threaten them physically and personally. After 'come on' he is almost encouraging – he ends on the least violent thought: 'If you'll stand fast we'll beat them to their wives, / As they us to our trenches. Follow me.'

The speech is explosive, but it has all the ingredients of word, rhythm and sense to hold you and control the rush of energy and passion. As you have heard me say time and time again, I believe that Shakespeare is tapping into human truths in his use of form. Caius Martius is furious, but still needs to make sense and pursue his need through his words. So Shakespeare never allows you to flounder, unless the character is doing so: he always holds the actor in the safety of his writing craft.

Cymbeline Act II Scene v

The Context

Posthumus has married Imogen, the daughter of Cymbeline, King of Britain. The marriage has not been consummated as the King doesn't approve of the match. Posthumus has gone to Italy. In Italy he meets Iachimo and is provoked by him to place a wager on Imogen's chastity. Iachimo reckons he can seduce her, Posthumus bets that he can't. Iachimo deceives Posthumus into believing he has lost. In fact, he's hidden in a chest which is placed in her room. Here, when she is asleep, he observes the detail of the bedroom and the marks on her sleeping body, and removes a bracelet from her arm. With this evidence, he convinces Posthumus of his success. Posthumus runs off and we meet him in this scene wracked by grief, pain and the desire for revenge.

Heightened Circumstances

Anyone who has faced a partner's infidelity knows how heightened this situation is, particularly if the partner seems so chaste – they are not what they seem. In addition, the distance between Italy and Britain heightens Posthumus' pain as he can't talk to her, which makes him feel even more powerless.

The Human

Another man has slept with your virgin wife! She hasn't slept with you but has immediately succumbed to Iachimo. Shakespeare has placed his finger on a universal male fear of being cuckolded that still gets women stoned around the world. Depressingly but typically, his rage is focused on women rather than on Iachimo.

Equally depressing is the fact that Posthumus has bet on his wife's chastity. Boys talk about their women and by doing that place the worm on the hook for other men to nibble at. The passion Posthumus feels sends him mad but in moments like this – and many of us can identify with it – such madness can seem the height of sanity.

Rationally speaking, it is mad to believe that all men are bastards because all women are unfaithful to their husbands but Posthumus feels it so deeply that for him it is real. Throughout the speech he believes he is seeing the realities of the world clearly for the first time. This conviction in his sanity is what makes him dangerous and unearths in him a dedication to hate all women.

It is also human to want to know the details of infidelity. It's not enough to know that someone is unfaithful, we need to know the details and it is these that both humanise and heighten the pain; the nature of the kissing, where it happened. In effect, Posthumus places a hand in an open wound and moves it around – he can't leave the gaping gash alone.

The Speech

Posthumus: Is there no way for men to be, but women
Must be half-workers? We are all bastards,
And that most venerable man which I
Did call my father was I know not where
When I was stamp'd. Some coiner with his tools
Made me a counterfeit; yet my mother seem'd
The Dian of that time. So doth my wife
The nonpareil of this. O, vengeance, vengeance!
Me of my lawful pleasure she restrain'd.
And pray'd me oft forbearance; did it with
A pudency so rosy, the sweet view on't
Might well have warm'd old Saturn; that I thought her
As chaste as unsunn'd snow. O, all the devils!
This yellow Iachimo in an hour – was't not?
Or less! – at first? Perchance he spoke not, but,
Like a full-acorn'd boar, a German one,
Cried 'O!' and mounted; found no opposition
But what he look'd for should oppose and she
Should from encounter guard. Could I find out
The woman's part in me! For there's no motion
That tends to vice in man but I affirm
It is the woman's part. Be it lying, note it,

The woman's; flattering, hers; deceiving, hers;
Lust and rank thoughts, hers, hers; revenges, hers;
Ambitions, covetings, change of prides, disdain,
Nice longing, slanders, mutability,
All faults that man may name, nay, that hell knows,
Why, hers, in part or all; but rather all;
For even to vice
They are not constant, but are changing still
One vice but of a minute old for one
Not half so old as that. I'll write against them,
Detest them, curse them. Yet 'tis greater skill
In a true hate to pray they have their will:
The very devils cannot plague them better.

The Givens

This speech – one whole scene of the play – is not one long rant, although it is violent and passionate. The balancing act is to keep the passion and use the structure, thought and the exact detail of his discoveries to focus and contain its tremendous emotion.

Mouth the text on full support but no voice. Immediately you will feel how the physical quality of the consonants helps you to hold the text in check. They control the breath you need to motor your way forward.

The rhythm of the lines is broken but there are fewer fractured lines than in *Coriolanus*. In fact, some lines are so powerfully driven by the rhythm that they become frightening. This could be the reflection of the ease with which Posthumus vilifies women. He blames them entirely rather than question himself. By the time he reaches the list of their vices, he is in full steam – uncensored prejudice has always been easy!

However, there are rhythmic blockages when he comes up against his unspeakable new understanding – a lid is slammed on top of the text: 'O vengeance, vengeance'; 'O all the devils!' And the motor splutters around – 'was't not? Or less! – at first?' before gathering steam again. There is also an unfinished line that creates a gaping hole – 'For even to vice, they are not constant' – and a rhyming couplet that should, in regular verse writing, end his journey, but it doesn't:

> Yet 'tis greater skill
> In a true hate to pray they have their will:
> The very devils cannot plague them better.

In this the speech seems to fizzle out unceremoniously. Here is an important acting clue. If you speak the whole text fully you will feel physically drained at the end. It is like a child who has a tantrum or a crying fit: they tire themselves out and end whimpering. In some ways, this is what happens to Posthumus. He works his pain out and is eased by the act of speaking and releasing.

This will be keenly felt if you walk the journey of the speech. Sharp turns are followed by extended and fast movements; you might be moved to run. Blood is pumping very quickly through this young man's body and at points you could become breathless, which is an accurate reality of what Posthumus is going through emotionally.

Notice too how just when you think you might topple physically out of control, Shakespeare breaks a line, stops you in your tracks and whisks you off in a new direction.

Sequence of Thoughts

Shakespeare is being courageous in the format of this speech – that's why you too need to have courage to jump in. He breaks rules. We have already seen that it ends unusually, but it also begins with a question which is not specifically answered – 'Is there no way for men to be, but women must be half-workers?' Posthumus doesn't answer, but it is implied as he leaps onto the assertion 'We are all bastards'. No, men can't create themselves without the half help – the womb – of women. Therefore, because women are so untrustworthy, we are all bastards.

This leap of logic is not only bravado writing but aligns with the kind of thinking that infects most of us when we are jealous. It gathers power as Posthumus realises his father wasn't his father. Another man made him, although his mother was held to be the most chaste woman of her time, as his wife is of hers. Posthumus is thinking through his passion very clearly – it might be faulty thinking but it's clear. His supposed father, his actual father, his mother, his wife. That order will hold you.

The arrival of his wife in his mind brings him to an explosion – or perhaps an implosion: 'O vengeance, vengeance'. It's interesting that he doesn't name her, his mother or his father. Only Iachimo is named, although he does transform into a fat, German boar!

The next thought is about how his wife restrained him from his lawful pleasure (sex) with such modesty that she was like unsunn'd snow (perfect, white and unsullied). That memory and the accompanying confusion of being so thoroughly duped leads him to his next outburst: 'O, all the devils!'

But he can't let it go – here he is digging into his pain. Yellow, off-colour, liverish, Iachimo in an hour, or less than an hour, or immediately on entering the room, perhaps not even speaking mounted Imogen like a fat pig, and the only opposition he found and she gave was the thing she should have been protecting – the only protection – her hymen. You can't get more vivid, in your imagination, than that. It's also, from a reasonable point of view, ridiculous to think that Iachimo entered the room, cried 'O' and mounted Imogen.

And yet it's not ridiculous if you are jealous and see the world from Posthumus' point of view. His vision is so out of control that he controls it. Therein lies your acting control, and the fearful fact of jealousy – you believe you're seeing things as they really are, and are in control.

It's perhaps because this vision is so vivid and shocking that Posthumus moves on from Imogen and Iachimo for the rest of the speech. What he sees and knows is so ghastly that he detaches from them, and it is obviously this detachment that enables him to plot her death.

Up to this point Posthumus' eye has moved through a list of people: from men, women, we – all men – being bastards, then on to his mother, the man he called father, his real father and his wife and finally to Iachimo and his wife. Then he wants to find out the half of him that's a woman, because it's the women's part that creates man's vice.

Now he leaves specific individuals behind and deals with man and woman generally. He revels in a detailed list of vices engendered by women and their parts. There's a wonderfully comforting pulse in 'hers, hers'. All faults known to man and hell belong in part or all to women. They can't be constant even to vice, so much do they shift by the minute.

He discovers the thing to do: he'll write against them, detest and curse them. But now he realises that it will be better to let them destroy themselves and pray that they have their will – vice, sex. That will plague them best of all.

Unlike the structure of thoughts in most soliloquies, what is intriguing is that we don't hear from his own mouth what he plans to do with Imogen. That plot is not devised in front of us. This is another indication that he is lost although he thinks he is found. He believes he understands the workings of vice – women. His calculations are clear, and that clarity must be in place to stop the actor wobbling off the text. The wobbles are written in.

The other anchor is the detail in the language. Speak the speech visualising and experiencing everything before you say it.

Through this exercise, you will find how sharply the world Posthumus sees now contrasts with the world he has left through the betrayal of Imogen. The venerable man he thought was his father was absent at his conception – 'his stamping'. Instead a coiner with his tools made him, and made him counterfeit. His mother seemed – she betrayed him too with that one word – a Dian (as chaste as Diana, Goddess of Chastity). His wife's modesty was so rosy that it could have warmed the furthest, coldest planet, Saturn. Again, he's been duped: 'I thought her'. How strong the picture of unsunned snow is. We have already discussed the vivid picture of Iachimo taking Imogen. Notice how clear the list of vices is.

If you see this language as you speak it, its structure will hold you safely.

King John Act III Scene iv

The Context

King John has seized the throne of England. Arthur, Duke of Britaine, is
the young son of Geffrey, John's elder brother, and therefore the legitimate heir to the throne. Arthur is championed by his widowed mother,
Constance. Constance has allied herself with King Philip of France to
seize the throne for her son.

   This scene takes place after the French have lost to the English forces.
Even worse, Arthur has been captured by the English. We are in the
French camp. King Philip, Lewis – the Dauphin – and Cardinal Pandulph
are discussing the rout they have just endured. Constance arrives, entering a male domain where she isn't expected, with her hair undone and
disordered. At first the men try to lead her away, to still her. They definitely feel embarrassed by her emotion but she insists on staying and
expressing her loss and pain. She is like a lioness defending her last cub.

Heightened Circumstances

This is a mother lamenting the loss of a child. She has probably crossed
the battlefield in order to find King Philip. Her distress has led her to
undo her hair and let it down. She will not be silenced, and goes to
extremes to have her loss recognised and witnessed.

The Human

Constance is displaying clear human needs. Arthur is not dead but lost.
There is still hope if she can engage enough sympathy. It is also human
to fear the worst, and this is heightened by not knowing where Arthur

is. At this juncture in her life, she is not afraid of kings or cardinals and challenges them without fear or respect.

I remember television footage of the mothers of sailors who were trapped in a Russian submarine. They were pleading with the government to mount a rescue. One woman begged death to take her instead of her son.

The Speech

King Philip: I prithee, lady, go away with me.
Constance: Lo now! now see the issue of your peace!
King Philip: Patience, good lady! Comfort, gentle Constance!
Constance: No, I defy all counsel, all redress,
But that which ends all counsel, true redress –
Death, death; O amiable lovely death!
Thou odoriferous stench! sound rottenness!
Arise forth from the couch of lasting night,
Thou hate and terror to prosperity,
And I will kiss thy detestable bones,
And put my eyeballs in thy vaulty brows,
And ring these fingers with thy household worms,
And stop this gap of breath with fulsome dust,
And be a carrion monster like thyself.
Come, grin on me, and I will think thou smil'st,
And buss thee as thy wife. Misery's love,
O, come to me!
King Philip: O fair affliction, peace!
Constance: No, no, I will not, having breath to cry.
O that my tongue were in the thunder's mouth!
Then with a passion would I shake the world,
And rouse from sleep that fell anatomy
Which cannot hear a lady's feeble voice,
Which scorns a modern invocation.
Pandulph: Lady, you utter madness and not sorrow.
Constance: Thou art not holy to belie me so.
I am not mad: this hair I tear is mine;
My name is Constance; I was Geffrey's wife;
Young Arthur is my son, and he is lost.
I am not mad – I would to heaven I were!
For then 'tis like I should forget myself.
O, if I could, what grief should I forget!

Preach some philosophy to make me mad,
And thou shalt be canoniz'd, Cardinal;
For, being not mad, but sensible of grief,
My reasonable part produces reason
How I may be deliver'd of these woes,
And teaches me to kill or hang myself.
If I were mad I should forget my son,
Or madly think a babe of clouts were he.
I am not mad; too well, too well I feel
The different plague of each calamity.

The Givens

The first textual note is that, unlike Coriolanus and Posthumus in their passion, Constance does not break the line up. She is riding a verse swell with few stops or hesitations. Beat the rhythm and, apart from some small breaks, the overall effect is of an unstoppable surge: she is venting fearlessly. Initially this evidence could encourage the actor to spew words out and lose control, so we have to find aspects of the text to hold us.

As you explore the speech, you will begin to realise that Constance gains more control as the scene progresses and, in doing so, begins to find some relief. Before this speech she has to above all say what she needs:

> *King Philip*: I prithee, lady, go away with me
> *Constance*: Lo now! now see the issue of your peace!

She doesn't respond here to Philip. Instead she challenges him – a king. 'Lo now! now' work for her in two ways to impose herself on the scene. First, the open vowels keep her passion and pain present; and second, the rhythm of the phrase nests and embeds her in it. She is not going to be pushed out.

Then 'see the issue of your peace' directly blames Philip, not only in meaning but in sound. The *s* alliteration hisses at him. She is both emotional and ready to slash out with sense.

He tries to answer:

> *King Philip*: Patience, good Lady! Comfort, gentle Constance.
> *Constance*: No, I defy all counsel, all redress,

But that which ends all counsel, true redress –
Death, death; O amiable lovely death!

In this exchange Constance does respond to him – she is listening, not lost in herself. 'No' is strong and stops her flow. The repetition of 'redress', 'counsel' and 'death' acts as an emotional pulse and also a firm place on which to rest. Sandwiched between her defiance and her request for death – both emotionally charged lines – is 'But that which ends all counsel, true redress'. There is a control in these first two words, which pivot in your mind but also have the *t*'s holding in the mouth. 'Then odoriferous stench! Sound rottenness' comes next; and although this description of death is vile, it is held by two multi-syllabic words that cannot be rushed and whose safety and harness lie therein.

Next follows a seven-line thought, which addresses death. The extremity of the thought and the fullness of the image are propelled by the repetition of 'And' which starts six out of the seven lines. There is a madness in this but the text does just keep you in control. With 'Arise forth from the couch of lasting might' she stumbles on 'Arise forth' into the thought, and the next two lines have words that hold you through their syllables and rhythm – 'prosperity' and 'detestable'. From 'And put my eyeballs' to the end of the thought she does reach extremes of rhythmical flow and content, but she reins herself in with 'Come, grin on me and I will think thou smil'st / And buss thee as thy wife. Misery's love / O, come to me!' The break on 'Come, grin' and the physical texture of the 'smil'st' both help to slow her down. The next line breaks and she doesn't finish it: Philip does so instead.

If we retrace this speech placing the concrete images firmly in place, we will find another series of anchors. Many actors are so intimidated by the images that they are tempted to skate over them – and yet they are born from her pain and frustration. Perhaps she is reaching for such extremities in order to convince these men of her real distress and to provoke their need for action. She addresses death and asks him to arise from his couch of lasting night – a brilliant image – and calling him the familiar 'thou'. Death might be hated and terrorise prosperity but Constance will kiss those detestable bones, even put her eyeballs in 'thy vaulty brows'. Notice how her living parts are offered for his dead ones – eyeballs, fingers, breath. She offers to 'buss' (kiss) death. Death is the love of those in misery.

This might be extreme but she sees and imagines the detail with horrendous clarity. 'O fair affliction, peace,' says Philip, but on being told by the king to shut up Constance responds with absolutely clear determination to stay at the edge of experience: 'No, no, I will not, having breath to cry.' Elaborating the refutation of peace, she wishes her tongue was in the mouth of thunder to raise those who cannot hear a woman's voice. She is very aware of her position as a woman amongst men.

Now Cardinal Pandulph steps in to silence her: 'Lady, you utter madness and not sorrow.' Quick as a flash she rebukes and challenges him. Remember, she is calling a grand churchman to order. He has said that she is mad: 'Thou art not holy to belie me so.' Her response is not that of someone out of control. She is familiar with him, calling him 'Thou', and suggests it is unworthy of his holy office to deny her pain.

Then the structure and content of the text move into very controlled utterances. She answers him with heightened clarity and sanity.

> I am not mad: this hair I tear is mine;
> My name is Constance; I was Geffrey's wife
> Young Arthur is my son, and he is lost.

She gives herself a test, a list that proves she is not mad. She takes the notion of madness further by saying 'I would to heaven I were!' If she were mad she might forget her grief. She challenges the Cardinal to preach philosophy to make her mad; he would deserve to be canonized for it. In this way, she displays both reason and irony. Her reason, she explains, makes her want to kill herself. With madness she could forget, or be satisfied with a rag doll for a son.

> I am not mad; too well, too well I feel
> The different plague of each calamity.

This 'I am not mad' is the third repetition of the phrase. Constance uses repetition to hold herself in check as well as to print the sanity of her being on those who won't acknowledge her agony.

If you put in place her images, repetition, the sequence of her reasoning and the way she answers Philip and the Cardinal, you will be held. She is heightened but not incoherent or out of control. She creates a chaos in this military tent, but she knows what she is doing and as the scene progresses she gets clearer in the specific description of her grief.

Part 5 Checklists

'And, most dear actors, eat no onions nor garlic, for we are to utter sweet breath.'

(A Midsummer Night's Dream, IV. ii)

'The rest is silence.'

(Hamlet, V.ii)

Checklists

Here are three checklists that you should work through before and during any rehearsal of Shakespeare. Add or subtract exercises according to your own strengths and weaknesses, the demands of your role, the input of the director and the space you will be performing in.

1. Preparing the Body, Breath, Voice and Speech

Body
- Release tensions in shoulders, neck, jaw and face.
- Release and move the spine gently.
- Unlock any holds in the upper chest and lower abdomen.
- Centre the body.
- Enter into the state of readiness.

Breath
- Avoiding any force or pumping in the breath, or tension in the shoulders or upper chest.
- Breathe in calmly without noise.
- Stretch the breath muscles.
- Side stretches and back stretch.
- Release lower breath by pushing a wall.
- Increase capacity on *s* and introduce *z* to develop control.
- Full recoveries: count five to seven on *z*.
- Fast recoveries: low and fast, count one, one-two, one-two-three, up to fifteen.

Warm Up Voice
- Hum: *oo* into *ha*.
- Intone to a point above eyeline. Feel it leave you on *ha* and stop it outside you so that you sustain it.

Warm Up Resonators
- Head, nose, face, throat and chest.

Warm Up Range
- Glide down through the voice on *ha* several times before going back up through the voice.

Warm Up Speech Muscles
- Release jaw, stretch tongue.
- Tongue twisters.

The above can take ten minutes. Take more time if you need to, but remember it's better to do a few minutes every day and not get bored, rather than several hours once a week.

Bridging Exercises

The next exercises can – and should – be used at any time during the work on a text. Return to them after you have done the work on the givens and the imaginative. Each time you do these exercises, you will have a different sensation and perhaps make different discoveries as you enter the text with new and varying levels of knowledge.

They are fundamentally technical voice exercises, but they will frequently release acting clues. I call them bridging exercises because they offer a bridge between the technical and the text and acting work. There are only two rules you must try to obey:

First, keep all the voice work in place. If necessary, be conscious of the body, breath, support and voice work. Second, each time you finish an exercise, go back to speak the text *before* you have time to think.

- Select a verse speech to work on.
- With full support and vocal freedom, intone the whole text. Then speak it.
- Defining every syllable and end of word, mouth the text. No voice, but feel the breath under the word and the energy of the consonants. Then speak it on full voice.
- Keep your throat open and on support and voice just speak the vowels. Now speak the whole text again.
- Build up any line you don't fully understand with the breath, word by word.

The next exercise stretches your full capacity and recovery system but it can also shift your habitual breath patterns, so after the exercise you can often experience a more organic breath recovery – one more suited to the thoughts and feelings of Shakespeare's character. It works in several stages.

- Speak one line, then breathe. Do this for several lines. You will feel how unnatural and constricting it is. Many actors use this pattern of breath because they have learnt the text line by line and not felt the energy of the thoughts. Doing it consciously will reveal the habit.
- Build up the breath energy by next taking a breath after two lines – keep this going for a bit (you will have to restart the speech several times during this exercise).
- Now extend a breath after three lines, then four, then five – and so on. Go as far as you can without losing support or pushing the voice. Go to your limit.
- At this point, return to speak the speech while letting the breath take care of itself. That is, try not to think of the breath but to communicate the intention of the speech.
- Not only has your breath been stretched, but the speech might be breathing you rather than you it. You have begun to breathe in the pattern of Shakespeare's character rather than your pattern.

The Rock

This is a great exercise to help you support the voice, stop any falling lines, physically connect to the state of readiness and begin to feel the forward thrust of the text. I have often said that when you speak a heightened text, it's like pushing a rock up a hill. You can push the rock slowly or quickly, you can pause, you can push it in different directions, but you have to hold the rock – you can't let it go.

- Use a partner to represent the rock. 'The rock' can be pushed around but must be active if it feels the speaker has pulled off the text.
- As you push, keep your shoulders free and the breath low, connect strongly through the floor.
- Push the rock around as you speak the speech.
- At the end of the speech come away from the rock and, without losing the energy you will have found, speak the speech again to your partner. It should be much more dynamic and alive – you might begin to feel the rhythm of the text and its natural energy.

Extending Range and Variety

This gives your speaking more variety and should give you more passion in thought and feeling. Keep free in the breath and voice as you do these three stages of the exercise:

- Deliberately speak the speech with minimum range.
- Deliberately speak the speech with an exaggerated range.
- Speak the speech with intention – the exercise should have given your voice and feelings more bounce and expression.

By doing these exercises, you will discover something of the physical power and structure of the text. They are a good introduction to the next stage of the givens in a text. If you do them before learning a speech, you will find they help you memorise the text more quickly and more physically and organically. The text will have entered your body and breath, not just your mind.

2. The Givens

When you first look at a speech, scene or whole play, check:

- Is it verse or prose?
- Look up the meaning of any words you don't know and research any references you don't immediately understand.
- Divide the speech into thoughts; then take yourself through the speech, understanding thought by thought.
- Be aware of the progression of the thoughts – the build of an idea and the resolve the character is pursuing.
- If it's verse, count the syllables in each line. Are there any odd lines?
- Beat the iambic: are there any trip-ups?
- Check the words that start and finish the lines.
- Do thoughts start at the beginning of the line or mid-line?
- Are there rhymes or repetition?
- What is the story up to this point?
- Is it soliloquy or are there other characters involved?
- How does the story move forward during the speech or scene?
- Are there any stage directions in the text, props, entrances or exits?
- What is the location?

All this work might seem dry and restricting but by the end of this checklist – which for a speech will probably only take you thirty minutes – you will know the text much better and understand some of Shakespeare's intentions.

Remember that the givens drive the thoughts and story forward. An actor who sees only the givens will give a clear rendering of a character, not an emotional one. The givens are the foundation stones that will hold you, the story and the comprehension of the audience.

3. The Imaginative

This is the shortest checklist, but it will take more time and research than either the preparation work or the givens. These are tasks you will probably never finish or be wholly satisfied with. The very nature of the work on the imaginative is ever-changing and growing.

Own Every Word and Image
- Understanding the word is not enough – you should have an experience of it.

Own Every Word and Image from the Character's Point of View
- People the text.
- Anchor the text.
- Heighten the text.
- Move the text.

Experiment with Focus and Energy
- Work with the text in First, Second and Third Circles.

•

Unless we apply ourselves to this work we could lose the ability to perform Shakespeare in his full and original form.

You have to remember that there is no short cut that can serve these plays accurately: only a dedication to the speaking of these texts.

No director's concept, no designer's design, no composer's music, no amplification can save or serve these plays alone. The only way is a company of actors connected to themselves and to each other in body, breath, voice, speech, mind and heart, serving and owning the words and forms, the story and the humanity within the plays.

- Work, work, work.
- Work on your body, voice, speech.
- Work on your language skills.
- Work on the experience of language in all its forms – intellectually, emotionally, physically and poetically.
- Work on memorising poetic texts accurately. Learn a text at least once a week, so that the language swims in your bloodstream.
- Focus training and time on craft work. Use repetition, don't fear it.
- Rehearse actively. Discussion is important but it is vital to do the play and get the physical memory of the language into your body, not just your head.
- Run scenes.
- Run the play – this releases its inner energy and momentum, and exposes sooner rather than later what technically it will take to serve the play.
- Encourage passion not cynicism in the rehearsal room.
- Be prepared to go up to great work. As you do so, it will lift you. Although the preparation feels hard, it eventually gives energy back and you will find yourself not alone with the work but in it and empowered by it.
- Freedom not fear.